# Endings and Aftermath

The final year of the Great War
& the conflicting demands of peace

Tom Ashworth

Shalliley Books
The Pavilion
30 Victoria Springs
Holmfirth HD9 2NB
01484 683196


© Tom Ashworth
26 Flush House Lane
Holmfirth
Published 2018
ISBN 978-0-9569814-9-3


Printed and Bound by
D&M HERITAGE LTD
T: 01484 534323
Unit 7, Park Valley Mills
Meltham Rd., Huddersfield
HD4 7BH

# Contents

# Acknowledgements

Books like this (particularly in my case) don't get written and published without substantial help from a wide variety of people, chief among them family and friends. Their support and encouragement has been invaluable as always. Likewise the staff at Huddersfield Library whose professionalism and sheer depth of knowledge never ceases to amaze me. Dave Walker at Shalliley Books has stuck with me throughout, always there with good advice and only occasionally sighing with exasperation. Alan Hicks proofed the book from his bed as he recovered from major back surgery. Sean Robertshaw found time in a busy life to write the Foreword and Professor Paul Ward was kind enough to write a book review, yet again.

And then there's the long list of people over the last couple of years who've simply expressed interest and asked 'how's the book going' despite knowing that they will then have to stand and listen while I rattle on about the latest piece of research.

I set out to write books about ordinary people living through extraordinary times. This is the third and probably the last. I hope you enjoy it.

# Foreword

Tom Ashworth's telling of these challenging years – (1917-1919) – in Europe is in parts traumatic but also both tender and majestic. I found myself sometimes arrested and weeping, at other times laughing out loud as I combed these pages. However, there is no hiding in this book from the stark reality of what is about to unfold in Europe, and consequently across these pages, 'There was little to celebrate at the beginning of 1918.' The opening pages begin to detail the deaths of six local soldiers, and one ordinary seaman. In retelling these lads' stories we gain a concise, often moving and valuable insight into their homes and families. Here we meet an author who demonstrates in his writing style a love for those who served and the village folk they belonged to. None more arresting than an example from Tom's own family: Private Thomas Ashworth, who enlisted into the North Staffs Regiment at Stoke-On-Trent 08.03.1912 and who after serving for five years and 67 days in the Army, was discharged – no longer fit for service - at 24 years and 5 months of age. Or the author's true northern salute to the men of the 5th Battalion the Duke of Wellington's Regiment who courageously marched and fought back the German offensive in the Kaiser battles. This is not a romantic tale about our 'Toms' giving it all. Rather, it is a story which is respectful of those people left behind at home and occasionally enquiring of those in positions of authority or command. Beyond the narrative account of soldier's lives and those of our allies and their battles and their leaders, we are treated to valuable and deeply insightful descriptions of the domestic war effort both at home and in Europe. These include the effects of rationing, suffrage and changing status of women in the mind of the nation. Not to mention, the poverty herein detailed of the working classes, the effects of influenza, mutiny and failures following the cessation of the war. This is a tour de force of some reckoning. A 'must read' for anyone who is interested in local and national history. The statistical analysis alone is breathtaking, and reveals the depth and detail to which this book reaches to present us with an accurate picture of these years. A truly extraordinary read.

Revd Canon Sean Robertshaw V.R. (Vicar of Christ Church, New Mill)

# Introduction

## How Did it End?

No-one, on either side of the conflict, had expected the fighting to end so quickly. Victory this side of Christmas 1918 was thought highly unlikely and the War Cabinet in London was busily making military plans for 1919. Germany, in fact, was quite optimistic about the progress of the war:

> Since the start of the war our situation was really never so good. The military colossus Russia is totally finished and pleads for peace. Serbia and Montenegro have simply gone. Italy is still supported only with difficulty by England and France and we stand in its best province. England and France are still ready for battle but already much exhausted (above all the French) and the English are very much under pressure from the U-boats.

> Colonel Albrecht von Thaer, German General Staff officer

And yet, just a few months later, by September 1918, the military and political situation had completely reversed and few German politicians or generals believed that the war could be won. But one man did - General Erich Ludendorff, by now the most powerful figure in Germany and the only man able to exercise a veto over national policy. He recognised that the losses of the previous March and April had left the German Army incapable of mounting any major offensive but he believed a victory (of sorts) could be won by a stubborn holding action and a strong defence, in the hope that the Allies would eventually tire of their high casualty list when attacking. Berlin politicians and most of his colleagues in the Army High Command did not agree. His was a minority view.

By now war weariness had engulfed the civilian populations of Turkey, Austria and even parts of Germany itself. Generals Hindenburg and Ludendorff, who by 1918 were virtually running both the country and the war effort (the Kaiser by now was largely an irrelevance) had already been warned that Austria-Hungary would not survive another winter and Turkey was going its own way to end the conflict in the Caucasus. August had been a disaster for the Germans in the Battle of Amiens against the

British, and Austria had lost all faith in the invincibility of its main ally and supporter and was desperate for peace before the weather changed.

It was at this point that Ludendorff suffered what was virtually a nervous breakdown. He had received alarming news from the East which, coupled with the years of stress of leading the country, caused him to physically collapse.

The telegram he received stated that on September 28th, 1918, Bulgaria, Germany's Central European ally, had requested an armistice from the Allies and was withdrawing from the war. The shock of the news overwhelmed him. He fell ill and, during his slow recovery, decided to seek a ceasefire for Germany. Bulgaria's defection, he told his closest confidants, meant that the war was lost.

He had a point. The terms of Bulgaria's armistice with the Allies, signed on the 29th, demanded that Bulgaria immediately demobilise and disarm it's army, evacuate its conquered territory of Greece and Serbia and, crucially, allow the Allies to occupy its home territory as a base for further operations. These 'further operations' would inevitably involve invading Romania, another German ally, and one which provided the oil supplies for the whole of Germany's aircraft, half of its lorries and one third of the fleet of U-boats. The German munitions industry, deprived of supplies of high-grade lubricants would inexorably grind to a halt.

Moreover, the Allies were now making co-ordinated attacks along the whole of the Western Front utilising their numerical superiority (now that the Americans were arriving in numbers) and enormous forces of artillery. The Meuse-Argonne offensive began with the French on September 26th, followed by the British attack at Cambrai the following day and the Belgian-British assault at Flanders on the 28th. With preparations for the attack on the Hindenburg Line in full flow, the German Army was in the process of not only losing its best positions in occupied territory but of being destroyed piece-meal.

### Paul von Hindenburg's Urgent Call for a Negotiated Peace, 3 October 1918

Berlin, October 3rd.
To The Imperial Chancellor:
The High Command insists on the immediate issue of a peace offer to our enemies in accordance with the decision of Monday, September 29, 1918.

In consequence of the collapse of the Macedonian Front, and the inevitable resultant weakening of our reserves in the West, and also the impossibility of making good the heavy losses which have occurred during the battles of the last few days, there is no prospect, humanly speaking, of forcing our enemies to sue for peace. The enemy, on the other hand, is continuing to throw fresh reserves into the battle.

The German Army still stands firm and is defending itself against all attacks. The situation, however, is growing more critical daily, and may force the High Command to momentous decisions.

In these circumstances it is imperative to stop the fighting in order to spare the German people and their allies unnecessary sacrifices. Every day of delay costs thousands of brave soldiers their lives.

VON HINDENBURG

Records of the Great War, Vol. VI, ed. Charles F. Horne, National Alumni 1923

By October 1918 the priority for Ludendorff and Hindenburg was to save the German Army not just from the Allies but - with the example of the Russian revolution before him - from the internal social chaos that was beginning to spread throughout Germany. Revolution was in the air and Germany desperately needed a unified and disciplined army to counter the Socialist / Communist threat to the Homeland. It would be unable to achieve that feat if the fighting on the Western Front caused it to collapse into a disorderly, retreating mob. Signs of unrest were already evident in the armed forces themselves and unreliable units - 'poisoned by socialist ideas' - were being pulled out of the line. Ludendorff confessed to his staff in an emotional conference that 'no confidence was possible in the troops'.

The Allies, in the meantime, were close to a 'wholesale breakthrough' and he convinced himself that an armistice at the very least would give his forces time to rest and recover. Naively and rather blindly, he argued that if it turned out that the Allies' peace demands were excessive, then Germany could simply renew the fighting.

In the event, his call for a break in the fighting merely provoked the very collapse of order and discipline that he had schemed so hard to prevent.

By October German Army censors were reporting that soldiers were demanding 'peace at any price' in letters home. Some troops in the front-line had already surrendered and stragglers and deserters in the rear areas had grown to alarmingly large numbers. One army commander reported that his men had decided that 'they would be stupid if they now still let themselves be shot dead'.

The German Naval Command took the opposite view and determined to have one last and final show of force before capitulation. So far, despite the huge sums of money invested in the building of capital ships since 1914, the contribution of the Navy to German victory had been disappointing to say the least. They had failed to inflict a decisive defeat on the British at Jutland two years previously and had proved impotent against the Allied blockade. In order to salvage some honour and prestige (and with an eye to securing some post-war future funding) it was decided that dramatic, drastic and desperate action was needed. Operation Plan No. 19 was based around a night attack by the whole of the High Seas Fleet in the waters between Scapa Flow and the Netherlands. The British Grand Fleet would be enticed out of home waters by a series of attacks on the coast of Flanders and in the mouth of the Thames and would be enticed to sail into newly planted minefields which would hopefully erode their numerical superiority. To the German naval officers, who realised that few of their ships or their crews would survive, this was 'death before dishonour'. To the ordinary sailors, who were expected to man the ships, this was a 'suicide sortie' and they openly mutinied and refused to co-operate. Already, relations between officers and men were at best distant and hostile and many of the most capable men had already been transferred to the U-boats. As the squadron chiefs were being briefed on the planned operation, sailors on three of the battleships announced that they would refuse to serve. The insubordination spread throughout the Fleet and, in a bid to contain the protests, the Fleet Commander decided to disperse his battleships to other ports. It was a mistake. Newly arrived battleships with mutinous crews provided the starting point for a countrywide revolution. When the Third Squadron reached Kiel the mutinous sailors were joined by dockyard workers. Their demonstrations were met by gunfire from the authorities killing seven and wounding twenty-nine.The whole city erupted and the revolt became openly political. Sailors addressed each other as 'comrade Bolsheviks' and demanded universal suffrage for men and women and an immediate peace with the Allies. The revolution spread within days to Hamburg, Bremen and Wilhelmshaven and then moved inland - 50,000 people marched in Munich and proclaimed a Socialist Republic of Bavaria. Berlin was in turmoil. Thirty nine army commanders were asked if their troops were ready to fight for the Kaiser and against internal Bolshevism - just one replied that they were.

That shocking message on November 9th finally jolted the Kaiser into abdication and the decision was announced to a waiting crowd from the balcony of the Reichstag's library. Germany was now a republic, and somehow the politicians managed to present it as a victory:

> The German people has triumphed everywhere. The old rotten regime has collapsed. Militarism is finished.
>
> M.Jessen-Klingenberg

The Central Nations were not simply defeated militarily in 1918, they were torn apart politically. Following the Bulgarian armistice King Ferdinand abdicated. Allied forces with the Serbs in tow, advanced 500 miles through the country liberating Belgrade, and began to threaten Turkey which by now was in terminal decline. Between 1.5 and 2.5 million Turks had already died in the war, many of them civilians, most of them succumbing to disease, wounds or starvation. This was a casualty toll equivalent to that of France in a country only half its population. With the Turkish Treasury bankrupt, the rail line to Germany (and the supply of military hardware) cut, and the British under General Milne advancing on Constantinople, the Turks decided to seek peace.

Germany's main ally, the Austro-Hungarian Empire, finally imploded under a combination of rebellions, revolts and nationalist uprisings within its own borders, coupled with military pressure from the outside. The fighting part of its army had shrunk to about 600,000 men with more than a million others either on sick-leave, at home, deserters, or prisoners-of-war. When the Italians attacked in October nearly 500,000 troops, mainly Austrian Hapsburg units, surrendered.

Part of the problem was that the Austro-Hungarian Emperor, Franz Joseph, had died in 1916 and was succeeded by his son Karl, who began to relax political controls on the many and varied nationalistic minorities that made up the Empire. By 1918 these minorities - the Poles, the Czechs, the Croats, and the South Slavs - were demanding independence.

These internal stresses and strains on the political and ruling system coupled with a crisis in feeding the population in 1918 - by June the daily allowance was cut to eight ounces of bread and three ounces of meat - exacerbated by paralysis on the railway system, runaway inflation, and a collapse in industrial production forced the country to disintegrate.

It was a similar situation in the Hungarian half of the Empire. Its neighbour Romania had re-entered the war, this time on the Allied side, and immediately invaded Transylvania. The Hungarian Army rebelled and its officers demonstrated for peace in Budapest.

Germany was now alone.

The very reason for Germany declaring war in 1914 was to support its main ally Austria-Hungary which now no longer existed. The Germany that signed the armistice was no longer a monarchy and was now a republic which had also lost its empire.

After almost four years and four months of unrestricted and bitter international violence the Great World War came suddenly to an end with the signing of an armistice at five o'clock, French time, on the morning of November 11, 1918.

The British public first heard the news in an announcement by the Prime Minister a few hours later at 10.20 am and then the Admiralty released a curt message from the French Government:

Marshal Foch to Commanders-in-Chief.
Hostilities will cease on the whole front as from 11 November at eleven o'clock (French time).
The Allied troops will not, until a further order, go beyond the line reached on that date and at that hour.

(Signed) Marshal Foch

For the rest of the day the country celebrated madly. The end of the war was even more popular than the beginning, despite the photographs of vast throngs of people outside Buckingham Palace in 1914.

By noon an enormous crowd, estimated at over 100,000, had packed the open spaces in front of the Palace and far up the Mall cheering, singing and crying out for the King. A whole stream of lorries brought women munition workers from their factories to join the celebrations. They had left behind their work headscarves and instead had knotted the ribbon of the Allies and small flags into their hair. Women as well as men clambered onto the tops of taxi-cabs or climbed the pedestal of the statue of Queen Victoria. Two American sailors were sitting on Victoria's knees

while others had climbed right to the top of the statue and were dangerously astride the wings of the Angel of Peace.

When it was time for the Changing of the Guard at Buckingham Palace
any woman in uniform was allowed into the Palace forecourt as a special
privilege but there were so many women in Nurses, Land Army, WAAF,
WRNS, and WRAF dress amongst the crowds that the gates were prematurely shut.

Eventually the King and Queen ventured out onto the balcony, as they
had done four years previously, and the King gave a short speech - though
it is unlikely that anyone, apart from his wife, heard a word:

> With you, I rejoice and thank God for victories which the Allied
> arms have won, and have brought hostilities to an end and peace
> within sight.
>
> Daily Telegraph

At one o'clock Big Ben, the massive bell of the Clock Tower of the Houses of Parliament, struck the hour for the first time since the beginning of
the war.

And the next battles began:

> Of all the problems which Governments had to handle during the
> Great War the most delicate and most perilous were those arising
> on the Home Front.
>
> Lloyd-George

# ENDINGS
# Seein' Him Off

Sitha! Trains comin' daan into th'station,
Tha'll afta get ready to start;
Let's hev hod o' thi hand whol thar wi mi,
And gi us a kuss afoor wi' part.
O'm husky wi talkin' so mitch, Jim -
(Now, lad, O'm nooan beaan to cry:
Bit o' muck gettin into mi eye, Jim) -
Nah, God bless yo, my son! - Good-bye.

Holmfirth Express January 5, 1918

There was little to celebrate at the beginning of 1918.

The previous two years had seen a catalogue of hard fought, slogging battles with their attendant butcher's bill - the trials of the Somme were followed by those at Passchendaele in 1917. There had been something to cheer for a few days in November when British tanks punched a hole through German lines at Cambrai and, just for a brief moment, it seemed like a great victory until the enemy reorganised and pushed the British back beyond their starting line. More bad news for the Allies came with the signing of an armistice between Germany and Russia allowing massive German forces to be transferred to the Western Front. Those forces would eventually be used against the Allied lines in the 'Kaiser Battles' during March and April, 1918.

Heard on a hospital ship in Southampton, 1917
"Are you downhearted?"
"No!!"
"Then you bloody soon will be!"

The first Holmfirth soldier to die in 1918, the final year of the war, was not killed on the battlefield but died of meningitis during training. Private **Norman Ricketts** of Outlane died in the early hours of January 2nd and is buried at All Saints Churchyard in Netherthong. He was eighteen years old and had succumbed to the illness at Cannock Chase in Staffordshire. His pal Bill wrote to Norman's parents:

I feel I must write a line or two to assure you that I am almost heartbroken over the sudden death of your son Norman. He and myself have been together since we joined up on May 10th, 1917. He has been the best of pals, and the last time I saw him was last Tuesday night. 'D' Company was isolated on Wednesday morning and Norman was taken to hospital at dinner time. I made enquiries the next morning and was told by his Captain that he had passed away the night before after a short period of consciousness. His loss will be seriously felt by all who had the pleasure of his acquaintance. I can assure you have my heartfelt sympathy in your terrible bereavement.

From his lonely pal  William

Norman Ricketts

The second was **Arthur Kaye**, son of Maria Kaye of Butterley. Maria was a widow and Arthur was one of five children. There is a little confusion about the date of death. It was recorded at the time as being on the last day of 1917, December 31st, but his headstone has the date January 2nd, 1918. Arthur was 38 years old and had been born and grew up at Hill Top, where he was known as a quiet, steady and industrious chap. He had been a collier for most of his working life but immediately before enlisting in April, 1916, he had worked for a lengthy period on the construction of Broadstones Reservoir. Apart from a short visit back home to recuperate from a sprained ankle, he had been in France since Christmas 1916 and served with the 2nd Battalion, Lincoln Regiment.

PTE. ARTHUR KAYE
LINCOLN REGT.

2

His mother received official notification of Arthur's death at the end of January and the following Sunday, February 3rd, came a letter from a comrade:

> No doubt you have heard by this time that the worst has happened to your son Arthur. Being an intimate friend of his, I thought it was my duty to let you know he was killed instantaneously by an enemy shell on the morning of the 31st of December, 1917. I can assure you he suffered no pain whatever, and all his friends join with me in expressing sympathy in the loss of your son. No doubt you will think I am late in letting you know but we have been very busy lately.

Arthur's body was never found on the battlefield and his name was finally added to the Addenda Panel at Tyne Cot Cemetery on 26th August, 1997.

**Harry Wood**, Ordinary Seaman, No J/74600. Royal Navy. HMS Louvain. Killed in action involving a submarine in the Mediterranean on January 20, 1918, just three weeks after joining his first ship. His brother had been killed a few months previously. Harry grew up in Dunford Bridge and worked there for the Great Central Railway Company. He was nineteen years of age.

Harry Wood

A few days later, on the Sunday of that first week in January, Holmfirth held a 'Day of Intercession', beginning with memorial services for four local lads who had been killed in France and Belgium just before Christmas.

First, **Harry Brook**, Royal Field Artillery, killed by a German shell while getting breakfast ready for his pals on the guns; he was a talented musician, playing euphonium and cornet with Hepworth Brass Band and married, with a small child:

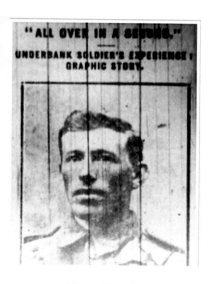

Harry Brook

You ask me about your husband's death. It is as hard for me to write it as it is to tell you, as we were the best of chums. Well, on Nov. 4th, Sunday morning, at 7.30, Harry and a young man named Denham went to the cook house to get breakfast ready for the men on the guns, only about two hundred yards behind, when Fritz sent a high explosive shell over. This dropped close to them and killed them both instantaneously, hitting poor Harry in the stomach and the other poor fellow in the face. We carried them about two miles on stretchers, and they were put away very nice and comfortable under the circumstances. Along with several of our chums, we had service over him and they are buried in the military cemetery at _____ . (Harry is buried at Menin Road South Cemetery, Ypres) I am sure that he did not suffer any pain, as it was all over in a second, and that is a lot better than lying in agony for days and then go.

Second, **Sam Earnshaw**, of 70 Dunford Road and Corporal in the Holme Valley Battery, Royal Field Artillery, killed while repairing telephone wires behind the front line. A comrade wrote to his family:

Such a cheerful fellow was Sam. He was beloved by all. The men under his charge put implicit confidence in his judgements, for, no matter what the task may have been, his affectionate spirit was endeared by everyone. It is in this respect that he was known more than a leader of men. Sam was a man amongst men.

Sam Earnshaw

Third, Sergeant **Ned Thorpe** of the Duke of Wellington's Regiment, played for Underbank football team before the war and was one of the first to enlist in 1914; killed during the fighting at Cambrai aged 23; they never found his body:

It is with deepest sympathy that I received the sad news of your son Ned having got killed. In fact, I can hardly realise it yet. It's three weeks today since I left him. I shook hands with him. That was when I left to come over to England and I have brought a souvenir across for him, which he got from a German officer. He said "Take it to our house for me." I expect to be coming home for seven days shortly, so I will bring it to you. I'm sure it will have been a sad blow to you all, for he would have been having leave shortly.

Ned Thorpe

Thomas Walmsley

Fourth, Sergeant **Thomas Walmsley**, son of Police Sergeant Walmsley of Station Road and proud possessor of the Distinguished Conduct Medal. In 1914 he had been a tram driver in Halifax and engaged to Alice. He was badly wounded during German shelling while attempting to reach and help his men who eventually managed to get him to a Casualty Clearing Station but he died almost immediately.

In a letter written to his mother to be opened in the event of his death he said 'Whatever happens Mother, don't think anything about it. It can't be helped.'

All public and licensed premises were closed for the day. It wasn't a good start to the year. Despite the constant bad news from the fighting front, Holmfirth put on a brave face over the New Year break. As usual, the wounded soldiers at the hospital were treated to a night of entertainment at the Drill Hall, and 'Grand Dances' were held at New Mill, Hade Edge and Thongsbridge. Married ladies had their own concert at Underbank Wesleyan Church and the Original Picturedrome in Holmfirth was showing Charlie Chaplin in 'The Emigrant'.

But what dominated conversation was food - or rather the lack of it.

The declaration of war in 1914 had created a wave of panic buying and food hoarding which in turn created steep price rises and nationwide shortages. These shortages continued as the agricultural, importing and distribution systems were disrupted. The situation grew gradually worse and became critical in January 1917 when Germany declared unrestricted submarine warfare. During February alone, 230 ships bringing food and other supplies to Britain were sunk. In April the Germans sent 880,000 tons of shipping to the bottom of the sea leaving Britain with just enough wheat to make bread for six weeks.

The situation was quite desperate and the Kaiser's intention to starve the British people 'until they, who have refused peace, will kneel and plead for it' was close to success.

Luckily, Lloyd-George finally persuaded the Admiralty to adopt the convoy system for shipping, a system that, up until then, naval chiefs felt was beneath the dignity of the Royal Navy. Baffled by the submarines' ability to hide beneath the waves, the Admiralty had attempted a number of solutions to the problem. They first appointed a psychic to tell them where the submarines were hiding, but unfortunately she couldn't. They suggested that seagulls could be trained to land on enemy periscopes and thereby give their position away, or even trained sea lions that would seek out the submarines, though what they would do when they found them is unclear. Reluctantly, they finally approved, what was to them, the radical idea of grouping merchantmen together and surrounding them with fast destroyers, capable of hunting down and eliminating any submarines that showed themselves.

Britain had become accustomed to plentiful food at relatively low prices before the war. Cheap(ish) food allowed the development of the country's huge industrial base by helping to keep wages down and all political parties emphasised the benefits of free trade. Improvements in transport at sea and by rail meant that the country was flooded with American and Canadian grain and the price of a loaf of bread was halved. Developments in the technology of cooling systems meant that frozen meat could cross the oceans from Australia, Argentina, New Zealand and the United States and arrive in Britain still (largely) edible. Sugar brought from the West Indies became commonplace as did tea from Assam and Ceylon.

The onset of war and the threat of German submarines quickly crippled this international trade and, with food supplies critically short by 1918, food had become a public obsession.

Before the introduction of rationing, the effort of finding and buying something to eat usually meant a tiring, time-consuming and demoralising round of queueing from shop to shop, a burden which fell largely on women. Initially it affected only the working classes but their ranks were soon swelled by more middle-class women who no longer had servants to queue for them.

How doth the little busy wife,
Improve the shining hour.
She shops and cooks and works all day,
The best within her power.
How carefully she cuts the bread.
How thin she spreads the jam.
That's all she has for breakfast now,
Instead of eggs and ham.
In dealing with the tradesmen,
She is frightened at the prices
For meat and fish have both gone up,
And butter too and rice has.
Each thing seems dearer ev'ry week.

Nina MacDonald, 1918 War-Time Nursery Rhymes

In Todmorden, just before Christmas, a giant queue formed which never consisted of fewer than 500 people at any one time and lasted from midday until late at night. The Times newspaper reported queues of over a thousand people in some parts of London during December, 1917.

Working class women suffered the most as they had less time to waste in queues and neither did they have the spare cash to splurge on 'under the counter' goods. The Society for the Prevention of Cruelty to Children raised the subject of young people waiting in the early hours of winter mornings to buy bread. Not surprisingly, tempers often flared and there were numerous violent incidents, sometimes against shopkeepers. Munitions workers in Leytonstone rioted and looted shops when their wives were unable to get food in January 1918.

Part of the problem (the government declared) was that the British were reluctant to change and adapt their eating habits. If only they would eat tinned fish instead of fresh, or more horse meat or eels, things wouldn't be so bad.

Here is a plate of cabbage soup,
With caterpillars in.
How good they taste! (Avoid all waste
If you the war would win.)
Now, will you have a minnow, love,
Or half an inch of eel?
A stickleback, a slice of jack,
Shall grace our festive meal.
We've no unpatriotic joint,
No sugar and no bread.
Eat nothing sweet, no rolls, no meat,
The Food Controller said.
But would you like some sparrow pie,
To counteract the eel?
A slice of swede is what you need,
And please don't leave the peel.
But there's dessert for you my love,
Some glucose stewed with sloes.
And now goodnight - your dreams be bright!
(Perhaps they will - who knows?)

Aelfrida Tillyard

Any number of initiatives were devised to counter the shortages - the Women's Land Army was formed to provide voluntary labour to replace the men who had been called up to fight. They were granted their own specially designed uniforms - slouch hat, knee length tunic, boots, breeches and puttees, and even had a marching song:

'The men must take the swords /
And we must take the ploughs /
Our Front is where the wheat grows fair /
our colours, orchard boughs.'

Farmers and farming communities of 1918 were fairly isolationist and many were initially appalled by the idea of mostly middle-class, city women invading their land. Utterly unfounded rumours of licentious behaviour and disgraceful morals preceded the women of the W.L.A. and, recognising the prejudice and dislike they were likely to meet they were carefully cautioned:

You are doing a man's work and so you are dressed like a man; but remember that just because you wear a smock and breeches you should take care to behave like an English girl who expects chivalry and respect from every one she meets. Noisy or ugly behaviour brings discredit, not only upon yourself but upon the uniform, and the whole Women's Land Army. When people see you pass...show them that an English girl who is working for her Country on the land is the best sort of girl.

The Government appointed a Food Controller, Lord Devonport, founder of International Stores - 'the Greatest Grocers in the World' - who spent most of his time exhorting people to eat less. People were urged to restrict themselves to 4lb of bread, 2.5 lbs of meat and 12 oz of sugar per week in a move designed to switch consumption from grain, which was imported, to meat, which was largely home produced. The advice was mainly ignored for no other reason than that the working class could never have afforded that amount of meat in the first place.

The really conscientious could wear a purple ribbon and badge with the inscription 'I Eat Less Bread' and the Holmfirth Express did its bit by imploring all its readers over the age of sixteen to sign a pledge that they would reduce their input:

The patriotism of this district cannot be doubted. We have given of our young men a goodly number, and over 160 have made the 'great sacrifice'* Are we going to take things easy and look on with a self satisfied air while others are doing all they can to help win the war ?

We wish every one of our readers to take a serious view of the Food question, and to make up his or her mind to do what is necessary to meet the present food scarcity.

We have been asked by Sir Arthur Yapp ** to bring the matter forcibly to our readers and we need only say we are willing to do all we can to meet his wishes.

With this end in view we propose to start a League of Food Economisers to be called the Holmfirth Express League of National Safety. We ask all our readers over 16 years of age to sign and return the pledge at foot, to the Express office at once. These pledges will then be forwarded to Sir Arthur Yapp who will cause a badge and certificate to be forwarded to the person signing the pledge.

* By the time of the Armistice Holmfirth had lost over 300 men.
** Sir Arthur Yapp was Deputy President of the YMCA and Director of Food Economy. He first made his name by calling for the voluntary rationing of beer before turning his attention to bread.

10

The King was asked to lend his weight to the campaign and issued a Royal Proclamation to be read out in churches for four successive weeks. It was, in fact, based on a proclamation by George III published over a century earlier and asked 'his loving subjects' to reduce their intake of bread by at least a quarter. At the same time (and this could only have happened in an age gone by) his wealthier 'loving subjects' were beseeched to eat more luxuries (it was said that tins of imported Larks were still occasionally available in London shops) and leave the bread for the stomachs of poor people:

The Food Controller and his department were diligent in their advice:

> Eat slowly, you will need less food.
> Eat less bread and victory is secure.
> Look well at the loaf on your breakfast table and treat it as if it were real gold because that British loaf is going to beat the German.
> The woman who wastes a crust wastes a cartridge.

When pleas to reduce consumption failed the bread was simply doctored. The milling process was altered to leave more wholegrain in the loaf and potato flour was added.

People were encouraged to grow their own food following the King's example - he had had his gardeners turn the herbaceous borders at Buckingham Palace into vegetable plots to grow turnips and cabbages which were then donated to a local military hospital. Local councils allocated public land, parks and verges, for allotments. Vegetables were grown anywhere there was space - golf courses, railway embankments, tennis courts, waste ground. By the end of the war there were thousands of allotments, most of which were quickly turned over to developers when hostilities ceased.

Cookery centres were set up to teach women how to make the most of available foodstuffs and introduce them to new ingredients, such as the hitherto undiscovered delights of lentils. Magazines offered patriotic recipes for 'war cake' or 'lentil loaf' which used no eggs, milk or butter and only a tiny amount of sugar. The benefits of pea-nuts, or monkey-nuts as the children called them, were stressed. Monkey-nuts contained more protein than rice, wheat, flour, Indian corn, starch, sugar or banana meal, it was claimed. They could be used as a 'palatable and nourishing' soup or, if roasted, were 'healthful and fattening'.

The National Food Economy League published a series of guides aimed at the various classes of consumers - *Housekeeping on Twenty-Five shillings a Week or Under* (price 1d); or *War-Time Recipes for Households Where Servants are Employed* (price 6d).

Newspapers were full of sound advice and the Holmfirth Express explained how simple it was for any housewife to make her own butter. This involved a quarter-of-a-pound of margarine (it had recently been resolved that the pronunciation of margarine should not be 'marjarine' - soft 'j' - but margarine - hard 'g'); three fair sized potatoes and a couple of

Oxo cubes. Boil the potatoes and mix all the ingredients together. Or, if that didn't appeal, skim the milk of its cream for four or five days and churn for forty minutes.

The Times suggested that the 'better classes' should save the tea leaves from the first brew, dry them and send them for distribution to the poor. Middle-class wives were firmly instructed that 'The woman who would feed her family well and yet reduce expenses, must first of all learn to cook, so that she may instruct her Cook in the best and cheapest methods of preparing food.' Presumably the Cook wasn't bright enough to figure that out for herself.

Fish was in such short supply that the Archbishop of Westminster gave dispensation to Roman Catholics to eat cheap cuts of meat instead of fish on Fridays.

A wide choice of food was still available for those who could afford it but, worryingly for the Government, signs of malnutrition were increasingly reported in some poorer communities.

And the young men were still getting killed.

**Horace Tolson.** 2nd Lieutenant. 6th Battalion The Royal Warwickshire Regiment. Reported missing, presumed killed February 29, aged 33. No known grave, his name is recorded on the Pozieres Memorial to the Missing.

Horace was born and brought up in Ryefields, Holmfirth. He trained as a teacher and taught in Liverpool. He enlisted soon after the war began and served in the Dardanelles. Commissioned in November 1917, he was in charge of a section of machine-guns when he was killed.

# RATIONING AT LAST

Manchester demonstration in support of rationing. 1918

Rationing was finally introduced in January 1918 as the only way to ensure a fairer distribution of available foodstuffs.

Everyone was issued a ration card (even King George and Queen Mary) which could only be used at certain shops. Families had to declare which butcher, baker, grocer they would be using and register with them, and the rules were strictly enforced. Cheats could be fined heavily or even imprisoned.

The first item to be rationed was sugar but by the end of April meat, butter, cheese and margarine had been added to the list. Some foods were still in short supply even after the war ended - butter remained on ration until 1920.

Butter and margarine were commandeered by the Food Control Committees of Honley, Holmfirth, Denby and Cumberworth, Shepley, Shelley, Thurstonland, Skelmanthorpe, Thurlstone, Kirkheaton, New Mill, South Crossland, Meltham, Linthwaite, Golcar, Slaithwaite, Marsden, and Mirfield under the direction of the Huddersfield Committee. From that point on, all butter and margarine coming into the Huddersfield area would be seized, pooled and distributed on a sugar card basis, i.e. only available with a ration book.

In Holmfirth there were shortages of just about everything - paper, food, coal and soap. Personal hygiene was an early casualty of the war. So many birds were being shot for food that the authorities finally had to point out that some of them were carrier pigeons on official business for naval and military purposes:

> The public are earnestly requested to exercise the greatest care to avoid repetition of such unfortunate incidents and are warned that persons convicted of wilfully shooting such birds are liable to prosecution.

> Holmfirth Express.

It wasn't just food that was carefully regulated. Fuel supplies, particularly that most common form of energy - coal, was part of a national system of fixed pricing, and those prices were meticulously observed. William Greensmith, coal merchant of Hinchliffe Mill, was prosecuted for overcharging his customers. The price of a single bag of coal, one hundred-weight - 112lbs of Best Hards - was set at 1s 11d and Mr Greensmith was found guilty of selling his at 2s 1d, making an extra profit for himself of 2d per bag. Moreover, once he had been informed that he was about to be prosecuted, he had visited all his customers and begged them to tell the authorities that he had only charged them 1s 11d. None of them did and all testified against him in court. He was found guilty and fined £6 10s.

Local Holmfirth farmers decided to strike when their request for an increase in the price of milk was refused. They were demanding a rate of 7d per quart to put them in line, they said, with other areas in the county.

Mr Fred Bramwell, Chairman of the Holmfirth Farmers' Association wrote to the Holmfirth Food Control Committee:

> At a largely attended meeting of dairy farmers held on the 9th inst. it was unanimously decided not to accept the price of new milk fixed and advertised by your Committee. We feel that you have dealt with us most unfairly and unjustly, and again reiterate our demand for 7d per quart. All that we ask for is to be placed

on an equal footing with the majority of our neighbours and unless you are prepared to grant this request before the 18th inst. we
shall cease delivery. In conclusion, gentlemen, we are prepared to
offer you our supply of milk at 1s 8d per imperial gallon at the
farm.

Holmfirth Express

The Divisional Food Commissioner was consulted and he gave his
agreement - the Holmfirth farmers got their 7d. New Mill farmers, who
were still receiving 6d per quart, were livid.

The average food bill rose by about 60% during the war to the dizzy
height of £2 per week for an average working class family. So too did
rents and rates until the Government put a freeze on increases. Coal
costs rose adding a further 2s to the household budget but alcohol consumption fell and tobacco consumption increased considerably. Most
of these rises took place during the first two years of the conflict and
caused widespread hardship as wages failed to keep pace. That situation changed as the war went on and family incomes either remained
steady or improved somewhat. Those families fortunate enough to have
children of working age (the legal age was fourteen but many children
started in employment much earlier) could take advantage of full employment, abundant overtime, a competitive labour market and regular
wage increases or government bonuses, and were becoming used to a
measure of unaccustomed prosperity.

Separation allowances for the wives of serving men were an added bonus and for those women whose husbands had been in irregular or badly
paid jobs before the war, a separation allowance was a real improvement,
'It seems too good to be true, a pound a week and my husband away!'
One unexpected side-effect of the payments was to reveal just how
many couples in the early twentieth century were living together but
unmarried and the War Office deliberated for some time before agreeing
to pay allowances to all women supported by their male partner before
enlistment. The ruling angered religious leaders but they were mollified
somewhat when restrictions were built in to the award system - wives
who were unfaithful to their serving husbands could have their allowances stopped, since '…the woman by her infidelity has forfeited the
right to be supported by her husband…there is no obligation on the State
to continue this payment.'

There was no mention of unfaithful men.

The police were urged to monitor women who spent their allowances 'unwisely', i.e. those who drank, or those whose behaviour gave rise to concern, confirming the prevalent attitude that women on their own were easily led astray and prone to immoral acts.

The sister of Field Marshall Sir John Denton Pinkstone French wrote to the newspapers to complain that:

> ...as the wife of a soldier she deeply resented the insults to her class which were implied by the ...instructions issued to the police to keep the wives and dependents of soldiers on active duty under police surveillance.

This was the formidable Charlotte Despard, Anglo-Irish suffragette, novelist, vegetarian, anti-vivisectionist and supporter of the early Labour Party.

In April the Meat Ration Card became obligatory. Of the four coupons available, three could be used to buy butcher's meat to a total of 1s 3d, or 5d per coupon, per person, per week. This applied to Beef or Mutton or Bacon or Ham. If you preferred to buy and eat offal - liver, heart or tripe - the value of your coupon rose to 10d. The fourth coupon in the book could be used to purchase venison or horse flesh or six sausages.

'Heavy Workers' - miners, steelworkers, munitions workers - were allowed a supplementary ration of extra bacon.

A family of four, comprising mother, father and two children under ten years of age were advised to use their ration cards thus:

Father (3 coupons) - Neck of Mutton, 13 ounces
Mother (3 coupons) - Sirloin of Beef, 12 ounces
Two children ( 4 coupons each) - Bacon, 1 pound
Father and Mother (2 coupons) - Tinned meat, 3 ounces.

### REMEMBER
Carry your cards with you.
Don't tear off the coupons yourself.
Register for bacon no later than today.

Holmfirth Express, April 18, 1918

Later on in the year, new meat ration cards were introduced reducing each person's allowance from 1s. 3d to 10d. The allowance now covered beef, mutton, pork, tongue, kidney, skirt, liver, heart and tripe. One coupon would allow a shopper to buy 5 oz of uncooked bacon, or ham with bone, or 4 oz. without bone, or a 2lb chicken, or a whole rabbit. Children under 10 were only allowed half the ration of an adult. Munitions workers retained their extra bacon allowance. In an ever-increasing world of regulation, even horses had ration cards.

The complex rules helped to create a den of crime in the food market and shopkeepers were prosecuted for hoarding food or for selling it at above prescribed prices. Consumers themselves were prosecuted for falling foul of the law. People were prosecuted and fined for feeding stray dogs or throwing rice at a wedding.

It became a crime for a workman to leave a loaf behind on the kitchen shelf of the cottage from which he was moving (£2 fine), for a maiden lady at Dover to keep fourteen dogs and give them bread and milk to eat (£5 fine), for another lady in Wales to give meat to a St Bernard (£20), for a furnace man dissatisfied with his dinner to throw chip potatoes on the fire (£10), and for a lady displeased with her husband to burn stale bread upon her lawn (£5).

William Beveridge, The Times, March 12, 1918

Matthew, Mark, Luke and John,
Guard the dish the butter's on
For we don't want a theft.
Four coupons I have left
One for sugar, one for fat
And two for liver for the cat.

Nina MacDonald, War-Time Nursery Rhymes

# Shortages in Germany

No matter how bad or inconvenient the shortages were in Britain, they couldn't begin to compare with what was happening in Germany, Turkey and Austria-Hungary, where the civilian populations were becoming increasingly exhausted and impoverished. The efficient and clinical coastal blockade by the British Navy off Germany's shores, coupled with soil exhaustion and rampant bureaucratic bungling resulted in terrible hardship. The first major hunger riots had taken place during 1916 in Hamburg where thousands of working class women had shouted for bread, looted bakeries and fought the police who had been sent to control them.

The situation grew even worse when a wet Autumn created the conditions for a fungus infection which devastated that year's potato crop, leaving the population reliant on turnips for sustenance. People who survived the notorious 'turnip-winter' of 1916-1917 were left looking lean and hungry - 'We are all gaunt and bony now' (Princess Blucher) and food riots became so serious that troops were deployed on the streets. There were cases of sabotage in key munitions industries as workers struck for better food rations, 250,000 strikers in Berlin alone, rising to a total of 500,000 nationally, and the capital city of Germany was declared to be under a state of siege. Strike leaders were arrested and large sectors of war industries were placed under military control. The situation was made far worse by the coal shortage. All non-essential parts of the economy - cafes, hotels, restaurants - were forced to reduce their consumption to one-third; lights went out in apartment blocks at 9pm. In Munich all public buildings, all cinemas and theatres were closed.

> One of the most terrible of our many sufferings was having to sit in the dark. It became dark at four…It was not light until eight o'clock. Even the children could not sleep all that time…And when they had gone to bed we were left shivering with the chill which comes from semi-starvation and which no additional clothing seems to alleviate.

John Williams - The Home Fronts: Britain, France and Germany.

Coal supplies depended totally on the railways for distribution but the German rail system, once a source of immense pride and the largest in

Europe, was falling apart. With so many skilled men serving in the forces, there were few workers left able to service the tracks or maintain the engines or rolling stock. Accidents increased and freight movement fell dramatically to 25% of normal.

Germany, then as now the powerhouse of Europe, was in slow decline and gradually disintegrating.

In Vienna, a quarter of a million people at any one time were on the streets queueing for food. In some districts lines began to form outside shops shortly before 10pm; anyone arriving after 3am was unlikely to get to the front of the queue before the foodstuffs ran out.

By 1918 the situation was desperate and evidence of severe malnutrition was widespread.

Bread had been 'diluted' with rye and potatoes ever since 1914 but as these essentials were exhausted more exotic materials were used - maize, lentils, peas, soya beans, chestnuts, clover and bran. When these in turn were unavailable the bakeries turned to sand and sawdust.

It was vile, 'You couldn't slice it, you broke it up with your hands. It was yellow, sticky, not good.' (Great War and Urban Life - Chickering)

German manufacturers blatantly cheated hungry customers. Egg substitutes were often nothing more than coloured maize or potato flour; 'coffee with sugar' was made mainly of sand; sausages became little tubes of an indeterminate slime; coffee could be made of walnut shells, plum stones, turnip heads and even tree bark. Many products were actually poisonous - 'flour' manufactured from gypsum was not uncommon. Keeping cats and dogs as pets was abandoned as people turned to more edible ones - ducks, rabbits, hens and geese. Goats became very popular, even with those city families who boasted only an apartment balcony as pasture. Malnutrition wreaked terrible damage on health, with children and young adolescents particularly vulnerable. On comparisons made with pre-1914 data, German children were found to be 2-3 centimetres shorter and up to 3.5 kilograms lighter by the end of the war. Children between the ages of six and thirteen simply stopped growing in 1918 and twelve to fourteen year olds resembled sickly eight to ten year olds. Food shortages and grinding war-weariness led to widespread illness throughout all sectors of the population and tuberculosis, pneumonia and other diseases of the lungs  became major killers. After the war, German authorities claimed that there had been 763,000 excess civilian deaths, many of them being blamed on the ruthless British 'starvation war' - the naval blockade.

There was certainly a blockade and British warships were stationed in the English Channel, the North Sea and off the Dalmatian Coast to prevent any supplies reaching the enemy by sea, but the process of denying resources flowing from neutral countries to the enemy was much more complex than that, particularly after a British Ministry of Blockade was set up in 1916. Britain used her international 'clout' to black-list companies trading with Germany. British firms were forbidden to do business with them and their ships were denied fuel - Britain owned most of the coaling stations on the major international sea-routes. If, somehow, their ships did make it to European waters they would almost inevitably be detained by Royal Naval patrols and their cargo confiscated. British law went even further. To prevent neutral countries from importing large quantities of, say, Argentinian beef and then re-exporting it across land borders and at large profit to Germany, those neutral countries were given lists of their pre-war imports and forbidden to import any increase on those figures. And finally, goods from neighbouring neutral countries - Norway, Sweden, Finland and Denmark - that had previously been bought by Germany were now compulsorily purchased by the Allies.

Britain bought goods purely to deny them to the enemy, with some unfortunate results. While German civilians starved, Norwegian herring was left to rot on the docks.

Rationing in Germany was introduced as early as January 1915 with a daily allocation of 225 grams of flour, quickly followed by the rationing of potatoes, milk, meat and fats. By 1916, all major foodstuffs were only available with a ration card, which worked well enough for things such as butter, sugar, flour or soup which required shops to be simply distributors of pre-packaged items. Problems arose when foodstuffs needed processing at shop level before being handed over to the public. Meat was a prime example of how the system could be abused. Carcasses were supplied directly to the butcher who then divided and trimmed the meat and sold it to the customer. If the authorities were too generous with the butcher's allocation, he would ensure that he had meat left over which could then be sold, under the counter, to favoured customers for a price. If the authorities provided too little, there would not be enough to go round.

This tended to be the case as the war progressed - the frequent una-vailability of goods on the ration card. With only sarcasm left, people complained that they had nothing to eat but the cards themselves.

---

Sunday Roast 1917

Take the meat ration card, coat it in the egg ration card and fry until nicely brown with the butter card. Steam the potato and vegetable cards until pleasantly soft and thicken them with the flour card. - As dessert brew the coffee card, add the milk and sugar card and use the bread card for dunking. - After the meal, wash your hands with the soap card and dry them on the ration coupon.

But we Germans see it through.
We do it gladly

---

Popular German postcard, 1917

Modern nutritionists recommend a daily total of 2,500 calories for an adult male. Germany's basic daily ration was set at 1,985 but dropped, to 1,336 and then in 1917 to 1,100. It was, as one contemporary expert pointed out, less than a sleeping person needs for life. Austrians were even worse off and their allowance had dropped to 830.9 calories by the time of the Armistice. A nutritionist noted that he had lost a quarter of his body weight in seven months on this regime and a woman in Upper Silesia summed up Germany's dilemma by declaring that the official ration was '…too little to live on and too much to die.'

Germany had decided from the beginning that allocating the same amount of food to everyone was not the answer, and that certain groups of the population would be recognised as having special needs. Breast feeding mothers, invalids and infants received a high milk priority - known as 'white gold' - until supplies fell dramatically. People were divided according to their occupation into producers or consumers. Farmers were designated as 'self-feeders' and their rations were set much higher than city dwellers - more bread and double the average meat ration. People working in the munitions industries and known as the 'heaviest workers' were allocated a supplement of 600 grammes of bread and a double ration of potatoes. Initially this applied only to men but after 1916 the list included women. At the same time, rations were cut for everyone else and, recognising the risk to public order as market places and shopping areas became unruly places, policemen were quickly added to the list of 'heaviest workers'.

On the whole, rationing failed and the authorities turned to a national system of soup kitchens, numbering 1,457 by mid-1916 and producing two million meals daily. The 'People's Kitchens' started well, serving meatloaf, pork belly, potatoes with a dessert of apple strudel and appeared to be the solution to all the supply, health and public order problems that rationing had created. But, inevitably, as food shortages began to bite even harder with the British blockade, the menus became dominated by a sort of colourless, odourless, gloppy stew known popularly as 'mass cow'. Moreover, these public kitchens were rejected by the lower-middle classes as being too reminiscent of Poor Relief. Dining in these mass halls or queueing in the street to buy a portion of stew from one of the many army-style 'goulash guns' was a step too far for a class desperate to maintain appearances, and instead they frequented separate 'middle-class' kitchens where the food cost twice as much.

(The 'goulash-guns' were mobile army kitchens which served a stew of horse meat and dried vegetables known as ' barbed wire entanglements' — mainly carrots, cabbage leaves, turnips and peas, supplemented by as many stinging nettles as could be harvested.)

In Vienna, where the food shortages were even worse, mass catering kept the population alive. In 1918, sixty-eight war kitchens were feeding an average of 150,000 people a day; dining halls fed 134,00 and charitable organisations handed out bread, warm soup and hot drinks to another 120,000. When the Armistice was declared, the Viennese soup kitchens had dispensed some 41,000,000 free meals in 1918 alone.

In some desperation, city authorities arranged for hungry children to be transported to the countryside to be fed on farms. The German Charity *Landaufenthalt fur Stadkinder* (Countryside Stays for Urban Children) sent nearly one million children on feeding holidays for between one and five months at a time.

In Britain, a system of school midday dinners had been in operation in State schools since 1906 serving solid, belly-filling meals with plenty of stodge - bean soup and bread, followed by treacle pudding / toad-in-the-hole, potatoes and bread / mutton stew and suet pudding / fish and potato pie, finished with baked raisin pudding - and over fourteen million meals a day were being served in 1914. Rationing and food shortages forced schools to cut back and they relied more on charities to set up soup kitchens serving cheaper food such as pea soup, fried fish, oatmeal and onion pudding.

Schools' midday meal

I said "I want a little tea,
A couple of pounds will do,
And sugar and bacon and butter and lard".
But the shopman said "Na poo!".
We stock the things that you ask about
But just at the moment we're quite run out".

I said "Then give me some margarine"
And he answered with honest pride
"We are selling that by the quarter-ounce,
Will you join the queue outside?".
But having no more than an hour to spare
I tried - with no better luck - elsewhere.

Holmfirth Express, April 1918

# What did the Army Eat ?

In the final year of the war there were more than 2.3 million serving soldiers on the Western Front and a mini-army of 320,000 men and 12,000 officers tasked with feeding them. Between 1914-1918 some three million tons of food had been transported to France and Belgium, not counting the millions of food parcels sent by friends and families to their loved ones.

As the war progressed, soldiers, just like civilians back home, had to get used to a deterioration in quantity and quality of the food supply, but in 1914 the official daily ration allowance for each soldier was impressive - to any new, urban, working class recruit more used to a meal of a slice of bread and jam it would have seemed the height of luxury. The army aimed to provide a soldier on active service with 4,000 calories each day, and the diet comprised:

1¼lb fresh or frozen meat, or 1lb salt meat; 4oz bacon; 20oz of bread or 16oz of flour or 4oz of oatmeal; 3oz of cheese; 4oz of butter or margarine; 5oz of tea, 4oz of jam or 4oz of dried fruit; pinch of pepper; pinch of mustard; 8oz of fresh vegetables or a tenth of a gill lime juice; half a gill of rum or 1pt of porter; maximum of 2oz of tobacco.

After a few years of increasing shortages, the soldier's front-line rations had shrunk somewhat and the diet had become fairly monotonous, consisting mainly of 9oz of tinned beef (bully beef), bread (which by 1916 had evolved into K-Brot, a dark brown concoction made of dried potatoes, oats, barley and even pulverised straw), and Maconochie tinned stew. It was this stew that gave rise to the oft-repeated soldier comment that the biggest threat to life was not German bullets but the appalling rations.

25

Maconochie's was named after the company in Aberdeen that made these meals of barely recognisable chunks of fatty meat and vegetables in a thin, gravy-like liquid. When served hot according to instructions, it was claimed to be barely edible; eaten cold, as it was more likely to be for days on end, it was said to be disgusting.

Additionally all troops carried biscuits (made from salt, flour and water and likened by the long-suffering troops to dog biscuits) produced under government contract by Huntley & Palmers, which in 1914 was the world's largest biscuit manufacturer. These notoriously hard biscuits were capable of breaking teeth if they were not first soaked in tea or water.

With food science in its infancy, this lack of variety and a shortage of fresh fruit and vegetables led to cases of vitamin deficiency; stomach infections were commonplace.

Wherever possible, soldiers moving into the trenches would also take with them cheese, tea, jam, sugar, salt and tins of condensed milk. If they were really fortunate they received bacon a couple of times a week which was cooked over a shielded candle, or a 'tommy-cooker' sent from home. The trick was to avoid smoke which might attract the enemy's attention.

Tea, of course, was vital in maintaining morale, keeping out the cold and helping soldiers to cope with difficult conditions.

And of course, there was always rum.

Out of the trenches and in the Reserve Line there was ample opportunity for the resourceful soldier to supplement his diet by poaching, scrounging and stealing from the local farms - activities that most officers turned a blind eye to. Loving families would often send food parcels of cakes, chocolates and biscuits that would be shared among groups of comrades ,and soldiers could use whatever wages they had to buy food locally.

French entrepreneurs quickly recognised a lucrative market and opened impromptu cafes - often in their own front rooms - called estaminets, which proved enormously popular with British and Commonwealth other ranks. French cuisine was 'out', and these cafes served platefuls of egg and chips and liberal quantities of cheap white wine - vin blanc - 'plonk'.

Officers, of course, had access to transport and the fine restaurants in most French towns and cities behind the lines.

# CHRISTMAS AT THE FRONT
## COLNE VALLEYITE'S EXPERIENCE

A few days previous to Christmas the weather was lovely. On Saturday evening a party of us walked into the next village, a distance of two or three miles to see 'The Fancies'. It was a very good show and the walk was delightful - crisp, frosty, a perfectly white countryside, and a lovely moon. In the evening we had steak and onions for supper and the usual sing-song. On the Monday - day before Christmas Day - I was chosen to go in a gig to a town twelve kilometres away for a final buy-in. It was a most interesting experience, for I have never been in that famous town before. (It was, in fact, Ypres) But oh! what a state it is in. Not thousands, but millions of shells must have done their deadly work in it. A few civilians have come back and opened shops, but it is a very ghost-like place. However, I was able to get evergreens, crackers, nuts, oranges, apples and cigars, so my foraging expedition was voted a success. the original menu for Christmas dinner was more elaborate than the actual one and included chickens, brussels sprouts etc., but the prices were prohibitive - about 2s 9d a lb. for chicken and 1s 5d a lb. for sprouts. Picture to yourself a large wooden hut, with three tables, each seating nine. The room was decorated with all kinds of evergreens and the tables had nice white tablecloths, shining cutlery, tumblers and floral decorations not to mention the type-written menu card.

### MENU
Leg of Pork
Forcemeat Stuffing
Roast Beef
Ham

———

Potatoes
Cauliflower

———

Christmas Pudding
Custard

———

Biscuits and Cheese, Dessert, Coffee

Mobile kitchens and army cooks were based in the Reserve Lines and, although they tended to produce fairly mundane dishes, they would often look to add nettles, dock leaves, wild mushrooms, or edible flowers as seasoning. They also pioneered the use of frozen meat, which was allowed to thaw during its journey from the French ports, and in true military fashion they were trained to avoid waste. All cooked leftovers were sold to French farmers as pigswill, while dripping was collected and sent back to Britain to be used in the manufacture of explosives. Bacon was made to go twice as far by the simple expedient of dipping it into flour or oatmeal to prevent it shrinking during cooking. Stale bread was either cut into slices, put into cold water and rebaked, or put into milk and put back into the oven to produce 'rusks'.

Curry became popular.

### ARMY WASTE —- AND ECONOMY

From waste fats collected from Army camps alone there has been produced tallow sufficient to provide soap for the entire needs of the Army, Navy, and Government Departments, with a surplus for public use, producing an actual revenue of about £900,000 per annum, and also 1,800 tons of glycerine for ammunition - sufficient to provide the propellant for 18,000,000 18-pounder shells. Well over £1,000,000 worth of military rags have been recovered and used in the manufacture of new cloths and blankets for the Army. Many thousand pounds worth of cuttings from cotton textiles have also been recovered and utilised in connection with munition and aeroplane requirements.

Colne Valley Guardian, January 1918

The culinary priority was to maintain a soldier's fitness to fight and there is no doubt that Allied forces ate far better than their German or Austrian counterparts, particularly in 1918.

### BRITISH ARMY DINNER TIME, 1918

**Recipe for Milk Biscuit Pudding (feeds 100 men):**

Ingredients: Biscuits (15lb), milk (3lb or 3 tins), sugar (5lb), currants (4lb), spice (a packet), candied peel (4oz)

Method:

Soak biscuits until soft, about three hours in cold water.

Cut up peel finely. Place biscuits, sugar and currants into baking dishes;

add milk and mix well with spice and peel. Place in oven until cooked.
Time: One hour.

**Recipe for Brown Stew**
Ingredients: Meat, onions, flour, mixed vegetables, pepper, salt, stock.
Method:
Bone meat, remove fat, cut into 1oz pieces.
Place 3lb flour, ½oz pepper, ½oz salt in a bowl and mix
Place stock in bottom of cooking vessel and dredge meat in flour.
Peel and cut up onions, wash and peel and cut up the mixed vegetables, add onions and vegetables to meat, mix well together. Barely cover with stock and place in oven to cook.
Stir frequently. Time: 2½ to 3 hours.

# THE 'DUKES'

The local regiment of the West Riding was the Duke of Wellington's, and their exploits, their triumphs, trials and tribulations were followed eagerly by people back home.

Originally known as Huntingdon's Regiment after its commander in 1702, it was disbanded in 1714 and re-raised the following year, this time entitled George Wade's Regiment. (One of Colonel Wade's descendants - also George - founded a pottery firm in Burslem, Stoke-on-Trent, in 1810 which remained open until the 1980's, famous for its manufacture of 'Wade's Whimsies'. The last owner of the pottery was Colonel Sir George Wade).

In 1782, Lord Cornwallis, who was at that point Colonel of the Regiment noted that:

> The 33rd Regiment of Infantry has always recruited in the West Riding of Yorkshire and has a very good interest and the general goodwill of the people in that part of the country. I should therefore wish not only to be permitted to recruit in that county, but that my Regiment may bear the name of the 33rd or West Yorkshire Regiment.

Recruitment parties were solemnly warned that they must not recruit Catholics (who were technically banned but joined up anyway), foreigners, boys, old men, idiots, the ruptured and the lame. They were reluctant to enlist 'strollers, vagabonds and tinkers' despite the entreaties of local magistrates who were keen to dump them on the Army. Instead, the recruiting officers were instructed to take only men 'as were born in the Neighbourhood of the place they are Inlisted in, & of whom you can get and give a good account'. Most of the new recruits were countrymen or discontented tradesmen picked up at county markets or hiring fairs, and most of them were between the ages of 17 and 25 - young men who had not yet settled to a trade or calling, and usually without family ties.

The King agreed the new title - 33rd (or the 1st West Yorkshire West Riding Regiment of Foot) and thus they remained until the title 'The Duke of Wellington's Regiment' was granted on June 18th 1853 on the anniversary of the Battle of Waterloo in the year following Wellington's death. This was the name that was retained under the Haldane Army Reforms of 1908.

These reforms created the modern Territorial Force composed of Volunteer Battalions under the parent regiment. The 'Dukes' 1st, 2nd and 3rd (Reserve) Battalions were the regulars, the professional soldier units, while the 1st Volunteer Battalion (The Territorials or part-time soldiers) was renamed the 1/4th Battalion and was based in Halifax; the 2nd VB became the 1/5th Battalion in Huddersfield (and Holmfirth - the carved title above the old Drill Hall reads - 2ndVBDWWRR); the 1/6th Battalion at Skipton (in 1908 Skipton was part of the old West Riding) and the 1/7th Battalion at Milnsbridge. All four Territorial battalions drew their volunteers from their respective areas and these men went to war together in 1915 and fought together as a Brigade until 1918. By then, of course, most of the battalions had been 'diluted' with men from most other parts of the country but they still retained their 'Yorkshireness' and their ties with the West Riding.

A glance at the Duke of Wellington's Campaigns Board in Huddersfield Town Hall confirms the notion that the history of the 'Duke's' is essentially the history of the British Army.

As the 33rd, the regiment fought with Marlborough in his European wars, and then later against the Americans during their Rebellion. In 1793, a young major by the name of Arthur Wellesley joined them and later became lieutenant-colonel and eventually the Duke of Wellington. They fought in Flanders, and in India, and against Napoleon (they were at Waterloo in 1815); they were decimated by malaria, dysentery and yellow fever in the West Indies; beat the Russians in the Crimean War, and won two Victoria Crosses assaulting Magdala against Emperor Tewodros II in Abyssinia, before being sent to South Africa and the relief of Kimberley.

WW1, THE REGULARS

The outbreak of World War One in August 1914 found the 1st Battalion as part of 2nd (Rawalpindi) Division in Lahore, India, and there they remained for the duration. The 2nd Battalion was serving in Dublin but were quickly transferred to the fighting and they landed at Le Havre, France, on August 16. The 3rd (Reserve) Battalion, which was a depot / training unit, responsible for supplying replacements to the other two battalions, remained in the UK during the war.

## KITCHENER'S MEN
West Riding men also volunteered to serve in 1914 in response to Lord Kitchener's plea 'Your Country Needs You'. These were the New Army men - the 8th (Service) Battalion, Duke of Wellington's Regiment, who landed at Suvla Bay in 1915 and fought at Gallipoli and the 9th and the 10th Battalions who served throughout the war on the Western Front. The 11th (Reserve) Battalion remained at home.

## THE TERRITORIALS
The Territorials of the Duke of Wellington's Regiment, the 1/4th, 1/5th, 1/6th and 1/7th battalions landed in France as the 147th (2nd West Riding) Brigade in the 49th (West Riding) Division in April 1915 for service on the Western Front and served together until the Armistice in November 1918. They saw action on the Somme, at Ypres, during the German Spring Offensive and the final Allied Hundred Days Offensive.

They were quickly followed by the formation of 'second line' battalions in September 1914 - 2/4th, 2/5th, 2/6th, and 2/7th - and then, as the need for more and more men became critical, the creation of third-line units to act as training / reserve battalions. These were known as the 3/4th, 3/5th etc.

These are the men this story follows during 1918.
But for the purposes of this particular book, the story begins in October 1917.

# Passchendaele - October 1917

The third British offensive in the area around Ypres began on September 20, 1917 and this time the objective was the ridge surrounding what had been the small town of Passchendaele. Beyond the ridge was terrain untouched by war, dry ground that could easily be crossed by a pursuing army and the Allies were keen to be there and out of the mud.

It would take seven weeks of fighting in the most appalling conditions, probably the worst of the war, before Australian troops finally captured the town. British losses for the battle had already reached 162,768 dead and wounded and even General Haig's two senior officers, Generals Gough and Plumer, were urging him to call a halt. He refused and ordered a new assault on a six mile front to begin on October 9th.

It was the turn of the Yorkshire regiments of the 49th Division. The Division (composed of the Duke of Wellington's West Riding Regiment, The King's Own Yorkshire Light Infantry, the Yorkshire and Lancaster Regiment and the West Yorkshire Regiment) attacked towards Passchendaele on October 9th and 10th against murderous machine gun fire from pill boxes and concrete blockhouses, half-hidden in a sea of mud and constant rain. As the assault began the Germans opened a massive artillery barrage of high explosive and mustard gas. Captain George Patton, later to become one of the Second World War's most senior American commanders, was present as an observer and later wrote to his wife:

> The Germans shoot a gas which makes people vomit and when they take off the masks to spit, they shoot the deadly gas at them. It is a smart idea, is it not?

Every battalion of the Division was involved; 146th Brigade (the West Yorkshire Regiment) attacked through the centre of the line with the 148th Brigade (the KOYLI's and the Yorks. and Lancs.) on their right. The Reserve Brigade was the 147th Duke of Wellington's and they were ordered to get ready within an hour of the attack opening. In those first sixty minutes of battle every officer and senior N.C.O. of the 1/7th Battalion West Yorkshire Regiment was either killed or wounded. Contact between Battalions, Companies and groups of men was lost within moments of the attack beginning, but somehow the troops continued the advance for two days before exhaustion took its toll.

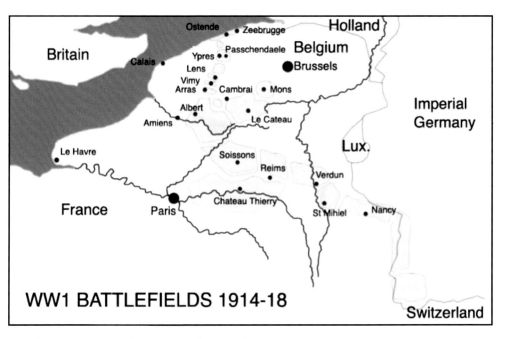

WW1 BATTLEFIELDS 1914-18

The casualty returns were horrendous.

The 1/5th Battalion, the Huddersfield and Holmfirth men, had been in the Reserve line at Zonnebeke, south-west of the ridge line at Passchendaele, and suffering under heavy German shelling since October 4th. On the 7th, the Headquarters dug-out of 'C' Company received a direct hit and the commanding officer, Captain Pinder, was killed. 'D' Company men were blown up in their trenches and buried, and survivors took shelter in shell holes - many of the men were waist deep in mud and water. At one point, German troops were spotted massing for a counter-attack in the trenches opposite but artillery was called for and the enemy force was effectively wiped out. The rain poured down incessantly and the trenches and ground conditions were appalling.

On the 9th, at 5.20am, the battalion waited in assembly positions behind the 146th and 148th Brigades who attacked on a front of about 1,200 yards.

Their orders were to take and hold a rather nondescript and quite scruffy, small Belgian village, Passchendaele, which lay on the top of a gentle sloping ridge. Not a very high ridge but in that flat, featureless landscape any feature more than a few metres high gave defenders a major advantage. And the Germans knew how to defend. They had sat there, making continuous improvements and building concrete blockhouses and pill-boxes for three years. Waiting for the British to come.

The attacking brigades, some five thousand men and boys (many of them were still teenagers), met stiff resistance almost immediately and at 7.20am the 1/5th were ordered to be ready to move on command. Orders to go over the top and advance came at 10.25am but the troops were late getting to their starting position through the sea of mud and lines of duckboards and there were immediate difficulties and some disorganisation. The objectives for the attacking troops were two successive German lines - lines on a map only, in reality they were mainly formed of linked up shell-holes and concrete pill-boxes - and by the end of the day the attackers had reached, captured and consolidated the first of them.

The 1/5th waited in the trench line below Abraham Heights ridge line for some hours, all the time under heavy shell-fire. They occupied a line of about 500 yards with 'B' Company on the right, 'C' Company in the centre and 'A' Company on the left comprising between five and six hundred men in a fairly confined space. 'D' Company was in battalion reserve, some 150 yards behind and with them was a detachment of one Trench Mortar unit and some of the Brigade's machine-gun sections. Troops had already been issued with their ammunition, Bombs, Rifle Grenades, SOS Rockets, flares and shovels - shovels which had been made in Holmfirth. They were under strict orders to return the shovels.

Passchendaele 1917. Google photos.

At 1.30pm orders were received to proceed through Waterloo trench to Fleet Cottage position. This they achieved despite suffering from accurate and sustained German machine-gun and rifle fire and proceeded to dig a line in the swamp where they then waited until 2.30am. At that appointed time, 'D' Company was ordered forward to support 146th Brigade and the rest of the Battalion moved up to help the beleaguered men of the 1/4th Yorks. and Lancs. As light broke it became impossible to move because of the incessant and sustained German sniper fire and shelling but finally at dusk they were relieved.

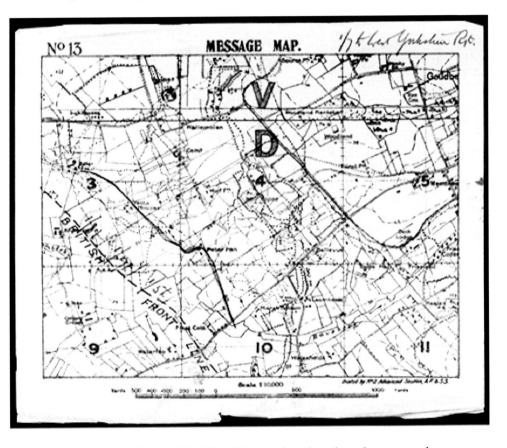

Message map of the 1/7th West Yorks. showing the advance made on October 9th 1917 from the British Front Line to the scribbled pencil line at Yetta Houses and Peter Pan between numbers 3 and 10.

The illustration below is one page taken from the List of Casualties pencil notes of the unit's War Diary written a few days after the action.

1/5 West Riding Regt.                                     Appendix. 15.
List of Casualties. October, 1917.

**Sept. 29 :-**
Wounded in Action :-
2Lt. R. JURY (Wounded by aeroplane bomb while on Signalling Course near DUNKIRK - since Died of Wounds).

**Oct. 5th :-**
Wounded in Action :-
200554  L/C. SKIRROW H.      B Coy.
202931  Pte. FIRTH A.R.      C -
200308   "   ALDRIDGE F.     A -

**Oct. 6th :-**
Killed in Action :-
204537  Pte. BLAKEY H.       C Coy.

Wounded in Action :-
200856  Pte. WEATHERILL J.   D -
200679  Spt. JUBB F.         B -
203662  Pte. FREEMAN W.      A -
240552   "   DICKENSON C.    A -
206103  ~~HARRISON W.~~
203558  L/C. OLIVER W.J.     C -
203208  Pte. ROWLEY F.       C -
203117   "   BOND F.E.       C -
29469    -   DENNIS I.       C -
15739    "   CATES A.        C -
203566   "   BUTT W.         D -
204203   "   FORDHAM A       B -

**Oct. 7th :-**
Killed in Action :-
235156  Pte. WHITTINGHAM J.E.  D -

Wounded in Action :-
203162  Pte. HARRISON W.     B -
16077    -   CASTLE F.W.     D -
201587   -   ROTHERY J.      D -

**Oct. 8th :-**
Killed in Action :-
203528  Pte. POLLARD H.E.    D -
Wounded in Action :-
202169  Pte. CLEGG T.W.      D -

**Oct. 9th :-**
Killed in Action :-
CAPT. A.E. MANDER           A Coy.
202736  Pte. INWOOD J.W.     A -
203511   -   DUGGAN J.       A -
24750    -   HARGREAVES J.   A -
201066   -   LEE H.C.        A -
306675   "   WEST A.W.       A -
203031   -   ARMSTRONG H.    A -
201550   -   ADDYMAN A       C -
203761   -   HEAP W.         C -
24668    -   BINNS E         C -

**Oct. 9th. (cont) :-**
Killed in Action (cont) :-
203222  Pte. EARLY P.        C Coy.
201820   -   WHITTAKER C.    B -
200267  L/C. MITCHELL T.     B -
14866   Pte. ROBERTSHAW J.   C -
202667   "   HILDITCH F.     B -
203461   -   FRANKLIN A.     D -
233304   -   RICHARDSON R.   A -
Wounded in Action :-
Capt. W.C. FENTON, M.C.
  -  H. GELDARD              D -
Lt. H.S. WILKINSON          A -
2Lt. R.E. STUBINGTON        B -
203653  Pte. BURFOOT T.      D -
268670  Cpl. JONES H.        A -
201745  L/C. GREENWOOD J.A.  A -
200117  Pte. KAYE H.         A -
24646    "   DAVIS J.        A -
203727   -   HOYLE G.G.      A -
242926   -   MELLOR A.       A -
201819   "   BELLSHAW V.     A -
30660    -   GARDINER J.W.   A -
30159    -   PRIEST G.W.     A -
200108   -   BROOKE A.       A -
203666   -   CARTER WE.      A -
203652   -   DELLAR S.F.     A -
203620   -   BARNARD C.      A -
203668   -   FLACK A.L.      A -
202698   -   THOMPSON J.     A -
200111  Cpl. GREEN H.        B -
203413  Pte. ANGLIS A.       B -
203821   "   PEARSON O.      B -
200295   -   BLACKBURN H.    B -
203441   -   HERON W.        B -
203271  Spt. YOUNG A.        B -
201782  Pte. POWELL H.       B -
200653  L/Sgt. BRUNT R.G.    B -
203401  Pte. SIMPSON R.      B -
204227   -   KITSON H.       B -
204757  L/C. FORTE P.        B -
203661  Pte. EASTWOOD J.W.   C -
268683  L/C. ROGERSON H.H.   C -
200180  Pte. BLANCHARD W.    C -
202926   -   COOK A.H.       C -
202636   -   FERGUSON S.     C -
200595   "   GARBUTT L.      C -
29117    -   GAMBLING S.     C -
203277   "   GOODMAN HM.     C -
262734   -   GUY T.R.        C -
31627    -   GREENWOOD A.    C -
203152   -   GREENWOOD V.    C -
203290   "   HARRISON H.     C -
202729   -   HUDSON E.       C -
203279   -   HARRISON P.     C -
202887   "   HARRIS G.W.     C -
241463   -   KETTLEWELL C.   C -
202731   "   KERSHAW H.      C -
                                (Cont.)

What was left of the Battalion eventually reassembled at St. Jean and were served tea, all ranks totally and utterly exhausted. For six days they had lived in a swamp, under constant shell-fire, soaking wet, without change of clothing in appalling weather and ground conditions and then fought for two days.

The majority of them involved in the fighting on October 9th and 10th would have been unlikely to have even seen a German, let alone fire their weapons. Their job was to occupy the captured positions and be prepared to repel any counter attack from the enemy, which in the event never came. In order to complete their task they were forced to endure the shelling and the gunfire.

Losses for the month of October numbered 193.

Their sister battalion, the 1/6th, had been moved forward from their own assembly lines to support the 1/7th West Yorkshires. Their orders were to clear the enemy from the new British line captured by the 7th up to the most advanced outposts between Yetta Houses trench and Peter Pan trench (see Message Map). They were faced with intense machine-gun and sniper fire from very well-concealed German positions as well as constant shelling and their casualty list for that one attack, lasting just a few hours, gives some indication of their difficulties.

After the trials and the losses of October the badly mauled 147th Brigade returned to the routine rotation between Front, Support and Reserve lines, gradually building up its strength again, both in numbers and in expertise. When not providing labour for other parts of the Front - they spent December 1917 salvaging war material and the dead from the Passchendaele area - they trained.

And, eventually, people at home learnt the news.

Private Samuel Booth, whose home is at Gully, Holmfirth has been wounded, and is in hospital in Nottingham.

Mr. and Mrs. D. Beardsell of Burnlee, have received a field card stating that their son, Private Frank Beardsell, has been wounded and was proceeding to the base.

Mrs. Walter Litton, of Bunker's Hill, Holmfirth, has received a letter from her husband stating that he has been wounded in the head and is in hospital at the base.

Trooper Thomas Wike, of Crown Bottom, Holmfirth is in a base hospital suffering from a gunshot wound to the leg. This is the second time Trooper Wike has been wounded.

Private Herbert Cartwright, of Winney Bank, Wooldale, son of Mr. and Mrs. Cartwright, of Wooldale Lane Bottom, has sustained a flesh wound in the right forearm, and is in hospital in Whalley (Lancs.)

Second Lieut. J. L. Vaitch, of the Royal Horse Artillery, son of the Rev. Robert Vaitch, and grandson of the late Mr. Alexander McClellan of Horsegate Hill, Holmfirth, is suffering from gas poisoning and is in hospital in Manchester.

Private Reginald Wagstaff, son of Mr. and Mrs. B. Wagstaff, Hollowgate, Holmfirth, has been wounded in the thigh, and is in hospital near London, and he writes to say that he is going on satisfactorily. Private Wagstaff crossed the Channel two days before his 19th birthday.

Private Ernest W. Hirst of Honley, formerly of Hinchliffe Mill of the Yorks. and Lancs. Regiment and son of Mr. and Mrs. Benjamin Hirst of Adeline Terrace, Hinchliffe Mill, has been gassed in the recent activities in France, and is in hospital in Surrey, where he is getting on as well as can be expected. Private Hirst has previously been wounded.

Holmfirth Express, April 1918

# The 'new' British Army

Contrary to what is often thought of as a moribund, plodding organisation, the British Army of the second half of World War One was in fact a complicated and increasingly successful machine. That's not to say that it was always used well, but in its organisation, its command of logistics and in the leadership of its battalion officers it was second to none. Officers generally were meticulous in their study of war. Every operation, whether of its own or the enemy's, was dissected for lessons to be learned - what worked, what didn't. Training of troops was constantly developed and adapted to take account of changes in technology or tactics in trench warfare. Training schools were set up so that experts could pass on knowledge or to update officers and soldiers in new aspects of waging war successfully. As the war progressed it spawned a range of technical specialities or equipment that demanded their own technical operators - tank drivers, aero-engine mechanics, flame-thrower teams, poison gas experts, wireless operators.

The basic infantry battalion had progressed from being an undifferentiated mass of riflemen at the beginning of the war to a far more structured and divided system of snipers, scouts, lewis-gunners, signallers, bombers, with each group needing its own training course, and theoretically at least, soldiers were expected to be proficient in most of these military skills.

At a higher remove there were machine-gun groups, trench-mortar teams, artillery cooperation leaders; and beyond them still were the air-to-ground liaison men, the counter-battery experts, artillery ranging, combined tank-infantry instructors.

The Yorkshire Territorials set great store in education and, wherever the division was based, training facilities were quickly established. Mining sections taught men the rudimentary skills of tunnelling while a Gas School gave lessons on the use and care of anti-gas appliances. Ambulance and first-aid courses were always popular. Newly arrived recruits spent their first few days in carefully constructed dummy trenches before being allowed to enter the real thing.

Lessons learned at the Front were applied to those men still in training back in Huddersfield or Holmfirth. Trench-digging, air-raid duty, gas drill, Lewis-gun courses were all practised and perfected back home under the supervision of recently wounded and recuperating officers.

Training was recognised as a vital, necessary and essential part of a soldier's life and was usually structured around three 'inductions'. The first was when a conscript joined the service and was instructed in basic military life - how to wear uniform, handle a weapon, how to march and obey orders. These basics were confirmed and developed upon his arrival in France at the 'bull-ring' or base depot and the new recruit would be instructed in elements of tactics and gas precautions. But the most important induction was when a soldier joined his unit and became part of the regular cycle of 'Jacob's ladder' - front line, support line, reserve line or totally out of the line altogether — successively moving closer to the Front, into action, and then further away again, spending a few days on each rung of the ladder.

Undoubtably, a great deal of informal training took place in the trenches where a new recruit's comrades, as well as his N.C.O's and immediate officers, would have instructed him on how to survive and quickly adjust to local conditions.

There were times when that wasn't enough. Private James Edward Mellor of No. 8, Flush House, Holmfirth had the misfortune to arrive as part of a draft replacement to the 1/5th Dukes just as they were preparing to attack the notorious German strongpoint of the Schwaben Redoubt. He was killed on his first full day in the trenches, unlikely to have even known the names of the people around him.

'Training' from 1916 onwards, was usually seen as a distinct activity that involved a much more formal course of instruction.

If the training was for a specific assault, or large scale raid on enemy trenches, the troops involved would be pulled out of the line to spend days studying maps, air photos and models of the area to be assaulted. They would rehearse their tactics and movements in fields marked out by tapes to the correct proportions. Problem solving exercises would be set - what happens if all the officers are incapacitated / if the creeping barrage moves too far ahead of the advancing line / if the enemy counter-attacks here - or here? In addition, troops would hone their specialist skills - bombers would bomb and clear mock trenches, machine-gunners and snipers would practise their marksmanship.

Things were rather quiet for the whole of January for the Yorkshire men. The 1/4th Battalion had only one man killed and ten wounded by shelling since Christmas, with a similar story for the 1/7th when one of their outposts outside of their front line was heavily targeted by German artillery which wounded seven other ranks. The 1/5th had completely lost four men, presumably by accident, during a night patrol when they simply disappeared. There had been no reported gunfire or noise, the four men just never reappeared in their own lines at the designated time.

All four battalions were busy providing working parties, labouring under the direction of Royal Engineers officers in building tunnels, repairing trenches and laying extensive fields of barbed wire, mostly in front of the Reserve Lines. Though the weather was bitterly cold and frosty with the occasional heavy fall of snow the trenches themselves were often flooded and muddy. Most men wore thigh length gumboots.

There were some distractions when out of the Reserve or Front lines - some men were marched to the divisional bath houses where they were deloused and given a change of underclothing while their uniforms and blankets went through the vermin destroyer. Troops in the 1/6th were able to have a mass washing of feet and a thorough dusting with camphor, but the best prize went to the 1/7th who were treated to a performance by 'The Tykes', the Divisional concert party. The word 'tyke', by the way, was originally a very rude Shakespearean term for a Yorkshireman.

The Tykes were a group of soldiers, performing mainly in drag or costume and singing well-known music-hall type pieces. They were enormously popular and most other divisions in the army had their own versions of the troupe. The 9th Division had 'The Thistles'; the 15th 'The Jocks'; the 20th 'The Very Lights'. The Australians and New Zealanders had 'The Shrapnels'. The 6th Divisional Troupe, 'The Fancies', had the extra attraction of two Belgian girls (real girls) in their party who were christened 'Lanoline' and 'Vaseline' (!) and who convulsed crowded houses each night with their rendition in hilarious accents of 'Which is the switch for Ipswich'.

But 'The Tykes' were special. They performed in almost every sector of the Northern Front, including Arras and in Cambrai during the advance of 1918 and their star performers were famous throughout the army. Lieutenant J.P. Barker, adorned in the latest fashionable hats and frocks, was reputed to have the most finely turned leg, more shapely than many a London chorus girl, while Private Moyes, another girl-impersonator, sang 'naughty' songs like 'Take a look at me now', 'Charlie

'The Splinters', Google photos

Chaplin's Walk', 'I wish I were a dog like you' and the much loved 'James William Maconochie'

> James William Maconochie ran a monarchy, on his own;
> Folks crowded to live on that island, with James on the throne.
> He loved them like anything, and a kindly king was to them;
> But the one he loved blindly, and treated most kindly, was - J.W.M.

Occasionally, mystified French civilians watched the performances from the back of the crowd as charming, very English 'girls' sang captivating songs to hardened troops who, on more than one occasion, had tears streaming down their faces.

It has to be said that the early months of 1918 found parts of the British Army in a weakened and demoralised condition. The B.E.F. (British Expeditionary Force) was holding some 100 miles of the Western Front with 47 'Home' divisions, 10 Dominion divisions, and 2 Portuguese, and were 100,000 men below strength in infantry alone. Forecasts of shortages for the rest of the year showed a gradually increasing imbalance of numbers - 250,000 by March, 1918; 460,000 by the end of October.

Despite holding a smaller section of the line than the French (a fact that the French continually referred to as evidence of the inequality of effort of the two nations, conveniently forgetting that large sections of their own line remained passive throughout the war), half of the German attacking divisions, eighty one of them, faced the British. Moreover, any enemy breakthrough of the British lines had the potential to produce far more damaging strategic effects on the Allies and their war plans.

The most pressing concern of all the Allied commanders - British, French, Italian and, soon to be, Americans - at the beginning of 1918 was manpower. Everyone, from General Haig downwards, recognised that the Germans were organising for an attack on the Western Front on a massive scale though this idea was dismissed by Haig's rival and Lloyd-George favourite, Sir Henry Wilson. Wilson represented the British Government at the Supreme War Council in Versailles and was a sharp critic of the British General Staff and their conduct of the war, particularly the strategy adopted on the Western Front. He was a keen advocate of 'war games' as a means of fathoming German military intentions - he insisted that those staff taking the part of German commanders in the games were obliged to wear their hats back to front - and his latest game in January had come to the conclusion that no military decision was likely on the Western Front in 1918 and the Allies would do better to concentrate their efforts against Turkey.

He was wrong. Very wrong.

And to understand why he was mistaken we need to look briefly at the war on the Eastern Front and the Russian Revolution.

# Germany's war with Russia

At the beginning of the 20th Century the Empire of the Russians was huge, covering one-sixth of the total area of dry land on the planet. When war broke out in 1914, Russia, which was allied to France against Germany, welcomed it as an opportunity to transform herself into one of the great European powers and a wave of patriotism and support for Tsar Nicholas swept the country.

Two years later, after a wave of military disasters, the mood had changed dramatically. Military casualties had reached 2.7 million by 1917 and between four and five million Russian soldiers were prisoners-of-war. After some success for the Russian Army in September, 1916 with the Brusilov Offensive against Austria, the news from the front resumed its more normal litany of successive defeats and retreats. By 1917 the war had magnified and aggravated the tensions and dividing lines in an already troubled Russian society to breaking point. The economy had collapsed and the food supply was almost non-existent. Eighteen million men had been conscripted into the army, most of them peasants, and two million horses had been requisitioned, leaving the countryside empty of labour and the harvest uncollected. The populations of Russia's largest cities lived under the constant threat of malnutrition and starvation.

The Tsar's secret police, the Okhrana, warned of imminent hunger riots and predicted that revolution was in the air. That revolution began in the northern capital city of Petrograd which had recently changed its name from the more Germanic-sounding 'St. Petersburg'. Early on the Thursday morning of March 8, 1917, 7,000 female textile workers staged a noisy protest against food shortages. As they marched through the streets they were joined by thousands of other workers until, by the end of the day, the crowd numbered some 120,000. The following day they marched again and this time the numbers doubled. On Saturday the numbers grew even greater to 300,000 people and by now the complaints were not just about the scarcity of food but were mixed with demands for democracy, an end to the war and vociferous criticism of the Tsar.

When news of the situation finally reached Tsar Nicholas he unsympathetically ordered the commander of the Petrograd military district - General Khabalov - to end the protests immediately, using force. As the demonstrations began again on Sunday the people were met by armed troops who opened fire and killed dozens of marchers. Nonetheless, over the next few days, the street protests flared up repeatedly and more and more troops were called in to regain control, but this time the soldiers refused to fire on unarmed protestors. The situation escalated on Monday when rebellious soldiers and workers stormed the prisons and released all the prisoners, before attacking the police stations, the offices of the Ministry of the Interior and the headquarters of the secret police. The Tsar's ministers in Petrograd resigned and fled as the whole country rose in rebellion.

Faced with a disastrous war situation, a broken economy and a nationwide uprising, Nicholas was persuaded to abdicate in favour of his slightly more popular brother, Grand Duke Mikhail Alexandrovich, who promptly and utterly rejected the proposal as a poisoned chalice. And suddenly the thousand-year old Romanov rule of monarchy was over. Russia was a republic. The shock waves reverberated around Europe. It was the first successful overthrow of an authoritarian European regime since 1789.

In order to fill the political vacuum, Russian politicians embraced the concept of democracy and formed a Provisional Government to run the country until someone or some party could make decisions about how to introduce a system of voting and hold elections. The deputy-chairman of this new government was the socialist lawyer Alexander Kerensky.

But there was a rival political power that had formed on the streets during the years of protests. These were followers of the political writings of Karl Marx and they developed a system of local representation - or Soviets - whose loyalty was to the people they represented, the people of their neighbourhoods. While the Provisional Government was composed of Liberal and Centrist politicians clamouring for democratic reform, the Soviets were controlled by the Far Left - the Mensheviks, Bolsheviks and Socialist Revolutionaries. The two power bases - centralised government and the streets - held fundamentally differing views on the direction the revolution should take, but for a time agreed to work together.

In a foretaste of what was to happen a hundred years later after the West's invasion of Saddam's Iraq, the Provisional Russian Government abolished the hated Okhrana and, for good measure, disbanded the Corps of Gendarmes, the police force. It then quickly dismissed all members of the Tsarist provincial bureaucracy. So, at the precise moment the country was descending into chaos, the government lost all means of policing or governing effectively.

The future of the country was also inextricably bound up with the continuing involvement in the European War and the Provisional Government made clear to its Western allies that Russia would honour all military commitments and continue to participate in the struggle.

This wasn't what millions of people on the streets wanted to hear. Promises of land reform and an end to war had been voiced and enthusiastically received. Serving soldiers, who were bitterly opposed to the war, were alienated and the rural population angered from the beginning. It wasn't a good start to a bright new future.

It got worse when Germany decided to stir the pot by introducing Vladimir Illyich Ulyanov - Lenin - into the mix. Berlin had long followed a policy of smuggling banned revolutionaries back into their own countries to foment unrest and had already compiled a list of exiled Russians with Lenin's name at the top. With the abdication of the Tsar confirmed, plans were made to transport Vladimir, his wife and entourage back to Petrograd in the sure hope that he would strengthen the anti-war Bolshevik faction.

Aged forty-six in 1917 Lenin was a seasoned revolutionary activist. His older brother had been arrested and executed for participating in a plot against the Tsar and Lenin himself had been banished to Siberia for three years for political agitation, after which, on and off, he spent the next seventeen years in exile. He was a follower of Karl Marx but disagreed with Marxist ideology on how a Communist society should be created. Whereas Marx was content to wait for a spontaneous uprising by the people against the bourgeoisie and the capitalist economic order, Lenin planned to seize power violently through a coup d'etat with a vanguard of well-trained, fanatical, professional revolutionaries. He intended to employ the existing workers' councils, the Soviets, to oust the old power structure by whatever means necessary and then to forcibly educate the illiterate peasants and workers in the Communist creed of class-consciousness.

As the train carrying Lenin and his party reached Petrograd station it was welcomed by crowds of Bolshevik supporters waving red flags, carrying flowers and singing the Marseillaise. Lenin was home.

He had arrived at an opportune time; the Provisional Government was finding it more and more difficult to fulfil the hopes, expectations and desire for change demanded by the people. The Allies had applied strong pressure on Russia to remain in the fighting and Kerensky, by now Minister for War, had gambled on channelling the new-found energy of the revolution into the army and a new offensive against the Austro-Hungarians and the Germans. At first, all went well but the attack petered out against strong German defences and the Russians were left with the usual massive butcher's bill. The demoralised army began to refuse to attack or move forward and units formed Soldiers' Committees to discuss orders from above. What had been a limited advance collapsed totally when the Germans counter-attacked in July and pushed the Russians back some 240 kilometres. Riga, the second-biggest port of the Empire surrendered. The Russian Imperial Army fell to pieces with units fighting each other, ransacking towns and villages as they retreated or simply deserting. The number of deserters reached 370,000 by the end of 1917.

Back in the homeland garrison troops ignored orders and flatly refused to be sent to the front. Increasingly they adopted a political stance and sided with either the local Bolshevik or Socialist Revolutionary parties. The first left-wing coup attempt was in July.

Members of the Bolshevik Red Guard, sailors from Kronstadt and soldiers of the Petrograd garrison stormed the Winter Palace, the meeting place of the capital's Soviet, where they fought with troops loyal to the Provisional Government, leaving some 400 dead before they were defeated. Lenin quickly went into exile again, this time in Finland.

In the second coup attempt, the situation was reversed. This time it was the army, led by the commander-in-chief, General Kornilov, in a putsch against the Provisional Government. They were defeated by workers from the Petrograd and Moscow Soviets with the help of the Bolsheviks. And it was the Bolsheviks who were the prime beneficiaries of this attempt. War Minister Kerensky, desperate for help from any quarter against the rebel army units, had enlisted their support to 'save' the revolution. He released the Bolshevik leaders from prison (though Lenin stayed safely in Finland) and armed them. By the time the threat was over, Kerensky had lost all political and military support and the country was in turmoil. In contrast, the Bolsheviks lost no time in promoting themselves as the saviours of the hour. And they hung on to their guns.

A unit of the Red Guards

Lenin, meanwhile, was still in Finland writing his essay *The State and Revolution* in which he rejected all forms of compromise with other political parties and advocated a complete destruction of the state by a 'revolutionary vanguard'. Only through the medium of that destruction, he argued, would the country finally see the establishment of the dictatorship of the proletariat and a classless society. His views mirrored those of another revolutionary, a man of ruthless ambition who argued for excessive force to crush all enemies of Bolshevism, and who had recently arrived in Petrograd from his exile in New York. This was the talented Lev Davidovich Bronstein, otherwise known by the name on the passport he had once stolen - Leon Trotsky. "You may not be interested in war" said Trotsky, "but war is interested in you". It was Trotsky, with his theory of 'permanent revolution' who formed the Red Guards, the well-trained and determined storm-troopers for the Bolsheviks.

And it was the Red Guards who played such a large part in the finally successful coup d'etat of October, 1917.

> The Provisional Government has been deposed. Government has passed into the hands of the organ of the Petrograd Soviet...The task for which the people have been struggling has been assured - the immediate offer of a democratic peace, the abolition of the landed property of the landlords, worker control over production, and the creation of a Soviet Government. Long live  the Revolution of Workers, Soldiers and Peasants!

> Lenin's 'Proclamation to the Citizens of Russia'
> November 9th, 1917

Compared to the slaughter taking place in the countryside as peasants took matters into their own hands and began to seize landowners' estates, the October Revolution in the Russian capital city was relatively peaceful.

Petrograd itself had been isolated for days with revolutionary soldiers and workers guarding the railway stations making train travel impossible. Eventually Kerensky borrowed a Renault car from the American Embassy in a vain attempt to contact military forces outside the city he hoped would support the Government in any conflict.

As Government Ministers in the Winter Palace debated what, if any, action they could take against the revolutionaries outside, they received a Bolshevik ultimatum to surrender. Groups of workers and soldiers had already occupied the last of the telegraph offices in the city cutting off any communication with the outside world and crowds had surrounded the palace. After a day of indecision, the Red Guards finally 'stormed' the Palace at 2.10am on 26th October, 1917. In actual fact, it wasn't so much a 'storming' as a simple case of accidentally discovering a back door that had been left unlocked. The first Red Guards entered the building and promptly got lost in the cavernous interior. After stumbling around for some time the group bumped into members of the Provisional Government in the Imperial family's breakfast room. Being illiterate the Guards had to order the politicians to compose, write and then sign their own arrest papers before being detained.

The Palace's defenders, consisting of some 3,000 teenage cadets, a few officers and Cossacks and 140 female soldiers of the Women's Battalion, had already left the Palace and returned to barracks or surrendered to the Red Guards. The 'storming' took place almost without resistance.

# EXTREMISTS' RISE TO POWER IN RUSSIA

## From Outset of Revolution They Have Thwarted Efforts of Moderate Governments.

## SAPPED KERENSKY'S RULE

### Supported Premier Only When the Korniloff Movement Filled Them with Apprehension.

Later official versions and films of the storming would show huge crowds and fierce fighting and were largely based on an historical re-enactment that was staged in front of a crowd of 100,000 in 1920. In reality, as opposed to the 'politically correct' story there were just two deaths and eighteen arrests and Kerensky managed to escape to the American Embassy disguised as a sailor.

It was, in fact, an excellent example of how to conduct a revolutionary coup d'etat and it was soon to become a familiar model in a number of European capital cities.

Despite this success, Lenin and his Bolsheviks had a very tenuous grip on power, and Russia was a cauldron of revolutionary groups, each attempting to gain control of the political structure. At this point the core membership of the Bolshevik Party probably numbered no more than about 15,000 and to gain time for his party to grow, Lenin agreed to general elections for the Russian Constituent Assembly in November. It was a poor decision. The much more moderate Socialist Revolutionary Party emerged as the undoubted winners, capturing twice as many votes as the Bolsheviks. Lenin simply ignored the result and dissolved the Assembly.

Stupidly, the Socialist Revolutionaries and the other main political party the Mensheviks, walked out in protest and left Lenin and his group in charge. It was the last political gesture they were allowed to make.

When political arguments failed to convince their opponents, the Bolsheviks resorted to more direct methods. Two members of the Kerensky Cabinet, M. Shengeneff who was Minister of Agriculture and M. Kohoshkin, State Controller were being treated in hospital after the fighting at the Palace. Armed men arrived and shot one of them as he lay asleep and when the other protested he too was shot dead.

Round about this time, the British philosopher and pacifist, Bertrand Russell, who was bitterly opposed to the European War was writing to a friend, 'The world is damnable. Lenin and Trotsky are the only bright spot.'

Lenin too, was writing to a friend:

> Comrade,
> Hang (and I mean hang so that the people can see) not less than 100 known Kulaks, rich men, bloodsuckers…Do this so that for hundreds of miles around the people can see, tremble, know and cry; they are killing and will go on killing the bloodsucking Kulaks…
> Yours, Lenin
> P.S. Find tougher people.
>
> Letter to a commissar, August 1918

Now in complete control of the State, Lenin's first major piece of legislation was to complete a massive redistribution of wealth and abolish private ownership of land.

His second was to end the war with Germany. He had recognised that Russia's military defeat at the hands of the Germans and Austrians was inevitable and in order to ensure the success of his Bolshevik revolution he needed to concentrate on fighting his internal, not his external, enemies. He was also confident that the war-weariness and shortages of food and other essentials in all the fighting countries of central and western Europe would create ideal conditions for the spread of his brand of revolution, perhaps leading to pan-European or even global Bolshevism. It was all heady stuff and on December 15, 1917, Lenin's emissaries signed an armistice. The peace conference itself began a short week later on the 22nd at the fortress city of Brest-Litovsk.

The fourteen members of the Central Powers delegation (five German, four Austro-Hungarians, three Ottomans and two Bulgarians) represented the power and the glory of the victors - the Foreign Secretary Richard von Kuhlman, General Hoffman, Count Ottar Czernin and Talat Pasha. The Bolsheviks, chosen by Leon Trotsky, were the exact opposite. Their delegation consisted of casually dressed workers, soldiers, sailors, a peasant and…women! The Germans were appalled and complained about their table manners.

Germany had three aims at the conference:

1. With one eye on the situation in the West, it wanted an immediate end to the war on the Eastern Front.

2. It wanted what would now be called 'buffer-states' between herself and Russia. These would be nominally independent countries but actually controlled by Germany.

3. Recognising that Russia was financially bankrupt, it demanded war reparations in the form of territorial annexations - Finland, Russian Poland, Estonia, Livonia, Courland, Lithuania, Ukraine and Bessarabia. In addition, it demanded that the provinces of Ardaham, Kars and Batumi would be returned to the Ottoman Empire. Unsurprisingly, these chosen territories, some 1.6 million square kilometres of land, effectively doubling the land mass of the German Empire, just happened to contain vital natural resources. Overnight, Russia lost 73% of its iron ore, 89% of her coal and a major part of her industrial heartland.

Lenin agreed to everything but he was opposed by Trotsky and most of the other leading Bolsheviks who, convinced that a Europe-wide revolution was only weeks away, attempted to draw out the negotiations.

Before long, the representatives of the Central Powers lost patience and signed a separate peace treaty with Ukraine, the 'bread basket' of Russia, who immediately agreed to provide a million tons of grain annually in exchange for recognition of the Ukrainian People's Republic and independence from Russia.

Trotsky, incandescent with rage, stormed out of the conference and refused further negotiations. Germany and the Austrians simply resumed hostilities. Within weeks, over a million troops were marching east, meeting little or no opposition, overrunning Latvia, Livonia, Estonia and Belarus.

Lenin threatened to resign as party leader and Chairman of the Council of People's Commissars if the Government refused to accept peace at any price. He eventually got his way and the Peace Treaty was signed on March 3rd:

Petrograd. Thursday.
We have entered upon an epoch of a series of wars, and are drifting towards a national and collective war. History tells of many similar crises. The terms imposed by Napoleon on Prussia and Germany were ten times heavier than those imposed on us by the Germans. Though placed in a similar position through the absence of an army, Prussia yet found strength to sign peace terms far more humiliating. Nevertheless, she rose later to the capacity of war.

We have concluded another Tilsit peace. We shall yet arise to victory and deliverance, even as Germany, after the Tilsit peace of 1807-1810, attained deliverance from Napoleon. The duration of Russia's period of probation will be shorter than was Germany's, owing to the swifter march of history.

Lenin

This moment was the closest Germany ever came to achieving its 1914 war aim of being the dominant power in Europe. It was an extraordinary moment of triumph.

The consequence of all this of course was that Germany, as the largest and strongest partner of the Central Powers Alliance, was now free to transfer huge numbers of hardened, experienced and disciplined troops across the continent to engage the Allies on the Western Front.
And they were coming not just to fight but to crush the British and the French and win the war before the Americans arrived in force.

It was a truly alarming and deeply worrying prospect for the British, possibly the worst crisis since the German invasion of 1914. Before the Peace Treaty was even concluded, the Germans began to move troops from east to west. In February 1918 they had 174 divisions facing the Allies; by March 3rd they had 182 divisions and by March 21st - the day they attacked - they fielded 192.

# HOME NEWS 1

To every civilian, therefore, I would say, 'Your firing line is the works or the office in which you do your bit, the shop or the kitchen in which you spend or save, the bank or the post office in which you put your bonds. To reach that firing line and to become an active combatant yourself there are no communication trenches to grope along, no barrage to face, no horrors, no wounds. The road of duty and patriotism is clear before you. Follow it and it will lead 'ere long to safety for our people and victory for our cause.'

Lloyd- George, New Year's Message to the Nation
January 1918

In blissful ignorance of German intentions, life in Holmfirth went on, and the women of the town had important issues to consider.

On the afternoon of Thursday, January 10, 1918, at Lane School in Holmfirth, some 200 women met to discuss and condemn the Matrimonial Causes Bill, recently introduced in Parliament. Mrs Hinchliffe was in the Chair and the invited speaker was Mrs Tupper-Carey, who had come all the way from Huddersfield.

After the opening hymn and prayers, Mrs Hinchliffe began the meeting. She was surprised, she said, that 'level headed men should consent to such an iniquitous act' and declared that women would not allow the marriage sacrament to be desecrated. Mrs Carey, speaking next, was adamant that this Bill was designed by men to encourage polygamy and was introduced in the interests of those men who, because of the war, had formed 'irregular unions'. The war had resulted in a shortage of men, she said, and the women of England were now expected to become concubines in order to replenish the stock:

Marriage, women believed, was lifelong, that death alone could separate. There were, unfortunately, cases of lifelong insanity, brutality and drunkenness but when they think of their marriage vows, that sentence 'Until death us do part', left no doubt as to the duty of a Christian.

The home life of England would be swept away, she claimed, 'a disaster greater than a military defeat' and, as the homemakers of the nation, it was up to them to rouse public opinion. She proposed the resolution:

In view of the suggested Matrimonial Causes Bill, this meeting protests strongly against its proposals and against any legislation which will weaken the lifelong bond of marriage, and endanger the happiness of homelife and the welfare of the children of the Nation.

It was carried unanimously. The Bill they were protesting about was a product of the social revolution produced by the First World War and was, in fact, part of a judicial process and a series of reforms to put men and women on a more equal footing.

Up until this point, the legal aspects of marriage and divorce had been based upon the 1857 Matrimonial Causes Act. At the time it was passed this was a ground breaking piece of legislation that for the first time involved the law in a religious sacrament. After 1857, divorce could take place in the courts instead of the House of Lords and adultery, the only ground for divorce, was no longer classed as a criminal offence.

Before the 1857 Act was passed there were only three ways a married couple could separate, all of them under the control of the Church of England, which insisted that separation or divorce from holy matrimony was an offence against God and should carry a heavy penalty. Considering that the Church of England had been created largely to facilitate Henry VIII's divorce, this seemed to some to be an odd position to take.

Under Church Law marriage could be annulled through reasons of insanity, impotence or potential incest. Couples could separate but any children would be deemed illegitimate. A second option was to prove that one partner in the marriage engaged in adultery, sodomy, bestiality, or physical violence. In this case, the couple would be allowed to separate but not remarry. The third option was to separate and then sue your partner on grounds of adultery. All three routes were long, lengthy procedures and only available to the very rich, out of reach of the majority of the population, as the Church intended it to be.

Wives were the property of their husbands and, in the eyes of the law, in the same category as lunatics, idiots, outlaws and children. A husband could lock up his wife; he could beat her; he could lock her out of the marital home and any children of the marriage belonged to him.

A prime mover of getting the bill passed was the attractive, witty and intelligent Caroline Norton who had found herself in an abusive marriage to George Norton, MP. George beat her regularly and servants were forced to intervene to protect her. She left him twice but returned for the sake of the children. When he lost a vindictive court case against a fellow politician, in which he had implied adultery by Caroline, he locked her out of the home and refused her access to the children. Engaging the help of a sympathetic MP, Caroline eventually succeeded in persuading Parliament to pass a law allowing a wife the right of custody to her young children.

It was the beginning of a system of reforms that eventually led to the 1857 Bill but there was still a long way to go. In addition to transferring jurisdiction from the Church to the civil courts, the 1857 Bill allowed women to retain control of their own bequests and investments - before then, all monies, investments or properties belonging to the bride passed to the husband at marriage - and was the first step on the road to financial and sexual liberty for women.

Traditionalists (men) were both disgusted and outraged. But, in legal terms, women remained second-class citizens. Up until quite recently women had no recourse against abusive husbands and a solicitor defending a husband in 1918 could argue that, 'In Blackburn and in Wigan it is the usual thing for the husband, when he comes home at night, to give his wife a kicking and beating.'

In 1918 children still belonged to the husband and if a couple separated, they were his, unless he had a previous conviction for assault. And adultery remained the only legal basis for divorce. As late as 1934, barristers would deliver the following advice to couples seeking a divorce:

> We are not here, Mr. Adam, to secure your happiness, but to preserve the institution of marriage and the purity of the home. And therefore one of you must commit adultery ... someone has to behave impurely in order to uphold the Christian idea of purity.

> A.P. Herbert MP Holy Deadlock (1934)

Churches continued to preach the sanctity of marriage and the damnable sin of fornication. The Archbishop of Canterbury condemned divorce as unchristian and was alarmed at the possibility of extending those facilities to classes other than those who already took advantage of them.

The Vicar of Leeds was outspoken, 'The passing of a law which makes marriage a temporary union constitutes an attack upon every married couple in the land.'

Local papers, meanwhile, were agog with the story of Archdeacon Wakefield who was accused of committing adultery at the Bull Hotel in Peterborough. The verdict depended on a chambermaid's evidence of whether or not the Archdeacon wore pyjamas or a nightshirt. The chambermaid said 'pyjamas'. Wakefield denied ever wearing pyjamas but lost anyway.

A few years before the war, the philosopher Bertrand Russell had spoken in the House of Lords for marriage reform. He argued for trial separations for couples, making both men and women equal in law, and allowing working class men and women access to the courts. He argued that the 1857 Matrimonial Causes Act was illogical and unjust and that it actually encouraged immorality by preventing a legal release from unhappy marriages.

The Lords reacted with horror, not least because Bertrand's elder brother had just been gaoled for bigamy. Bigamy wasn't that unusual.

A Royal Commission was appointed to consider reforms in the divorce laws. When it reported three years later in favour of quite drastic reform, all of its proposals were criticised and resisted by the established church. The argument was overtaken by the declaration of war and the whole issue was shelved by the Prime Minister, Herbert Asquith, until the conversation began again in 1918.

It was these preliminary discussions on changes to the marriage laws that so upset the women of Holmfirth. The clergy joined in. A meeting at the Drill Hall in Holmfirth, addressed by the Vicars of Wakefield and Huddersfield, saw a capacity crowd fill the main room with people congregating outside the doors, unable to get in. Canon Walsh explained that the Bill comprised three clauses, all designed to make divorce easier:

The Bill consisted of three clauses, the third of which was of the greatest importance. Under this clause a husband or wife, after being separated for three years, could by mutual agreement, re-marry. The second clause - to allow judicial separation to have the same effect as a decree absolute - was bad enough, but he did not think there had been anything so absolutely outrageous as the third clause. The effect would be to enable a husband and wife who had got tired of each other or who wished to have a fresh partner, after separation for three years, to get a decree pronouncing that they were divorced and their marriage dissolved, and then they would be at liberty to enter into marriage with someone else. It meant that a man who had got tired of his wife could leave her. It was not necessary that the separation should be mutual.

Holmfirth Express, January 1918

# BIGAMY AT LINTHWAITE

Alfred John Dearlove (38), engine driver, 11, Ramsden Hill Lane was charged with bigamy.

Elizabeth Dearlove, 23 Aslett Street, Wandsworth, said that she was married to prisoner on October 1st, 1908, at the Wandsworth Registry Office, London. After the marriage they lived together at 74 Garrett Lane, London, and in August 1914, prisoner was called up to the army as a reservist. During the time he was in the army, prisoner visited her when he was on leave, and made her a separation allowance. There were five children, one having been born before the marriage, and the youngest was two years of age. She saw her husband at his mother's house on Christmas Day, 1916, when he assaulted her, and did not see him again until June 1917. In consequence of something coming to her knowledge, she communicated with the police authorities at Huddersfield.

Emma Waters, munition worker, living at 11, Ramsden Mill Lane, said that she made the acquaintance of prisoner in the summer of 1916, at the place where they were both employed in Huddersfield. They began to keep company, but owing to a rumour which subsequently came to her ears, she asked prisoner whether he was a married man, and he replied "No". On the 3rd of February, 1917, they were married at the Registry Office, Huddersfield, and since then had lived as man and wife up to his arrest.

Police Sergeant Jenkinson stated that he arrested prisoner at 7.30 pm on the 27th December, 1917, and took him into custody. On the warrant being read over to him and asked what he had to say, he replied: "Nothing".

The magistrates committed prisoner for trial to the Leeds Assizes. Bail would be allowed of £50 or two sureties of £25 each.

While life in the Holme Valley may have changed little, despite the war, the mood in the rest of the country had transformed. Young people smoked and drank. Women wore lipstick in public; a kiss no longer automatically signalled an engagement. Contraception was far easier to obtain and Marie Stopes had published her book on women's sexuality. It was rumoured that in London one girl in ten carried a contraceptive in her vanity case. There was a recognition that tens of thousands of wartime marriages had been conducted in haste and perhaps for the wrong reasons and were about to end in failure - were those young people condemned to lives of unhappiness? More pragmatically, failed marriages meant fewer babies and Britain, given the losses of the war, desperately needed a population boost. And though the war was still in full flow and about to get much worse, there was, nonetheless, a sense of looking forward to when it would all be over. Discussion was already taking place on how to solve the hypothetical problems of the peace.

In 1918 there were more divorces than ever before; in 1919 there were half as many again.

Meanwhile, Councillor Brook still presided over the Holmfirth Military Tribunal along with Councillors Barber and Quarmby, Mr. Tommy Pickles and Mrs. Walker. They had a new member, Mr Holdsworth, who represented agriculture, and Mr. Varley on behalf of the military.

The first case of the day was a single, eighteen year old 'putter-up' - a strapping lad - who had been medically classed as Grade 'A'. He sought exemption on the basis of having three brothers already in France, but as Mr Varley quickly pointed out, even having four serving brothers was not sufficient absolute reason for granting an exemption. The committee compromised and granted three months exemption.

A father spoke on behalf of his 19 year old son. There were three other sons in the army, two had been wounded and the third was in hospital:

> I can see families in this district where they have as many sons and only one has gone. I think if there is a man doing his share it is me. And I think I have proved myself an Englishman in front of you.

His son was granted conditional exemption.

Another father claimed his son was physically unfit for the army and had a weak heart. When he was medically examined by the army he was classed as C2, just one grade above the absolute bottom line of physical ability. He had employment as a shop assistant and the Tribunal ordered him to find work of greater national importance - munitions - and to report back to them.

The same judgement was given against a salesman of fish who was blind in one eye.

---

### FACTS FOR THE FAIR SEX

All women realise that they can scarcely expect to escape, from time to time, suffering which men are not called upon to endure. But not all women know - though the fact might easily suggest itself - what is really behind all these miseries is something wrong with the blood.

Most often, especially when a girl is entering womanhood, the one cause of pain, low spirits, backaches, and slow development is anaemia. This miserable condition of health - too little blood, or blood that is thin and poor - is sometimes the cause of decline, leading to consumption, at this age. In full womanhood the miseries come to some women, due again to a scarcity of good blood; and when middle age approaches , the penalty which has to be paid is the punishment which Nature exacts for neglecting the blood.

---

Dr Williams' Pink Pills for Pale People
advertisement, Holmfirth xpress

At the beginning of the war in 1914 medical examinations of recruits were based on a comprehensive check-list:
- That the recruit is sufficiently intelligent;
- That his vision, with either eye, is up to the required standard;
- That his hearing is good;
- That his speech is without impediment;
- That he has no glandular swellings;
- That his chest is capacious and well formed, and that his heart and lungs are sound;
- That he is not ruptured in any degree or form;
- That the limbs are well formed and fully developed;

- That there is free and perfect motion of all the joints;
- That the feet and toes are well formed;
- That he has no congenital malformation or defects;
- That he does not bear traces of previous acute or chronic disease pointing to an impaired constitution;
- That he possesses a sufficient number of sound teeth for efficient mastication.

General conditions of rejection
- Indication of tubercular disease;
- Constitutional syphilis;
- Bronchial or laryngeal disease;
- Palpitation or other diseases of the heart;
- Generally impaired constitution;
- Under standard of vision;
- Defects of voice or hearing;
- Pronounced stammering;
- Loss or decay of teeth to such an extent as to materially interfere with efficient mastication;
- Contraction or deformity of chest or joints;
- Abnormal curvature of spine;
- Defective intelligence;
- Hernia;
- Haemorrhoids;
- Varicose veins or varicocele, if severe;
- Inveterate cutaneous disease;
- Chronic ulcers;
- Fistula;
- Or any disease or physical defect calculated to unfit them for the duties of a soldier.

By 1918 the rules had changed considerably and at least one British general complained that some of his troops were either blind, deaf or lame.

# Food Hoarders and Other Criminals

By the end of January all local stores and most of the private traders had registered their customers on the card rationing system. The cards were designed for family use and had a life of six months, regulating sugar, tea, bacon, flour, butter, margarine and lard. Meat rationing used a separate card. When purchases were made, the shop assistant would either rubber stamp or use a solid steel punch to mark the appropriate week, and, as people were already using a similar system for buying sugar, the introduction of rationing passed largely without incident. There were still queues but it was hoped that rationing would end the practice of certain individuals, usually wealthy ones, hoarding food. Food hoarding was viewed not just as a crime against the State but as a moral offence against one's friends and neighbours and was punished quite harshly. Naming and shaming in the press was common, offenders were prosecuted and some were imprisoned.

One particular Member of Parliament, Mr. W. J. McGeagh MacCaw, was visited in his London town house, 103 Eaton Square, by Mr. James Hill, an inspector from the Ministry of Food. On inspecting the pantry, Mr. Hill found 53lbs of tea, 54lbs of semolina, 155lbs of rice, 132lbs of tapioca, 58lbs of oatmeal, 435lbs of flour, 29lbs of sago, 100lbs of biscuits, 34lbs of golden syrup, 22lbs of honey and 11lbs of sugar. In court, Mr. MacCaw pointed out that his house contained his wife, himself, two grown-up daughters and fifteen indoor staff. He entertained frequently and he had had reassurance from no less a person than Lord Devonport that it was acceptable to maintain a 'reasonable supply' of foodstuffs. He was fined £400 and 35 guineas costs for breaches of the Food Hoarding Order.

> Mrs. Jessie Klaber was, on nine of fourteen summonses, convicted of food hoarding and fined £10 and costs on each. It was stated that her store cupboard contained nearly a ton of food…It was evident, that Mrs. Klaber was a very wealthy woman. Mr Ernest Jackling, the Food Control Executive Officer, recited the 'list of food-stuffs (apart from margarine) which he found on the premises. Defendant, giving evidence, said there were always at least fifteen persons in her house hold, and if she included the gardener, the chauffeur, and their families, and two dress-makers, the household comprised twenty-six persons. In cross-examination, she ad-

mitted that, having forty-seven tins or packages of cornflour in the house, she went to Selfridge's to buy more. She did so because she was using cornflour very freely. She also bought more golden syrup, although she had a lot in the house. Notwithstanding that she had a lot of sugar in the house...During the hearing Mr. Oliver stated that while the possession of a hoard of food before the promulgation of the order was not an offence, the order was designed to dissolve hoards. If people with a quantity of food in their possession bought even a pound of food on top of that it would be 'acquiring food in excessive quantity.'

The Maitland Weekly Mercury, 4th May, 1918

Things could have been a lot worse. According to a report from Rome published in the Huddersfield Daily Examiner, the Austrians in Belluno had begun to publicly hang in the town square all Italian citizens found to have concealed food supplies. An Austrian order declared that all foodstuffs were to be handed over within six hours, all money was confiscated and every man and woman of the district was forced to dig trenches and erect wire entanglements.

Lord Rhondda

Eventually the Food Controller, Lord Rhondda, declared a seven day amnesty for those persons who had hoarded food 'inadvertently'. Offenders could report and surrender their stock to the local Food Control Committee who would sell it on at a fair price to the more needy of the community such as the elderly. Half the money raised would be returned to the person surrendering the foodstuffs.

Even more despised than the hoarders were the profiteers. Trades Union newspapers called them 'The Vampire on the Back of Tommy' or characterised them as the 'Brit-Hun'. Profiteers ranged from the local shop adding a penny over and above the stated government price to the cost of a pound of tea, to shipping firms and Lord Rhondda's armaments companies making enormous profits from government contracts.

Mrs. Amy Thomas complained to the Food and Drink Committee that a local fish and chips cafe had given her short measure. She had sent a girl to the shop for two portions of chipped potatoes and peas for which she paid sixpence each. Seeing that the portions were small she sent the chips back to the shop and made a complaint. They were produced in court (they had been kept in the icehouse) and the cafe owner insisted that the value of them was eightpence. The committee found that a mistake had been made and Mrs. Thomas got her shilling back.

On a bigger scale, the Western Daily Press newspaper reported that Henry Thompson, a Lincolnshire farmer, had been fined the colossal sum of £1,800 (about £90,000 today) for selling potatoes above the maximum allowed price.

Despite restrictions on pub opening hours, 'treating', and Lloyd-George's antagonism, distillers and brewers did very well out of the war. People complained that the strength of whisky had been halved while the price had doubled. Beer suffered the same fate and the quality reduced - according to one Holmfirth connoisseur to 'minus nothing'. Nevertheless, share prices jumped. Allsopp's share price increased ninefold in 1918.

But when it came to really big business the potential profits were enormous. By 1918 the Americans were fully involved in the war and it wasn't long before an accountancy firm with links to the arms industry calculated that it cost the military around $25,000 to kill each enemy soldier. The same firm pointed out that in the world of private enterprise - New York criminal gangsters for instance - the average cost of a single killing rarely exceeded $100.

The biggest arms manufacturer in Germany was the firm of Krupp. One of its major trading partners before the war was Vickers, an English firm who, among many other different armaments, made shell fuses for the British Army - shell fuses designed and patented by Krupp who received a royalty payment for each one made. With the onset of war, all payments to Germany were suspended under the terms of the Trading With The Enemy Act and royalty payments were paid instead to the 'Custodian of Enemy Properties' Department. After a while, Vickers not only stopped paying the royalties to the Custodian but included the royalty payments in their invoices to the Government instead of paying them out of their own profits. The Government unwittingly paid 1 shilling 2 pence of royalties to Krupp on every fuse it bought and fired on Germany until 1916 when the contracts between the two firms were officially suspended. Between 1914 and 1918 Vickers were paid £11 million by the UK Government (over £200 million in today's money) including £300,329 of royalties (calculated as a percentage of fuse prices). Those overpaid royalties were clawed back at the end of the war but Vickers still received a final settlement of £1,250,000. Managing Director of Vickers, Basil Zaharoff, received a knighthood in 1919.

After the war had ended Krupp demanded over £300,000 in unpaid royalties between 4th August 1914 (the day the war began) and September 30th 1917 plus interest on the unpaid sum. Arguments between Krupp and Vickers and between Vickers and the Government dragged on until 1926 when Vickers finally agreed to hand over to Krupp the relatively small sum of £40,000. Most of that money went to fund Germany's secret military rearmament programme.

As an aside, most of the weaponry and ammunition used by the Turks to kill or wound 141,547 British and Irish, French, ANZAC, Indian and Newfoundland troops in Gallipoli was made and supplied by Vickers.

# Back to food !

Spending on food in working-class families rose by about 60 percent during the war to a little under £2 per week. Whenever the price of a particular foodstuff increased or a shortage occurred, the cry of 'profiteering' was heard, but more usually the cause was failures in administration or planning or even enemy activity. One week in January saw some 18 merchant ships of 1,600 tons or more sunk by U-Boats before they could reach port.

Shortages could also be caused by more local issues.

A committee appointed in 1918 by Lloyd-George to investigate whether or not living standards were declining reported that while the war had led to a change in what people ate, the amount they ate remained pretty much the same. More milk, potatoes, bread, flour and oatmeal were consumed by families; meat was replaced by bacon and white bread had been replaced by the more nutritious brown bread - though most people hated it.

> ...the working classes as a whole were in a position to purchase food of substantially the same nutritive value as in June 1914. Indeed, our figures indicate that the families of unskilled workmen were slightly better fed at the later date, in spite of the rising cost of food.
>
> Sumner Report, p.9

A food supplies amalgamation of all the townships in the Huddersfield district had already taken place with the aim of equalising distribution but it was taking some time to properly organise the rationing system and occasionally there were shortages, especially meat.

> For the first time in their lives scores and hundreds of local households have had to make shift without their Sunday joint. They couldn't get it. It wasn't there to be got. A few managed to get a rabbit or a fat hen and so managed to save the situation...Ham is being sold at local stores in rashers but to get a share it has been decided that customers shall fetch it — no orders can be taken. The result is a long queue. In view of the danger to health, the waste of time and the consequent neglect of home duties , it is a wrong and unfair procedure. Some people cannot go and stand. They haven't time. They are working. Others will not go and stand

— they would rather go without…It's no use seeking to abolish butter queues and setting up meat queues.

Colne Valley Guardian, February 1918

Huddersfield fixed the price of beef sausages at 1s 4d per lb., pork sausages at 1s 6d per lb., and proprietary sausages, such as Palethorpe's at 1s 8d per lb. Meals ordered in restaurants, hotels, boarding houses or clubs were very carefully regulated by law under the Public Meals Order:

- No breakfast could contain meat and there should be two meatless days each week;
- milk was limited to children under ten and invalids;
- meat at lunch or dinner was reduced from 5ozs uncooked to 3ozs; 2.5ozs of poultry or game is reckoned as 1oz of meat;
- the daily allowance of fat per head, including cooking, was 1.25oz;
- an increase in the bread allowance of 1oz for breakfast and dinner was balanced by a reduction of 0.5oz in the allowance for tea.

Basically, it was all the fault of the farmers. The Food Controller had set a price for cattle that they thought too low and, until they got the price they wanted, they refused to sell their livestock. At the Wednesday cattle market in Wakefield there were only 120 cows for sale compared to the usual 800 to 900 beasts. The majority of the ones available were Irish cows, considered to be very poor quality. The day before, at Leeds market, there were only 14 cows. Usually, some 300 West Yorkshire butchers attended at Wakefield, all looking for beasts, but most of them went home empty. Once 26 cows had been allocated to Wakefield butchers the rest of the stock was balloted for, but only to those butchers who were regular customers.

The question was raised about soldiers on a fortnight's leave who were entitled to meat. What about their meat ration? Lord Rhondda was contacted immediately and replied:

All soldiers and sailors on leave are entitled to assistance from Food Offices to obtain civilian ration in force in district. Any who, after leave, return to service abroad or service afloat, are entitled to assistance in obtaining total meat ration of eight ounces a day or thereabouts.

## THE FOOD TANGLE

Last weekend the Colne Valley had its first experience of a shortage of meat. There had been butterless, lardless and tealess days, but last week there was not enough meat to go round. Butchers shops were in many cases closed all day on Saturday because they had sold their week's supply. Then on Monday and Tuesday they were again closed as a consequence of the shortage and a notice exhibited in the shop windows. The situation is still serious, but with reason and moderation in buying there is enough for all to have a share. Owing to the regulations regarding the sale of cattle the supply will again this week be very short, but there will be plenty of mutton. No butcher can now approach a farmer and buy his cattle direct as formerly. Farmers must send their beasts to a market, where they are graded into first, second and third classes, and sold by ballot or without, to those on good terms with the auctioneer. Because a herd of cattle may be placed in the second or third class at a diminishing price the farmer keeps his cattle at home until the Food Controller gives him more money. Up to the present sheep are not controlled, with the result that butchers are buying large quantities of sheep direct from farmers at big prices. The retail price is fixed and how the butchers get their own back, let alone a living profit, is something of a mystery. Before many days are passed it is expected that the Food Controller will issue an Order making Wednesdays a meatless day. It is essential therefore that housewives should arrange for the hundred and one different ways of making vegetables, fish, fruit, etc., into appetising and wholesome meals.

Colne Valley Guardian, January 4, 1918

Wages, of course, rose too. Average earnings doubled, but it was those who were the poorest paid before the war who benefitted most. Unskilled workers in the building trade who were lucky to get a little over £1 per week in 1913 were getting three times that in 1920. Agricultural workers were getting well over twice their pre-war wage, and the same was true for unskilled workers in the munitions industries. The wages of skilled workers was increased but not by the same margins. Unemployment virtually vanished during the war years while jobs tied to the war economy, particularly munitions, paid especially well to those on piece-work or payment by results. Just about everyone was expected to work overtime; on average men worked at least ten hours and women seven to eight hours each week on top of a working week of between 49 and 52 hours. Family income was also boosted by the fact that many young women and boys, who might not ordinarily have gone out to work, found ready employment. For those fortunate families who were receiving far better wages than before the war, rationing enabled them to purchase more and better goods than they had ever been able to previously.

Robert Roberts was thirteen years old in 1918 and later wrote about his life growing up in Salford. He remembers the customers in his parents' corner shop:

> …slum grocers managed to get hold of different and better varieties of foodstuffs of a kind sold before only in middle-class shops and the once deprived began to savour strange delights. This brought the usual charge of 'extravagance' from their social superiors. 'But why shouldn't folk eat their fancy?' my mother said. 'They work for what they get'.
>
> One of our customers, wife of a former foundry labourer, both making big money now on munitions, airily inquired one Christmas time as to when we were going to stock 'summat worth chewin'.
>
> 'Such as what?' asked my father, sour faced. 'Tins o' lobster!' she suggested, 'or them big jars o' pickled gherkins!'.
>
> Furious, the old man damned her from the shop. 'Before the war', he fumed, 'that one was grateful for a bit o' bread and scrape!'

A Ragged Schooling, Robert Roberts

Some fishermen in Grimsby, according to their local M.P., were paying tax on incomes of £6000 to £7000 and over. Boats were coming back to port carrying cargoes of fish worth over £500 a time, with the skipper on a bonus of 10%. It was claimed that skippers' wives wore the finest fur coats and finest diamonds and had nest eggs in the form of War Bonds. Despite the dangers of U-boats, Mr. Tickler said, there was no shortage of recruits for the trawlers given the wages to be made, and more fish were being landed every day than pre-war.

In Huddersfield market, fresh herrings were fetching 8d per lb - about four to the lb. The week before they had cost 5d each. Sprats were good value at 6d per lb.

The finances of working class households also benefited from a variety of State provisions, as mentioned previously.

There were three kinds of payments:

The first was separation allowances for families of men on active service, awarded according to family size. From October 1917, the wife of a soldier with a child under the age of 14 received 23s per week. With four young children she received 40s 6d.

Widows of soldiers killed in the conflict received pensions according to the rank of their deceased husbands. A Private's wife got a flat-rate payment of 13s 9d per week, while the widow of a junior officer was paid about £2 a week, in addition to a third of that sum for each child up to the age of 18 for a son and 21 for a daughter. Widows of officers of higher rank received considerably better pensions.

For those men unfortunate enough to be discharged from the army with disabilities, payment was made dependent on the degree and severity of their wounds and on their ability to support themselves and their families.

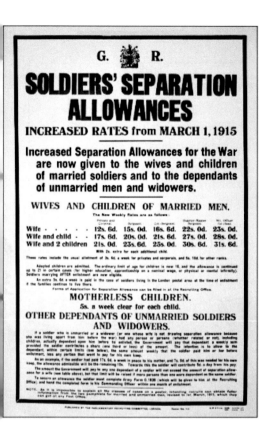

G. ꙮ R.

# SOLDIERS' SEPARATION ALLOWANCES

## INCREASED RATES from MARCH 1, 1915

**Increased Separation Allowances for the War are now given to the wives and children of married soldiers and to the dependants of unmarried men and widowers.**

### WIVES AND CHILDREN OF MARRIED MEN.

The New Weekly Rates are as follows:

|  | Privates and Corporal | Sergeant | Col.-Sergeant | Quarter-Master Sergeant | Wt. Officer 1st class |
|---|---|---|---|---|---|
| Wife · · · · · | 12s. 6d. | 15s. 0d. | 16s. 6d. | 22s. 0d. | 23s. 0d. |
| Wife and child · · | 17s. 6d. | 20s. 0d. | 21s. 6d. | 27s. 0d. | 28s. 0d. |
| Wife and 2 children | 21s. 0d. | 23s. 6d. | 25s. 0d. | 30s. 6d. | 31s. 6d. |

With 2s. extra for each additional child.

These rates include the usual allotment of 3s. 6d. a week for privates and corporals, and 5s. 10d. for other ranks.

Adopted children are admitted. The ordinary limit of age for children is now 16, and the allowance is continued up to 21 in certain cases (for higher education, apprenticeship on a nominal wage, or physical or mental infirmity). Soldiers marrying AFTER enlistment are now eligible.

An extra 3s. 6d. a week is paid in the case of soldiers living in the London postal area at the time of enlistment if the families continue to live there.

Forms of Application for Separation Allowance can be filled in at the Recruiting Office.

### MOTHERLESS CHILDREN.

5s. a week clear for each child.

### OTHER DEPENDANTS OF UNMARRIED SOLDIERS AND WIDOWERS.

If a soldier who is unmarried or a widower (or one whose wife is not drawing separation allowance because she was living apart from him before the war) had any person or persons (whether related or not, including children, actually depended upon him before he enlisted, the Government will pay that dependant a weekly sum provided the soldier contributes a share (one third or less) of the amount. The intention is to allow to the dependant, within certain limits (see below), the same amount weekly that the soldier paid him or her before enlistment, less any portion that went to pay for his own keep.

As an example, if the soldier had paid 17s. 6d. a week in peace to his mother, and 7s. 6d of this was needed for his own keep, the allowance admissible will be the remaining 10s. Towards this the soldier will contribute 5d. a day from his pay.

The amount the Government will pay to any one dependant of a soldier will not exceed the amount of separation allowance for a wife (see table above), but that limit will be raised if more persons than one were dependent on the same soldier.

To secure an allowance the soldier must complete Army Form O.1836 which will be given to him at the Recruiting Office, and hand the completed form to his Commanding Officer within one month of enlistment.

NOTE. As it is impossible to explain all the classes of cases on a poster, intending recruits can obtain fuller information from the two pamphlets for married and unmarried men, issued on 1st March, 1915, which they can get at any Post Office.

PUBLISHED BY THE PARLIAMENTARY RECRUITING COMMITTEE, LONDON.

In addition of course, all soldiers automatically qualified for health insurance which allowed their wives to claim maternity benefit and sickness benefit, and all people over the age of 65 received a small old-age pension, whether they were in employment or not. There was also a sizeable and dynamic charity movement operating both locally and nationally for relief of war-related distress. The biggest was the Prince of Wales Relief Fund to help servicemen's families and those out of work due to trade dislocation. In the Holme and Colne Valleys there were any number of groups dedicated to raising funds for soldier's hospitals, war widows or refugees.

Despite the shortages, privations and occasional disruption to the food supply, the population at home never suffered the kind of starvation rations endured by enemy civilians. In fact, though actual quantities may have declined, overall nutritional values increased. All British governments recognised that the success of the war economy depended on feeding the population at home, a stratagem that resulted in a rising standard of living, especially marked in those parts of the country that had been significantly poorer before the war.

The German war economy, by contrast, failed dismally.

Sapper Alfred Davies used to be a cloth scourer at Bottom's Mills before the war. On New Year's Eve, 1917, he was one of 2,200 troops and 160 VAD female nurses on board HMT Aragon sailing to reinforce the Egyptian Expeditionary Force in the war against Turkey. Escorted by the cruiser HMS Attack, Aragon was within sight of Alexandria when she was torpedoed by a German U-boat, UC-34. The torpedo struck on the

# ARTIFICIAL CONDITIONS

One of the greatest anomalies of this war is that the men who are fighting to save the country and the democracies of the world are being paid a bit of pocket money. They are enduring discomforts unknown to the people at home, daily risking their lives, and in hundreds and thousands of cases giving them. On the other hand young folks at home — both boys and girls — are drawing more wages that their parents got married on and set up housekeeping, and still they are not satisfied. Last weekend the City of Bradford had its business disorganised by a strike of girl tram conductors, who demanded 55s. a week. We are also told of girl typists of eighteen who ask 41s. a week, and we know that boys in the Colne Valley not yet old enough for military service are drawing more in wages and bonus than their fathers reared a family on. We do not for a moment suggest that the old wage of the father was enough. It was not, and will never again in our time at least menace the happiness and health of respectable homes. But we do say that these lads' wages are too much. They are not only entirely artificial, they are detrimental to the well-being of the lads and an injustice to the families of soldiers. There is no doubt that the war has brought a great and welcome change in the mind and heart of the people in general, but this is one of the weak spots in our wartime outlook. The parent's wages will remain when the war is over, but these young folk will find that as soon as the war ends, their occupation and their state of opulence will be gone. It is intolerable that these lads and lasses should be enabled to spend money recklessly and wantonly while the wives of soldiers and sailors are worried to get enough food to feed their children, and still more puzzled how to pay for it and other things out of their separation allowances.

Colne Valley Guardian, February 1918

port side and almost immediately the ship began to sink and lifeboats were launched. The female nurses were given priority on the lifeboats but some protested and one, apparently, pleaded 'Let us take our chances with the Tommies'. HMS Attack closed up on Aragon to take survivors aboard as quickly as possible while the soldiers on deck were heard singing 'Keep the Home Fires Burning' and 'By Jove! It Took Some Doing'. One soldier, Trooper James Magnusson, saw a comrade struggling in the rough sea and dived overboard to rescue him, managing to hold on to him before getting him placed in a boat. He then swam back to rejoin his unit on board the sinking Aragon and went down with the ship.

With its decks now crowded with approximately 300 to 400 survivors from the sinking troop ship, HMS Attack was, in turn, torpedoed, broken into two pieces and sank in minutes. The explosion ruptured the ship's oil bunkers, spilling hundreds of tons of thick, black bunker fuel into the waves. Many of the men in the water died from the fumes.

Of those aboard Aragon, 610 were killed or drowned including six of the nurses and Sapper Alfred Davies.

A few days previously there had been a similar incident closer to home when a Mersey pilot-boat, cruising near the bar to meet incoming vessels, struck a floating mine and sank, resulting in the death and drowning of 41 of the 43 on board, all within sight of land. The loss included nineteen of the best known Liverpool pilots, eight apprentice pilots, one wireless operator, the engine room staff of five and the cook. The explosion happened about 3.15 in the morning. It was a bitterly cold night and the sea was choppy. The mine struck amidships, near the coal bunkers, and the boat went down so quickly there was no time for anyone from below to reach the deck. Three survivors were rescued from the water - two of them apprentices - but the third survivor, Mr. Davies, died from exposure before reaching land.

There was also talk of making an attempt to raise the Lusitania which still lay 300 feet below the surface off the Old Head of Kinsale. If that proved impossible and it became too difficult to beach the vessel on the Irish coast then, at the very least, attempts would definitely be made to recover the treasure in the strong room on one of the upper decks.

Despite the desperate need for food imports, the dangers of U-boats and the losses at sea, the Liverpool Journal of Commerce for January 1918 listed some interesting items that had recently arrived on the dockside. Amongst a variety of imports it mentioned ornamental feathers worth £14,899; an as-

74

sortment of furs costing £656,791; 1,394,388 pairs of gloves; £328,802 of embroidery; £95,556 of furniture. Unnecessary goods - thundered the Holmfirth Express - to the value of £2,697,387 for that month alone - £32,000,000 each year. The list included fresh flowers to the value of £4,617, needed, the Express declared sarcastically, to place on the graves of the seamen who risked their lives for these 'playthings'.

Tragic deaths weren't confined to the battlefield or the water. Young Joseph Brook, a 14 year old 'clever little lad of studious habits', had been intrigued by a science demonstration at his school where a metal tray had been 'silvered'. He was keen to have a go himself and spent his lunchtime buying sulphuric acid and mercury from the chemist which he mixed together in a bottle. The shaking produced an explosion which severely burnt his face, eyes and hands. He remained fully conscious but died hours later at the Huddersfield Royal Infirmary.

Clifton Battye, a twelve year old Holmfirth boy and a pupil of Almondbury Grammar School, left home as usual to catch the 8.00am train. Friday was a 'drill day' at school so he was wearing his cadet's uniform and carrying his rifle and a box of 46 cartridges. For some never to be known reason he played truant and his body was found later at Ramsden Rocks. He had shot himself through the head. In a sign of the times, no-one thought it unusual that a twelve year old should be carrying a loaded rifle to school and no-one ever knew why he had committed suicide.

Children who fell foul of the law were taken in hand by Mr. Thomas Grundy, the Huddersfield Probation Officer:

I have little chance with a juvenile from an extremely bad home unless a change can be wrought within it, which is sometimes possible. Where this cannot be done, institutional treatment is the only hope of the child's salvation. Punitive or repressive measures, such as imprisonments and birching, in these cases cannot bring much success. A sound birching for the right subject has done good. The boy likely to benefit most therefore is the one who has been coddled or pampered. Generally, those committed to my care have not been spared the rod; others I have known might have done better with a little more encouragement and less buffeting. They have taken their whipping without shedding a tear, and in more than one instance when stripped for their chastisement, they have presented bodies already black and blue, indicating that to such corporal punishment is nothing new.

Report from the Huddersfield Probation Service 1917.

In Gloucestershire, magistrates agreed to raise the age at which a child could be birched to sixteen. For some magistrates that wasn't severe enough. Colonel Noel declared that:

> 'nowadays' boys didn't care tuppence for half-a-dozen strokes of the birch rod and that the only way to prevent juvenile crime was to do what they did in China - birch the father.

Wainhouse's Tower in Halifax came up for sale again, this time at auction. It was regarded as the finest architectural example in the district but with no practical use. As the bidding reached only £400 the property was withdrawn.

# Sex, Drink and Health

Henry Douglas-Irvine, of Holmfirth, wrote a strident letter to the Holmfirth Express condemning proposals that had recently been made in Parliament. A Scottish M.P., Mr. Macpherson,, had called for the setting up of 'maisons tolerees' in France to cater for the 'natural needs' of British soldiers. He was not at all sure, he said, '…human nature being what it is, that it was such a bad thing to have certain houses in which women were registered and kept clean'. These houses would also be a safeguard against the spread of venereal disease, he claimed.

The President of the National Union of Women's Suffrage Societies Millicent Fawcett, no less, contributed to the Holmfirth debate.

I say nothing for the moment of the degrading sex slavery which this implies though, of course, I feel this deeply, even passionately… The countries which have had the system in operation for the longest time are riddled through and through by venereal disease, and its prevalence is largely caused by persuading tempted men that a security can be given which cannot be given. This policy therefore tends to spread the race poison which it is desired to destroy.

Letter to the Holmfirth Express,
Millicent Fawcett, March 2, 1918

Venereal disease was not just confined to the services (some 400,000 men were treated for the disease during the war) but was rife throughout the population as a whole. Class, status, wealth or age formed no barrier. (There has long been suspicion that Vladimir Lenin died of syphilis, along with Frederick Delius, Al Capone, Idi Amin and Jawaharlal Nehru).

The Royal Commission on Venereal Disease which reported in 1916 declared that over ten percent of people in all the larger cities and towns suffered with syphilis. The proportion with gonorrhoea was even higher. Their evidence confirmed that on the eve of the Great War somewhere between 26 percent and 32 percent of the entire male population of the country would have had an infection of either syphilis or gonorrhoea by the time they reached their mid-thirties. As this was the prime marrying time for men, the potential social, cultural and demographic consequences were extremely worrying.

The Commission sat for 64 days, taking evidence from 80 expert witnesses who answered 22,296 questions filling 758 pages of testimony and 191 pages of appendices. It concluded:

> … syphilis is most prevalent amongst the highest and lowest of the five social classes dealt with, and the three great industries of textile manufacture, mining and agriculture are exceptionally free from the disease.

The combined toll on the national life, health, wealth and efficiency of the nation was crippling. Typical symptoms of syphilis included:

> 'paralysis (hemiplegia and paraplegia), blindness, deafness, loss of speech. loss of memory, mental enfeeblement, epileptiform convulsions, locomotor ataxy, optic atrophy and general paralysis of the insane'.

Numerous deaths which were recorded under another name were directly linked to the disease. Hereditary syphilis had even more harmful consequences, since it attacked developing foetuses in the womb during pregnancy.

> It is a frequent cause of ante-natal death, producing abortion, miscarriage or stillbirth. The less fortunate infected mothers bear not dead but living children, who may be blind, deaf, 'ricketty', mentally deficient, or otherwise unfit for the battle of life.

Statistics quoted by the Commission showed that in a sample of 34 syphilitic mothers, 175 pregnancies produced only 30 'apparently healthy' children. There were 104 premature births, still-births, or deaths in infancy and 41 'seriously diseased' babies. Of the 30 'apparently healthy' children, some would be likely to display symptoms of the disease as they matured.

Of 22 married women suffering from syphilitic dementia, 7 were sterile and only 10 children survived from 69 pregnancies. Doctor Yearsley, one of the examining Commissioners, studied 49 infected families. He reported '289 pregnancies, 38 miscarriages, 87 died in infancy, 168 living, 54 deaf and blind, and 13 born before syphilitic symptoms showed in the parents.'

Gonorrhoea was said to be the commonest cause of absolute and relative sterility in women. Over twenty-five percent of blindness in infants was attributable to gonorrhoeal ophthalmia. When children died of the disease doctors rarely put the true cause of death on the certificate, either to spare the family from a degree of shame or from knowing that the insurance company would have refused to pay up if the real reason had been declared. Instead they wrote 'marasmus', or 'atrophy' or 'congenital debility'.

> It is notorious that medical men do not—they simply cannot afford to—state such facts candidly on open certificates of cause of death handed to the relatives and copied on to public records carefully preserved for the information of any interested party.
> Hence, most certified deaths from syphilis appeared to occur among workhouse, infirmary and asylum inmates, specifically among the illegitimate infants of single pauper mothers, where the doctor's potential income was unaffected by his certification choices.

In our antibiotic age we forget that this killer disease was more common than cancer is today. One-in-ten of the population - that is men, women and children - had syphilis; ten out of every hundred people cared for in psychiatric institutions (in the vernacular of the day - 'lunatic asylums') were there because of syphilis; 50% of children suffering from blindness were blind because of the disease inherited during their mother's pregnancy; those unfortunates who contracted the disease in their nose or throat would eventually and slowly have those parts of their body eaten away.

The National Council for Combatting Venereal Diseases, which was set up after the Royal Commission published its findings, held a meeting in a packed Huddersfield Town Hall in October 1918 with some heavy weight speakers including the Lord Mayor, and the Director of the Bristol Training School for Women Police Patrols - Miss Peto. The principal speaker though was Sir Francis Champneys, Bart., M.D. The audience, it was noted, was almost exclusively women.

Sir Francis declared from the start that he would call 'a spade a spade'. He wasn't there to talk about the 'hidden scourge', or the 'white plague' but

Syphilis and Gonorrhoea. The diseases, he said, were a moral as well as a medical problem and the solution was religion. Both forms of the complaint were acquired through 'impure intercourse', though he did admit that children could be born with syphilis, or infected while suckling, and it could spread through dirty towels, bed linen, utensils, forks, spoons or pipes. Nonetheless, wives or husbands who had been untrue to the marriage pledge, or who had married before being cured of the disease, were capable of transmitting the problem to unborn children and this was 'tainting the race'.

But, he declared to the great and the good women of Huddersfield, the biggest cause of the spread of the disease was in the behaviour of girls aged 14 to 18. They were called 'flappers' and they were a national danger. He quoted statistics to prove his point. In a hospital specialising in the treatment of venereal disease, it was found that out of 100 men, 78 of the cases had come from non-professional women! These 'flappers' earned high wages and were out of their parents' control, but if only they could be 'kept on the rails' they would eventually come out of their 'flapper-hood' and become perfectly sane persons.

In her speech, Miss Peto blamed the drink. The first social cause of venereal disease was intemperance, she said, 'Persons who took too much drink lost their moral sense, and too much drink stirred physical passions. Girls were taking to drink as they never did before.'

So, there we have it - this horrible and horrendous disease, which threatened not just the future of the country but of the whole Empire, was entirely the fault of women!

It was a pragmatic age and the public were scandalised by the amount of public money involved in coping with this epidemic. The Commission published figures that demonstrated that it cost ten times as much to educate a deaf child as one with normal hearing; seven times as much to educate a blind child. The biggest crime, it was felt, was that these children would be unlikely to grow into productive workers:

> The education of the mentally deficient child, again, is exceedingly costly, and cannot be expected to produce a self-supporting worker...Prisons, hospitals, asylums, workhouses, alike bear witness to the positive loss of waste, as well as to the negative loss of non-productiveness, and we shall all agree with the Commission that the resulting total must be enormous.

Overlying everything was the unspoken fear that the war had decimated the male population of the country. The birth rate was already declining and the matter of public health and population growth could no longer be left to chance.

Some aspects of state control had been introduced at the very beginning of the war and these had gradually been extended into other areas until rules and regulations touched most aspects of people's daily lives. Public health had improved considerably with the shortening of opening times for pubs, weakening the alcoholic strength of beers and spirits and forbidding the practice of 'treating' others to a drink or buying rounds. Lloyd-George, who was desperate to introduce complete prohibition, claimed the credit:

> We have reduced the drinking to an extent that would have been incredible before the war. Not only have hours been severely curtailed, but the actual amount of alcohol has been enormously reduced.
>
> The proposal for rationing sections of the people has been frequently considered, but is more complicated in execution than the beer saved could justify. The whole problem has been constantly before us, and has been periodically surveyed, and the Government would not hesitate to take any action if it were thought materially to assist in the successful prosecution of the war.
>
> Lloyd-George replying to a parliamentary question.

In Golcar they were keen to go much further. There, in a well-attended public meeting at the Baptist schoolroom, a resolution calling upon the Government to impose countrywide prohibition was passed unanimously. Sixteen pints of beer was equivalent in calories, they said, to 2lbs. of bread, and the man who drank two pints each day was consuming the same as a bread ration. Mr. Wilkinson proposed the motion 'That this meeting urge the Government to prohibit the manufacture and sale of intoxicants for the period of the war and during demobilisation.'

Despite all the restrictions, the total figures for consumption, distilling and brewing were still impressive. Excluding the drink sent for export and the rum for front-line troops, distilleries produced, in 1917 alone,

18,549,406 proof gallons of spirits for home consumption. That year also saw 28,620,800 bushels of malt, 61,200 cwts. rice, 6,200 cwts. of maize, and 1,613,700 cwts. of sugar used in the production of 16,133,800 barrels of beer. And people were still very fond of the stuff despite the reduced strength. Landlord Ben Ellis of the Cross Pipes Inn was fined £5 and £1 6s 6d expenses for permitting drunkenness in his establishment. Five miners, after drinking at the bar, wandered outside and immediately lost their way. One fell over a wall, fractured his skull and died. Mr. Ellis maintained that they were not drunk, merely 'fresh' or 'market fresh'.

Huddersfield Police Superintendent McDowell objected to the renewal of the licence of the George Tavern in Scammonden. The beerhouse was owned by Messrs. Bentley and Shaw, the Lockwood brewers, and was sited close to 'The Upper Royal George' and 'The Lower Royal George' and was not far away from 'Nont Sarah's Hotel'. In addition to these four fully licensed premises there were four further 'refreshment' houses with seating for 400 people. Considering that the total population of Scammonden numbered 341, and the George Tavern already had three

## LICENSED TRADES ASSOCIATION.

# Beer Rationing.

On and after Thursday next, March 28th, all Licensed Houses in the districts of Marsden, Slaithwaite, Linthwaite, Golcar, Longwood, Milnsbridge, Longroyd Bridge, Paddock, and Manchester Road, will be OPEN for the SALE OF BEER (where practicable) between the hours of

WEEK-DAYS: 12-30 to 1-30 noon, and 8-0 to 9-30 at night
SUNDAYS. 12-30 to 1-30 p m, and 7-30 to 9-0 p.m.

Customers are earnestly requested to assist the License Holders to carry out the above scheme, so that Beer may be on sale from day to day.

convictions against it, Superintendent McDowell felt that it should be closed. The magistrates agreed.

In his report to the annual licensing sessions, he mentioned the decreasing numbers of prosecutions in the Huddersfield area for public drunkenness - 1913/1914, 184 convictions; 1914/1915, 213 convictions; 1915/1916, 126; 1916/1917 92; 1917/1918, just 46. The Chairman went back even further and pointed out that in 1904 there had been 531 convictions!

The latest one to appear before the magistrates was Fred Rawnsley, a motor steerer, who was summoned for being drunk in charge of a motor-car. After being detained at the Royal Oak, Mr. Rawnsley was incapable of steering the vehicle and had to be taken home. When questioned by P.C. Hawkes, he replied that he "had had nowt to sup".

Huddersfield Town's first game of the new year was home to Grimsby on Saturday, January 5 and despite an impressive team list, were a little nervous about the fixture given the Fishermens' record at Leeds Road. Town fielded: Mutch, Parton, Rogerson, Harvey, Lindley, Watson, Etherington, Elliot, Hall, Mann and Wooding. They won 2-0 but lost the following week 1-0 playing Grimsby away.

Their most convincing win of the season was against Sheffield Wednesday in March with Buchan, by now a regular member of the team, scoring a hat trick and Hall adding to the total. Despite some vigorous attacking play in the first half, Wednesday were outplayed after the interval and were completely worn down when Elliot's header rebounded off the crossbar directly to Buchan who scored easily to increase the lead. Elliot was involved a few minutes later when a fine pass to Hall resulted in a third goal, and it was left to Buchan to deliver the fourth from a pinpoint accurate corner from Etherington. Town played them at Sheffield the following Saturday and lost 3-1.

Crowds at home averaged about 2000 to 4000 each Saturday and they attracted a record gate of 15,000 at Birmingham at the end of January. They finished 8th in the Midland League at the end of the season.

Football success wasn't confined to men back home. Over in France, various teams from the machine-gunners, signallers, mortar-batteries, A.S.C. men, and battalions of the Duke of Wellington's, played a knock-out competition for the Brigade Cup. Victory went to the Milnsbridge men of the 1/7th Dukes.

Larrett Roebuck

Huddersfield Town lost a number of their players during the war. The first to be killed was the left-back Larrett Roebuck, in fact he was the first English Football League player to lose his life in the conflict. He was killed in action during the First Battle of Ypres in October 1914 just six months after helping Town win against Leicester. The Club had been sending Larrett's wife £1 a week since he had enlisted but, on hearing of his death, the Club's Secretary-Manager, Mr. Fairclough, wrote to say that, because of Town's weak financial state as wartime restrictions began to bite, the payments would have to cease. Directors of the Club sent her ten shillings each week out of their own pockets for the next month and, in addition, the players had a whip-round and sent £2 and five shillings.

Before he enlisted in the Coldstream Guards, Charles Randall played sixteen times for the Terriers during their first ever two seasons as a non-league club in 1908/1909 and the following season 1909/1910 scoring five goals. He also played in three FA Cup ties, scoring once. He was killed on September 27, 1916.

Private Jack Cameron of the Cameron Highlanders lost his life in early 1916. He had played twice at centre-forward (scoring once) early in the 1911/12 season.

The goalkeeper Leigh Roose had played five times for Town towards the end of the 1910/1911 season and died, serving with the Royal Fusiliers, on October 7, 1916.

Sergeant Sidney James Headington played at centre-forward and centre-half before the war and went on to play thirty games in the first 'wartime' season of 1915/1916. Killed in action April 9, 1917.

Ernest George Kenworthy was an outside-right who made twenty appearances for Huddersfield scoring six goals in the 1909/1910 season. He had started his football career playing for Matlock Town, then Bradford

City and Heckmondwike. After joining Town he secured his place in history by scoring twice in the 11-0 thrashing of his former club, Heckmondwike, a club record that still stands. He retired from football due to injuries and returned to teaching before enlisting in the Royal Garrison Artillery as a gunner on the outbreak of war. Aged 29 he was killed by German shells on November 10, 1917.

George Kenworthy

Edward Didymus made thirty appearances for Town in the 1908-1909 season, playing on either wing and scoring five goals. He joined Blackpool on leaving Huddersfield and ended his career playing for non-league Burslem Port Vale. He was a tram-driver in Portsmouth when war was declared and he enlisted with the 8th Battalion Middlesex Regiment, a Territorial unit. He was killed in action in France on April 12 1918 leaving behind his widow and five young children.

Many of those spectators at the games - small numbers compared to pre-war attendances - would, by 1918, be men who were working in protected industries and were exempt from the 'call-up'. Given the hours they would be expected to work during the week, watching sport on a Saturday afternoon would be a welcome relief. Responding to Government exhortations to increase output, workers produced more of just about everything. The figures for coal, steel, textiles, had risen prodigiously each year, despite the numerous strikes and walk-outs in all these industries. The latest figures for mineral extraction had just been published and showed a rise in total value to £214,034,524. Coal output reached 256,375,366 tons, over 3 million tons more than the previous year. Prices had risen too - pithead coal was now 15s 7d a ton, up from 12s 6d. Iron ore extraction totalled 13,494,658 tons and Scotland produced over three million tons of shale oil, each ton yielding twenty gallons of oil.

But for most employees, work was a constant battle between wages and prices. In March the National Association of Unions in the Textile Trade, representing about a quarter of a million workers in the woollen and worsted textile industries of Yorkshire, Lancashire, Derbyshire and Leicester, wrote to the employers:

> We are directed by your employees to draw your attention to the fact that the cost of living has now risen to 90 percent, and the cost of food, when obtainable, to 113 percent over the prices ruling in July 1914. It is pointed out that there are no indications that there is a general falling-off in profits; on the contrary, we are pleased to observe that generally, profits are increasing. We are therefore directed to make application for a substantial advance in wages to all operatives, male and female.

They asked for a wartime bonus of 72 percent for day workers, and 61 percent and 58 percent for men and women piece-workers. The employers couldn't make any promise until the Government gave approval and the problem was referred to arbitration at Bradford Town Hall. The workers won their case and got their bonus.

By mid-1918 most of the local mills were still heavily engaged on government work - blankets, uniforms - not just for the British services but for many foreign governments too. Trade with France was still good but there was some slackening off of exports to the United States which held out the promise of releasing machinery for cheap domestic tweed goods. At the end of March, Sir Charles Sykes, Director of Wool Textile Production, was able to announce that the 6s 9d cloth for men's ready-made suits, the 5s 5d cloth for boy's suits and the 7s 9d cloth for Scotch overcoating was now available. As a bonus, about 1,000,000 yards of the expensive 9s 10d blue and black worsted could be made into one and a third million ready-to-wear suits.

Bank Bottom Mills in Marsden had welcomed some very distinguished guests - King George and Queen Mary visited the mill on their way to Huddersfield and were shown finished khaki and grey cloth, some of the nine million yards that had been made at that mill alone since the beginning of the war. The King and Queen were then escorted between the deafening looms until the engine was slowed, the noise quietened and the weavers doffed their hats.

Meltham Military Hospital - 25 pairs socks.

Miss Weston's Sailors' Home - 50 pairs socks, 10 scarves, 11 pairs mittens; total 61.

2nd Lieut. C.S. Floyd - 30 pairs socks.

Holmfirth Auxiliary Hospital - 12 shirts, 37 pairs socks, 6 bed jackets, 14 night shirts, 15 many tailed bandages, 50 roller bandages; total 134.

British Red Cross Society - 6 shirts, 6 pyjamas, 14 pairs hospital socks, 3 pairs bed socks; total 29.

Capt. Keith Sykes, M.C. - 80 pairs socks.

Lieut. Gerard Shaw - 30 pairs socks, 20 pairs mittens, 10 scarves; total 60.

2nd Lieut. Norman Butterworth - 24 pairs socks, 13 pairs mittens, 12 helmets, 12 scarves, 6 pairs gloves; total 67

Lady Smith Dorien - 70 hospital bags.

Lieut. Brown, Holme Valley Battery - 50 pairs socks.

Royal Mission to Seamen - 42 pairs of socks, 17 scarves, 15 pairs mittens, 5 pairs mine sweepers gloves; total 79.

Soldiers at the Front and Home - 111 shirts, 227 pairs socks, 66 scarves and helmets, 52 pairs mittens and gloves, 1 vest, 1 pair pants; total 458

2nd Lieut. Norman Lawton - 30 pairs socks, 2 pairs gloves, 20 pairs mittens, 6 scarves; total 58

Sir W.E. Ward, D.G.V.O. - 25 many tailed bandages, 100 roller bandages, 20 pairs socks, 12 pairs gloves, 22 pairs mittens, 70 scarves; total 249

The Navy League - 6 shirts, 24 pairs socks, 6 pairs pyjamas, 16 scarves, 6 helmet scarves, 6 pairs mittens, 6 pairs hospital slippers, 112 roller bandages, 9 packets hospital dressings; total 191.

Articles sent away — — — 1641
Sent away before — — — 5684

Total — — — 7325

S.H. SYKES,        President
R. BLANCHE MELLOR
BERTHA SYKES      Joint Hon. Secretaries
TERESA TINKER     Hon. Treasurer

In Marsden there were constant complaints that street lighting hadn't been restored despite the fact that the danger from Zeppelin raids was now non-existent. Aeroplanes might just penetrate as far inland as the West Riding but it was considered doubtful, and even if they did get that far, there was a well organised body of special constables, volunteers, ambulance workers and others who could assist in extinguishing lights. Slaithwaite Council had managed to keep the light outside the Star Hotel illuminated for pedestrians so why couldn't there be a similar one in Marsden, they asked.

There were numerous other groups involved in making the less official parts of soldier's uniforms. These were the various ladies groups of the valley that were involved in the knitting and making of 'comforts' for local serving men and they had been even busier than ever in 1917. They proudly published their accounts and lists of items and their assorted destinations (see previous page).

# THE WAR GOES ON
## Re-Organisation and Disruption

In Westminster, and largely unknown to the good people of Holmfirth and Huddersfield, there was serious disagreement between the military and the politicians on how the war should be conducted in 1918.

Three issues arose in January that had far-reaching consequences for the British Army. The first was the difficulties caused by the alarming losses sustained throughout the previous year - British casualties had reached almost 900,000 in 1917; secondly, there was the growing worry of the threat posed by the transfer of German forces from the Russian to the Western Front and the imminent assault; lastly, there was the major problem of the shortening of the line held by the French (their losses too had been severe in 1917 and some elements of their army were on the edge of mutiny) and its takeover by the British - another 28 miles of fighting front had to be manned and defended.

The Army, in its proposals for action in 1918, asked the Government for 615,000 extra men. Lloyd-George, who disagreed with General Haig on almost every aspect of the Army's conduct of the war, and who chaired the Cabinet Committee on Manpower allocated them only 100,000. These were Category 'A' men and, to soften the blow, he added 100,000 men of lower medical grades.

> The British Army had of course been fighting hard on the offensive all through 1917; but as it was to stand on the defensive for the early part of 1918, the Committee considered that the military estimate was likely to prove unduly large.
>
> Lloyd-George.

The Navy, the Air Force, food production, ship building, munitions, timber-felling and the provision of cold-storage accommodation would all have priority for manpower over the Army.

Moreover, the Committee insisted that if the British Expeditionary Force in France and Belgium was undermanned as General Haig claimed (which it, frankly, doubted) then it should be re-structured instead. Over-riding the angry and vehement objections of General Haig and the Army

Council, Lloyd-George demanded that British divisions should be reduced from twelve to nine battalions and brigades from four to three battalions. Two out of the five cavalry divisions were completely disbanded. Tellingly, none of the governments of Australia, New Zealand or Canada would have any part of this scheme and kept their forces intact.

The consequence was that, at the precise moment that the German forces were preparing for a massive attack on British lines (they would attack in March), the Army was thrown into the chaos of wholesale reorganisation. Divisions, Brigades and Battalions were diluted, disbanded or amalgamated - the process took months.

One of the first units to be broken up was the 1/5th Battalion, Duke of Wellington's Regiment. These included those few men who were left from the group of Territorial volunteers who had marched from the Drill Hall and up Station Road, Holmfirth to go to war in August 1914. Keith Sykes, a young lieutenant that evening in 1914 and in charge of the men of 'F' Company, the Holmfirth men, (the designation was changed to the more normal A, B, C and D companies later), was still with the battalion as Adjutant and a Captain and would survive the war. His close friend and fellow lieutenant that day in 1914, 2nd Lieutenant Edgar Clapham would not. Lieutenant Clapham served for four years with the Duke's and was killed on November 5th, 1918, one week before the end of the war. His mother asked for the phrase 'He laid all on the altar of duty, his life' to be carved on his headstone at Awoingt British Cemetery, near Cambrai. After four years of war he was still only twenty-three when he was killed.

On the evening of January 27th they returned from a long, cold day re-building fortified outposts to find instructions to send 26 officers and 640 other ranks to other battalions. The Orderly Room and Headquarters staff worked throughout the night and for the following two days to complete all the necessary arrangements:12 officers and 234 men to 1/4th Battalion; 8 officers and 195 men to 1/6th Battalion; 8 officers and 172 men to 1/7th Battalion, leaving a nucleus of 13 officers and 200 other ranks who were sent to join 2/5th Battalion. The Brigade was reduced from 4 to 3 battalions and the Commanding Officer of 49th Division came to say 'goodbye' to the whole battalion on parade.

Two days later, the 2/6th 'Dukes' was broken up and 10 officers and 220 soldiers were sent to the 2/4th Battalion. On the same day in the West Yorkshire Regiment, the 2/5th welcomed 7 officers and 150 men from the 2/6th Battalion, which was then disbanded. The pattern was being repeated throughout the British Army, all Divisions being reduced from 12 battalions to 9. In effect, the army was now expected to defend a longer line with fewer men, and moreover, defend that line against an all-out German offensive expected sometime in the early spring.

So the men trained when they could, but above all they laboured. When they were not in the line they provided working parties. They dug railway cuttings, laid rails, built roads, improved trenches and dug-outs and constructed communication systems.

There were no enslaved populations who could be turned on to such work. For months before the attack the troops were digging incessantly. Indeed the remark has been made that their military efficiency was impaired by the constant navvy work upon which they were employed.

Sir A. Conan Doyle - The British Campaign in France and Flanders: January to July 1918

We were in the reserve trenches; of course when a battalion is in reserve it has to do all fatigues for those up in the front line. We went one night to carry rations and water etc., for our comrades up in the front. The weather was extremely wet on this particular night, and we were many times up to the middle in water in the trenches going up, and we were wet through and through, and of course we had to sleep in our wet clothes, as we have no suit to change like we have in civil life. However, we accomplished our task, and the next night we were on the same job.

Now this night was brilliantly fine, with a good moon, but the communication trench was practically impassable, so we went over the top up the front line, to within thirty yards of Fritz. All went well until we were within fifteen yards of our journey's end when the ever-watching Boche must have spotted us. You talk about shells! He put them all around us and scattered us to a trench - which was about four feet deep in water - for cover. We had six men wounded and one poor sergeant killed. The latter, by the way, was with us for the first time since being very badly wounded last April. Out of these six wounded men there were three or four stretcher cases which had to be carried right back. And let me here tell you that although we were all dead beat, still there were quite enough volunteers to help our unfortunate comrades to safety. And I must give a word of praise here to our enemy, as it was broad daylight when the last man was carried out, and to his credit he did not fire a single shot at those who were carrying the stretcher.

Soldier's letter home, Holmfirth Express

91

# Russia leaves and America joins.

'War is a disciplinary action by God to educate mankind'

Kaiser Wilhelm, February 10, 1918

The first three months of 1918 saw momentous events happening on both fighting fronts - the Western and the Eastern. As one ally, Russia, abandoned the conflict, another ally, America, joined it.

## Russia leaves and…..

By February 17, the long-drawn out peace negotiations between Germany and Russia had broken down as the Russians decided that Germany's demands were far too harsh and couldn't be met. The Germans immediately prepared to continue the war and fifty-two divisions crossed the ceasefire line and moved eastwards, following the main Russian railways.

> Tomorrow we are going to start hostilities against the Bolsheviks. No other way out is possible, otherwise these brutes will wipe up the Ukrainians, the Finns, and the Balts, and then quickly get together a new revolutionary army and turn the whole of Europe into a pig-sty.
>
> General Hoffmann, diary entry.

Three days later the Germans entered Minsk, taking 9,000 Russians prisoner. German troops described their advance as being like civilians on a holiday excursion rather than an invading army, using the Russian railways to advance step by step, meeting no resistance.

> It is the most comical war I have ever known. We put a handful of infantrymen with machine guns and one gun on a train and push them off to the next station; they take it, make prisoners of the Bolsheviks, pick up a few more troops and go on. This proceeding has, at any rate, the charm of novelty.
>
> General Hoffmann, diary entry.

In two weeks of fighting the Germans advanced to within eighty-five miles of Petrograd, took 63,000 prisoners and captured 2,600 artillery pieces and 5,000 machine guns, weapons that would be used later against the Allies when the Germans attacked on the Western Front.

Lenin and Trotsky finally gave in and wrote to the Germans agreeing to all their demands and conditions, but Germany, seeing the territorial disintegration of Russia that was taking place all around them, simply demanded more. On February 24th, during a bitter and argumentative session of Lenin's ruling council, Lenin threatened to resign unless the council accepted Germany's latest ultimatum. Eventually they agreed and he won the vote 116 to 85. He then had to persuade the Central Committee. This time it was even closer - 7 votes to 6. One of the men watching and listening that day was a newcomer, Joseph Stalin.

Russia conceded vast areas of the western and southern parts of the country to Germany so that they could formally withdraw from the European war in order for the Bolsheviks to concentrate on the internal and bloody civil conflict that followed. The two largest combatant groups in this purely Russian war were the Red Army Bolsheviks, led by Lenin, and the White Army, made up of monarchists, capitalists, and alternative socialist factions. To complicate matters, there were also rival militant socialist groups, and a Green Army and a Black Army of anarchists, all of whom fought both the Red and the White Armies. To complicate matters even further, eight foreign nations intervened in the conflict, including the Americans.

Gradually, the Red Army gained the upper hand, defeating the White Army in Ukraine and in Siberia by 1919, and the remnants of their opponents in Crimea in 1920. Minor skirmishes continued for another two or three years until the Bolsheviks felt strong enough to declare the formation of the Soviet Union. Even then resistance in Central Asia wasn't completely crushed until 1934.

There is no agreement on the eventual butcher's bill, which has been calculated as somewhere between 7,000,000 and 12,000,000 people, most of them civilians.

## .....America joins.

On Saturday, February 23, 1918, two American officers and twenty four of their men volunteered to take part in a French raid on German trenches at Chevregny, south of Laon. The London Times newspaper later called it, 'one of the dates that will always be remembered in the history of the war.' The raid lasted half an hour and resulted in the capture of twenty-five of the enemy. It was the first time that American troops had been involved in offensive action against the Germans. Three days later while observing a similar French raid, the Chief-of-Staff of the American 42nd Division got carried away with the occasion and joined the French troops in their attack. He was awarded the Croix de Guerre, the first member of the American Expeditionary Force to win an award. His name was Colonel Douglas MacArthur.

The Americans had originally planned to have one million armed troops in Europe by the summer of 1918, but quickly realised that the plan was far too ambitious. The most that could be hoped for was 525,000 men by May, but even then there were not enough available ships to supply and feed them adequately until early 1919. For the British it was a bitter disappointment. Lloyd-George pleaded with the United States to send as many troops as they possibly could and immediately incorporate them into British and French units. General Pershing, Commander of the American Expeditionary Force, who was committed to keeping the American force as a complete and separate fighting unit, was adamant that this would not happen. In the event, he compromised slightly and agreed that four regiments of black soldiers should serve alongside the French, which they did for the rest of the war.

On January 18, 1918, the first full American Division took over a section of the front line in the St. Mihiel Salient but was not allowed to initiate any offensive action. The Germans, meanwhile, launched raids and ambushes on the Americans and killed, wounded and captured a number of them. Propaganda was used extensively. The German wireless news broadcast the result of the first interrogations of captured American troops.

> They are strong fellows but do not seem to have much desire to fight. To them it is an enterprise undertaken by New York financiers. They hate but respect the English. With the French they are on good terms. They have not the slightest idea of military operations and seem stupid and fatalistic in comparison with the war-accustomed Frenchman. They were glad to escape further fighting.
> French officers do not conceal their disillusionment over the value of American troops who were entirely incapable of carrying out independent operations.

# March 21st. The Germans attack.

> Our overall position requires the earliest possible blow, if possible at the end of February, or the beginning of March, before the Americans can throw strong forces into the scales.

> Ludendorff in an address to German army commanders,
> November 11, 1917

Shortly before dawn on the morning of March 21st, without warning, 6,473 German guns (including 2,435 heavy pieces) opened fire on the southern part of the British front line south of Arras. Their destructive power was augmented by 2,532 mortars and a storm of gas shells - in the first two weeks of the assault some two million gas shells alone were fired on a 40 mile front of the British lines. In the opening barrage lasting some five hours the guns fired 1.16 million shells of high explosive compared with the 1.5 million shells fired by the British over seven days at the Somme. The first targets were British artillery and command posts followed quickly by the British front line before lifting to a rolling barrage as the infantry attacked. It lasted just a few hours but it severely damaged the British ability to respond.

The opening barrage mixed high explosive with phosgene shells and a newly developed lachrymatory gas which was so intense in its effect that men would tear off their gas masks to relieve the pain and to ease the irritation to their eyes only to expose their lungs. In the air above it all, the Germans fielded 361 fighter and bomber aircraft.

It was one of the most intense barrages of the whole war and in just a few hours it had blown holes in the defensive line, holes which allowed German infantry to pour through. By the end of the first day, the British Fifth Army, commanded by General Gough, had lost 600 guns and sustained 38,512 casualties including 21,000 soldiers taken as prisoners while being driven back four and a half miles. During the following five days they were forced back more than forty miles and twenty-five of the defending sixty British divisions had been decimated.

The 16th Battalion Manchester Regiment under the command of Lieutenant-Colonel Wilfrith Elstob, were part of the British front line at a place appropriately named Manchester Hill when the attack began. The order quickly went out that the position must be defended to the last round and to the last man. By 11.30am the Germans had broken through all around them and they were surrounded. Wilfrith moved from position to position encouraging his men and at one point was seen driving off a German attack on his own using hand grenades and his service revolver. During the afternoon, as the Germans mounted a large attack he was slightly wounded, and then during the next few hours was wounded three more times, once by the nearby explosion of a shell that blew him five yards through the air. Finally, with sheer weight of numbers, the Germans broke into the Manchester's trenches and the carnage degenerated into hand to hand fighting. Wilfrith was shot dead in the act of throwing a hand grenade and the surviving members of the 16th Battalion surrendered at around 4pm.

No-one knew what happened to his body. It wasn't until September the following year, 1919, that the Army finally accepted that 'considering the length of time that has elapsed' he was dead. His life insurance company took another twelve months to reach the same conclusion.

Lieutenant-Colonel Wilfrith Elstob was posthumously awarded the Victoria Cross on June 9, 1919.

For most conspicuous bravery, devotion to duty and self-sacrifice during operations at Manchester Redoubt, near St. Quentin, on the 21 March 1918. During the preliminary bombardment he encouraged his men in the posts in the Redoubt by frequent visits, and when repeated attacks developed controlled the defence at the points threatened, giving personal support with revolver, rifle and bombs. Single-handed he repulsed one bombing assault driving back the enemy and inflicting severe casualties. Later, when ammunition was required, he made several journeys under severe fire in order to replenish the supply. Throughout the day Lieutenant-Colonel Elstob, although twice wounded, showed the most fearless disregard of his own safety, and by his encouragement and noble example inspired his command to the fullest degree. The Manchester Redoubt was surrounded in the first wave of the enemy attack, but by means of the buried cable Lieutenant-Colonel Elstob was able to assure his Brigade Commander that 'The Manchester Regiment will defend Manchester Hill to the last.' Sometime after this, the post was overcome by vastly superior forces, and this very gallant officer was killed in the final assault, having maintained to the end the duty which he had impressed on his men – namely, 'Here we fight, and here we die.' He set throughout the highest example of valour, determination, endurance and fine soldierly bearing.

It was the worst defeat of any army, Allied or Central Powers, on the Western Front up to that date. But it was much more than just a military defeat. Since 1914 the Germans had been on the defensive in France and Belgium and had been content for the last three years for the British and the French to exhaust themselves and sacrifice their troops in a series of assaults which rarely made any strategic advance. Now suddenly and dramatically, within just a few days, the Germans had broken through prepared lines of defence - lines which themselves had been modelled on German examples - with what appeared to be consummate ease. The blow was as much psychological as military and the British Army reeled.

## How had it happened ?

As the fighting in Russia came to an end, Germany realised that she would be  in a position to take the offensive on the Western Front for the first time since the invasion of France and Belgium in 1914. With the Americans beginning to build up their forces in Europe, time was pressing and if they were to defeat the British and win the war the attack needed to be done quickly. Planning for this massive assault began in earnest in 1917.

This time the focus of the assault would be the British, not the French. The British were seen as the softer option, not as clever in military matters as the French and less committed to holding ground which didn't belong to them.

Germany's previous hope for victory in 1917 had been pinned on the U-boat offensive and the adoption of unrestricted submarine warfare. Holtzendorff, one of just six Grand Admirals of the Imperial German Navy, had argued that if the U-boats could sink 600,000 tons of British shipping each month for five successive months, Britain would be on the verge of starvation and would be compelled to seek peace. They achieved their target, indeed they exceeded it - they sank 860,334 tons in April and again in May and June. But by then, British countermeasures, including the use of the convoy system, had turned the tide against them and the American Navy was now involved. More British destroyers were at sea, and destroyers carried wirelesses which meant that they were able to receive the latest and most up-to-date intelligence on the movement of German submarines (British Intelligence had cracked the German naval coding system some time earlier).

Holtzendorff had gambled that the U-boat threat would deter neutral shipping from trading with Britain, forgetting that London controlled the world wide shipping insurance market and determined freight rates. Despite the dangers, world shipping would be forced to follow the money which was controlled by the British. Neutral shipping began instead to limit supplies to Germany's own trading partners, exacerbating the shortages in Austria-Hungary and Romania.

The naval plan to win the war had failed. Now, in 1918, it was the German Army's turn again. This was the first major battle on the Western Front for the new high command of Generals Hindenburg and Ludendorff, fresh from their Russian victories, and many thought that they underestimated the difficulties of fighting in France. As Crown Prince Rupprecht, commander of the army group earmarked to make the assault, pointed out to them, 'fighting the Russians was not the same thing as taking on the British or the French.'

Germany had made some tentative peace overtures the previous year to President Wilson, the American leader, but these had foundered on Germany's insistence on retaining their occupation of Belgium and Alsace-Lorraine in any peace agreement, something Britain and France would never agree to. In fact, President Wilson had ruled out even talking to Germany until they deposed the Kaiser and embraced democracy.

But, incredibly, German military High Command had already begun planning for the war following this one! The plan, still in its very early stages, was to fight the present war to a stalemate, with all protagonists exhausted, but leaving Germany in occupation and control of Belgium. German military forces in Belgium would be the key to threatening Calais and Paris. Only thus, said the High Command, would the Western Allies be deterred from attacking Germany in any future war.

And now, faced with the failure of the Navy to bring Britain to her knees, the fact that the Americans were arriving in force, a waning industrial base, allies that were close to collapse and with reserves of manpower running low, Germany had one last chance for victory.

Even then the political aims were rather vague. Ludendorff wanted an offensive to force Lloyd George and Clemenceau, Prime Minister of France, to the negotiating table before the Americans arrived in strength. Even if the offensive failed, he argued, it would encourage the army to try again in the next war, and for that he was willing to lose 'a million men in the effort.' (Crutwell, History of the First World War.)

The place to attack, as all the German 'Westerners' agreed, was in Flanders, due west, aimed at cutting off the British in the Ypres salient and threatening the channel ports. The British Army would be compelled to retreat to defend the ports, without which they couldn't continue the war in France.

But Flanders was too wet in the early part of the year and the attack couldn't wait. Ludendorff looked further south, from Arras to St Quentin, the old battlefield of the Somme. The difficulty here was that the Germans would first have to attack south-west to eliminate the Cambrai salient and then re-organise themselves in mid-battle, change direction and attack north-west towards Arras and Vimy Ridge.

Arras was too strongly defended by the British so Ludendorff decided to strike in the less densely garrisoned section of the line between Cambrai and St Quentin. Here the land was dry and flat and though there were no important objectives to be taken it would be relatively easy for him to move his forces north-westwards to divide the British from the French and push them towards the coast. The irony of the strategy was that it repeated the same error that the British had made in 1916 on the very same territory - that is to attack into a featureless void, and when finally halted, to be in possession of land with no strategic or worthwhile significance.

Tactically the Germans were on much surer ground. The High Command - the OHL - distilled the lessons learned from recent successes at Caporetto, Riga and Cambrai and published them at the beginning of the year in a new manual *The Attack in Position Warfare*.

Every officer down to battalion commander was expected to have read the book and be able to put its 'rules' into practice. These advocated 'eating through' the enemy defences, keeping the opposing troops off-balance, constantly pressing the attack and always being ready to reinforce success. There were instructions to the artillery - they were to surprise the enemy, to neutralise and disrupt communications and counter-batteries, and to provide a creeping barrage for the infantry to follow. The infantry should set the pace of the advance with front units pressing forward regardless of casualties.

Ludendorff recognised the poor quality of some of the troops under his command and viewed many of them as being little better than 'a militia'. Some fifty-six divisions were brought out of the line during the winter of 1917-1918 for training, with the emphasis less on the skills of the infantryman as on the morale of the individual. Intensive training lasted three weeks, covering basic drill to re-emphasise discipline, marksmanship, fast, long-distance marching for fitness, fighting on the move and storming mocked-up enemy positions under live fire.

Not all his soldiers were good enough, fit enough or young enough to be stormtroopers leading the attack, so those that were - about a quarter of the younger and fitter men aged between twenty-five to thirty-five - were selected and organised into 'attack divisions'. These men received priority in rations, provisions, equipment and training and were instructed to fight in small units of nine riflemen or light machine-gunners under the command of an N.C.O. This was the Gruppe or section and they would be followed in the attack by more specialised squads carrying flame-throwers and heavier machine-guns. All soldiers of the German Army were expected to have read and to be familiar with the newly revised *Training Manual for Troops in War* which explained assault squad methods.

There was no shortage of rifles and ammunition and all stormtroopers received the newest and latest equipment. Priority was placed on the excellent MG08/15 light machine-gun and the heavier MG08. Attacking troops carried the Minenwerfer - light mortars - to destroy any determined resistance and they were followed by units carrying medium mortars. Aircraft production had lagged behind schedule but there were still more than double the numbers available during 1917, and some 2,000 were available for active service on the Western Front. Moreover, most of them were brand new, made of metal and single winged. Their crews were trained in ground attack as well as reconnaissance.

What they didn't have was tanks which might have made the breakthrough even easier with fewer losses but Ludendorff made no apology for the lack of them. He was sceptical about their usefulness and wanted production concentrated on other weapons. Neither was the German Army equipped for mobile warfare despite forward movement forming the core of the plan of attack. It owned 23,000 lorries but very few of them had the advantage of rubber-tyred wheels. Their steel wheels simply chewed up the road surface and eventually made them impassable. The Allies, in contrast, had over 100,000 lorries, all of them with rubber tyres.

Morale boomed among German soldiers as they switched from defence to attack mode and with the end of the war in sight. Troops were told they were going to win the war with this attack and that marching west was the quickest way home. What they weren't told was that their High Command described this operation as 'a last card'. If it failed, said Ludendorff, Germany must go under. It was a huge gamble, the last roll of the dice.

German attacking forces were increased with the transfer of troops from the East, where armies were stripped of their best units, including the guards divisions, and all men under the age of thirty-five as well as most of their horses. Eight German divisions were transferred from Italy and contingents came from the Macedonian Front. For the first time, Austro-Hungarian forces moved to the Western Front. Germany was also able to call upon the 1899 conscript class which came into the line early in 1918. And the war industries - the vital war industries - had been subjected to a 'comb-out' to make up for the losses in manpower. Reserves were being called up at the rate of 58,000 trained and 21,000 untrained men each month.

On March 21st the German Army in the West numbered 136,618 officers, 3,438,288 men and 710,827 horses. Their total of 191 divisions faced an Allied force of 178. For the first time since 1914 they held numerical superiority.

Based on their successes in Russia, Ludendorff and Hindenburg adopted a 'let's attack - see what happens - and then exploit any opportunities' formula.

There was no decision made as to the goals of the battle when the breakthrough occurred, or, in the event of failure, a contingency plan. When his army commanders questioned the lack of operational or strategic orders Luddendorff stated, 'I object to the word 'operation'. We will punch a hole into their line. For the rest, we shall see. We also did it this way in Russia!'

Considering the stakes involved - failure could lead to total and utter defeat - it was a high risk strategy.

# Operation Michael.

The first wave of waiting *sturmtruppen* left their trenches at 8.40am and, taking every advantage of the low-lying fog which obscured the battle-field, moved through the gaps in the British machine-gun posts. 'We honestly could not see each other, it was that thick with the German guns and the fog,' wrote Corporal Ted Gale.

The main blow of Operation Michael (named after the patron saint of Germany) fell on the British Fifth Army, commanded by General Sir Hubert Gough. Gough's army lay either side of the Somme river and was attacked by forty three German assault divisions of the Second and Eighteenth Armies. A further nineteen divisions of the Seventeenth Army attacked further north on the British Third Army sector.

Hindenburg and Ludendorff had gathered their most capable and in-novative army commanders to lead the assault. The Seventeenth Army, under General Otto von Below, who had triumphed at Caporetto, at-tacked towards Bapaume; the Second Army, led by General Georg von der Marwitz, who had thrown back the British at Cambrai, went south-west towards Albert, and the Eighteenth Army with the victor at Riga in command, General von Hutier moved forward from a base-line at St Quentin.

By now the war had settled into a conflict dominated by trenches and fortifications. Artillery had become the king of the battlefield. No at-tack could be made on enemy lines unless those lines and the protecting barbed wire had first been pulverised. No attack could succeed unless the opposing troops in their trenches had either been eliminated or shocked into stupefaction. No attackers were able to advance and occupy the enemy's lines against unsuppressed machine-guns without suffering cat-astrophic losses. Only artillery could fulfil all those tasks and yet the very destructive power of high explosive meant that any attacking force would struggle to advance over a destroyed terrain and would find it al-most impossible to maintain communications or move supplies forward quickly enough to break through enemy lines before the enemy had time to 'plug the gap'.

After the fluid battlefields of 1914 had settled into static warfare the technology of defence became superior to the technology of offence. And there it stayed until March 21st, 1918.

What the Germans re-discovered with Operation Michael was the power of the infantryman. The Stormtroopers were a force to be reckoned with, aided undoubtably by the ground fog and by the fact that the British hadn't had enough time to improve the trench lines recently taken over from the French. Well trained, encouraged to use their own initiative, equipped with a formidable array of portable firepower, including bangalore-torpedoes and flame throwers, they were able to deal with any strongpoint that threatened their advance without having to wait for artillery to deal with the problem. They were trained to attack in small, mobile units instead of en masse and infiltrate Allied lines, bypassing centres of strong resistance. They were not to worry about whether or not they had support on their flanks, their job was to penetrate 'quickly and deeply' into the rear areas. Success was dependent on a continuous forward movement which would dislocate and disrupt the whole of the enemy's defensive system.

Private Knott of South Lane, Holmfirth, serving with 61st Battery Machine-Gun Corps, managed to get a postcard home to his parents some time after the battle:

> Myself and all our gun team have been taken prisoners and all are in Germany. We were captured at _____ on March 21st. Most of our company have been either captured or killed, including nearly all the officers. The morning we were captured was very foggy, and we could not see many yards in front of us. Despite this, we fought hard until we were surrounded by the enemy and forced to give in. I thank God I have been spared my life, but it has been a very near thing. I am going on very nicely, for we have been treated very well indeed.

Neither did the Germans have to overcome the difficulties of a blasted landscape. Bruchmuller's artillery barrage was massively intense but short-lived and many of the shells fired contained gas rather than high explosive. It was a form of blitzkrieg but without the tanks. And it worked.

The British had known for months that an attack was coming and that it would be against them rather than the French. General Haig's biggest fear was that the Germans would attack around Ypres in Flanders where room for retreat was limited and any mass movement to the rear by his forces could result in a catastrophic defeat for the Allies. He recognised the weaknesses in the juncture between the British and French lines in the south but reasoned that, if forced to, General Gough could retreat slowly and wait for French reinforcements before the Germans could reach the vital transport and communications hub of Amiens.

Taking all this into account, Haig distributed his forces: starting in the north and working south - Second Army with 14 divisions defended 23 miles of front; First Army with 16 divisions covered 33 miles of Front; Third Army, 14 divisions, held 28 miles; leaving General Gough and Fifth Army with just 12 divisions to defend 42 miles of front-line trenches. Moreover, a good part of these lines had just been taken over from the French and were found to be in poor order, the British were unfamiliar with the terrain, and communications with their French neighbours were patchy at best and poorly co-ordinated. 'Never before had the British line been held with so few men and so few guns to the mile; and the reserves were wholly insufficient.' (British Official History)

The Fifth Army was recognised as being the weak point of the British line, though that particular piece of military knowledge was shared only by those at the top of the High Command, the rest of the army were left in ignorance. When Gough's new front was formed in late 1917 and then extended southwards in January 1918, divisions were transferred from the northern sector. Not one of those divisions came from the elite Empire armies - the Australians, Canadians, New Zealanders or South Africans, neither were there any Regular troops or any of the First-Line Territorial divisions. Instead, his command was composed largely of New Army and Second-Line Territorial men, backed up by a few cavalry divisions who were unused and untried infantrymen. The defence system was largely unfinished and undeveloped. Worst of all, Gough was out of favour with General Haig and had only just escaped being ordered home to England as a failure. Haig regarded the Fifth Army as low priority and expendable in the forthcoming battle.

The British and the French had spent the last four years concentrating on offensive actions. The move to defence wasn't just a matter of readjusting the trench lines - though that in itself was a mammoth task - it was also a change in mindset and tactics that required thorough training and preparation.

British troops didn't think defensively; they had never been encouraged to do so. Most of the front lines that they held at the time were the limits of previous offensives. Wherever they had been stopped by the enemy became the next front. A new military philosophy was called for.

Haig decided on a system of defence in depth as used by the Germans at Passchendaele, knowing just how difficult an obstacle that had proved to be when attacked by his own forces the previous year.

Under this new system, what had always been the front defence line became the 'Forward Zone'. This was essentially an outpost line, held with just enough men to force the Germans to bombard it and be forced to assault it with attacking troops. The defenders, meanwhile, would concentrate on inflicting the maximum number of casualties before withdrawing to the main defensive line, which was to be called the 'Battle Zone'. This was anything between 2,000 - 3,000 yards behind the outpost line and almost as deep.

British artillery and machine-guns were 'zeroed-in' on the terrain between the two lines and would be expected to destroy any forces that attempted to cross it. Which might, of course, include German tanks. To counter that particular threat minefields were created using 'toffee apples' - the spherical, 60-pound trench mortar bombs - which were buried just under the soil where they would be activated by the weight of the tank. As an added precaution, batteries of 18-pounder field guns were hidden just behind the front line to act as anti-tank weapons, and finally, ditches were dug across the battlefield wide enough to prevent any tank being able to cross them. That was the theory.

Unfortunately, the construction of fortified forward redoubts and designated battle zones, the siting of huge quantities of barbed wire, and digging miles of obstacles proved too much for the limited amount of labour available and most of the lines were unfinished when the battle began. Many observers looked back at Lloyd-George's decision to withhold troop reinforcements earlier in the year.

Soldiers too had to learn an unfamiliar method of fighting. Defence in depth entailed basing relatively small numbers of men in the front lines, who would be trained to give ground and draw attacking troops into killing zones where they would be destroyed by heavy artillery fire and carefully sited machine-guns.

> Depth in defensive organisation is of the first importance...The economy of forces in the front line system is most important in order that as many men as possible may be available in reserve. The front line should generally be held as an outpost line covering the main line of resistance a few hundred yards in the rear.

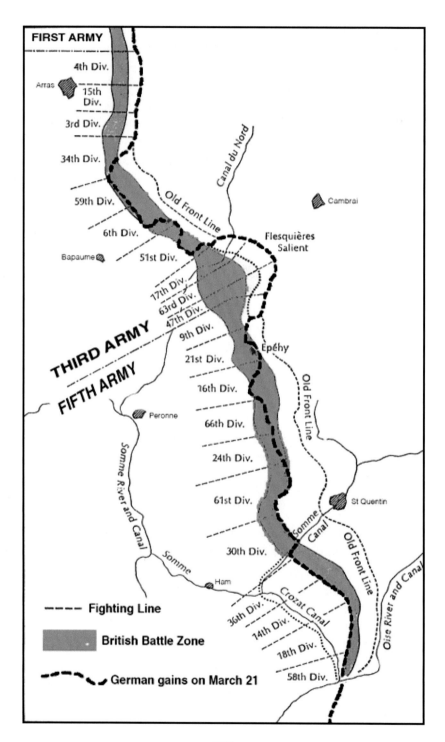

FIRST ARMY

4th Div.

Arras

15th
Div.

3rd Div.

34th Div.

59th Div.

6th Div.

Bapaume

51st Div.

Canal du Nord

Cambrai

Old Front Line

Flesquières
Salient

17th Div.

63rd Div.

47th Div.

THIRD ARMY

FIFTH ARMY

9th Div.

21st Div.

Epéhy

16th Div.

Peronne

66th Div.

Old Front Line

24th Div.

61st Div.

St Quentin

Somme

Canal

30th Div.

Somme River and Canal

Old Front Line

Somme

Ham

36th Div.

Crozat Canal

Oise River and Canal

14th Div.

– – – – Fighting Line

18th Div.

British Battle Zone

58th Div.

German gains on March 21

107

The Forward Zone, protected by barbed wire was little more than a number of scattered outposts and trenches, sometimes manned by a platoon of 40 to 50 men, but more often by a section of 12 to 15 soldiers.

Just behind the front line but well forward of the Battle Zone was a series of strongpoints, or 'redoubts'. These were designed as all-round defensive positions, usually sited on some raised natural feature and bristling with riflemen, bombers and Lewis-gunners.

Each Brigade in the Fifth Army sector would normally base one battalion in the Forward Zone, one in the Battle Zone and one in Reserve. Half of the battalion in the Forward Zone would occupy the front line outposts and the other half the much larger redoubts. Battalion headquarters would normally be positioned behind the Battle Zone, which meant, of course, that almost as soon as an artillery barrage began (particularly one as intense as March 21st) all effective communication with forward units would be lost.

Control of the coming battle would devolve on the men in charge of the redoubts or the outposts - the Company Captains, or the platoon officers, (usually young 2nd Lieutenants not long out of school) or sergeants and even corporals.

No-one fully explained to these men that their positions were never intended to be permanent. The new defensive philosophy stated that as soon as the initial German assault had been 'blunted' i.e. enough of the enemy had been killed or stopped, then an orderly withdraw could take place to the next prepared positions. What no-one really thought about - or if they did, they kept it to themselves - was what would happen if their redoubts were surrounded and isolated by infiltrating enemy soldiers. Their only chance of survival then was if counter-attacks were quickly mounted from the Battle Zone to their rear. Unfortunately, the new defensive policy made no provision for counter-attacks to recover any territory lost in the Forward Zone or to rescue trapped units.

By default, the men facing the Germans in the initial stages of the battle were expendable.

I was very worried about the scanty way the front line was held. The trenches were poor and shallow and the wiring in front consisted of a single strand of barbed wire held by screw-iron stakes here and there and, in stretches, this was on the ground forming no defence at all. All we had in the company front-line trench was a pair of sentries about every hundred yards on a long stretch of front. To impress the enemy of our great strength we had orders that the officer on trench duty was to take a Lewis gunner with him and put the gun over the parapet and fire a few rounds every twenty-five yards or so. He would go one way and then travel back a few yards, fire again, and then move once again and repeat the performance. I do not think the enemy was very impressed.

Captain E.P. Hall, 2nd Leinsters

German units in their own front line were told nothing of the impending attack in case they were taken prisoner but, secretly, the Germans had been preparing for months.

From March 1st nearly a million men were moved to their allotted sectors opposite the British Front line from their rest and training areas along the whole of the Western Front. They were packed into every available building in dozens of villages in the German-occupied areas; guns, vehicles and horses were hidden in forests and woods and all movement was forbidden during the day. Pioneers and engineers strengthened bridges, improved roads and built airfields - all in secret. The zones to be attacked had previously been occupied by the Germans themselves and had already been fully surveyed so that all road and rail junctions, main trench lines and likely positions of command posts were known and pinpointed. Artillery firing plans were able to be calculated using maps, no need for preliminary targeting which might give the game away. By night, huge assembly shelters were dug in the front lines to accommodate the thousands of attacking infantry, and storage was found for hundreds of wooden bridges which would be used by the artillery and supply units to cross captured British trenches. Each day at noon precisely, a German observation balloon was sent aloft with a large black ball suspended beneath it. After ten minutes the ball was hauled sharply upwards and then the balloon descended. It was a way for every German unit within visible distance to synchronise their clocks and watches.

When the onslaught finally began the British defenders were shocked by the ferocity of the German bombardment and struggled to cope with the sheer quantity of gas shells fired amongst them. Their view of the battlefield was greatly limited by the ground fog, the smoke of battle and the difficulty of wearing gas masks.

The gas mask was actually a gas helmet incorporating a nostril-clip, a mouthpiece and eye-pieces which restricted visibility. Breathing through the filter required some effort and any prolonged use sapped men's energy levels. British soldiers wore their masks for some hours that day. Even horses had gas masks.

By this stage of the war, gas was a relatively common weapon and procedures were usually in place to counter the worst of its effects. On the 21st, the Germans were firing three types - chlorine gas with its very distinctive smell, phosgene which had a smell similar to rotting flesh or rotten fish, and a lachrymatory gas which smelled of pineapples. In theThird Army sector the Germans also fired mustard gas.

> A party of us, four or five, were in a shallow dug-out about ten feet square and two feet below ground. The entrance had no curtain. We had been asleep and awoke with daylight. By then gas from gas shelling that had been going on had seeped into the dugout and I had absorbed a certain amount.Somehow the others were not affected. The way it took me was at both ends at the same time - diarrhoea and vomiting. As shelling was still going on, one could not go outside but one's pals advised using one's groundsheet, which could be cleaned later, for a lavatory.

> Private Robins.

The British front line forces were outnumbered by the attacking German troops who were following a rolling barrage just ahead of them, lifting and moving forward 100 yards every two or three minutes. The British had carefully laid some 6,000 machine gun posts in the Forward and Battle Zones (compared with the 200 the Germans had used to such devastating effect on the opening day of the Battle of the Somme in 1916) but their teams of gunners were largely blinded and most of their artillery batteries had already been destroyed and put out of action. Those guns that survived the bombardment received little information about what was happening in front of them and were unable to assist in the defence.

Within the first hour of the German infantry attack some fifty miles of the British Front Line had been overcome. The Flesquieres Salient was still largely intact but for eleven miles north of it and thirty-eight miles south of it the British forward lines didn't exist. There had been no military success like this, by any army on the Western Front, since the earliest part of the war. The effectiveness of the bombardment, the attacking skills of the German infantry and the fortuitous fog had enabled the Germans to overwhelm and inflict serious casualties on the defenders. They advanced to attack the main positions of the Forward Zone - these were the support and reserve trenches and the redoubts and outposts, which were expected to provide a much more difficult series of obstacles. Each one of these defended positions had Lewis guns, light trench mortars and heavy machine-guns in addition to infantry rifles; some had artillery observers, hopefully still in touch with whatever guns in the rear that were still in action.

This was the point, according to the new defence policy where the carefully sited and mutually dependent strongpoints would stop, or, at the very least, seriously delay the German advance. The fog and the fact that the Germans had infiltrated the Front so quickly and completely meant that the British Forward Zone was now no more than hundreds of small groups of men in a trench, or an outpost or a redoubt, isolated and unable to communicate with comrades around them.

The Germans too were affected by the fog but most of their infantry companies were accompanied by buglers who were trained to sound twenty-four different calls, enabling commanders to address individual units. The most common call that day was one ordering units to advance and most German soldiers remembered it by the rhyme:

| | |
|---|---|
| Kartoffelsuppe, kartoffelsuppe. | Potato soup, potato soup |
| Den glanzen Tag, kartoffelsuppe | All day long, potato soup |
| Und kein Fleisch | And no meat |

In total contrast to the experiences of the British at Passchendaele just a few months previously the German troops moved over ground that was:

> ....old fields but no crops, dry underfoot, some short grass or simply bare earth with a few old weeds flat on the ground. It was only March and there was no new growth. It was mostly level ground and flat, a few new shell holes.

Many of the British strongpoints were simply bypassed by the first groups of Stormtroopers who were under orders to avoid the main defences. For many of the defenders the first sight of the enemy were the 'battle groups'. These 'follow-on' groups quickly surrounded the British positions and gradually brought to bear their heavier weapons - mortars, machine-guns and then mobile field-guns - to suppress and reduce the position before moving on to the next:

We watched over the top - no movement, no rifle or machine-gun fire - don't seem to be coming this morning. Got a fire going to brew up and fry the bacon. I stood on the fire-step with my canteen and bread and bacon and my back to the front line, watching the heavy gunfire in the back areas. Quite casually I turned round to face the front line. 'Christ almighty. The bloody Jerries'. About eighty yards away there was a loose bunch of sixty to eighty Germans advancing towards us. I noticed that they were big blokes and they all had new uniforms.

Private Leedham, 1st Leicesters

The forward defence zone fell apart quite quickly, particularly so in the southern sector where the Fifth Army was weakest and badly prepared. Within the first few hours of the attack the Stormtroopers, who advanced in groups rather than waves, had infiltrated the battle zone and were threatening to break through into the British III Corps area. Most strong-points that had been bypassed surrendered once they realised they were surrounded and had little chance of being relieved. Others fought on and were simply wiped out or taken prisoner by the following German units.

The right flank of the Fifth Army was forced back and units started to withdraw to the Crozat Canal, but having received the order to retire they went further and faster than General Gough intended. By evening the situation was critical.

Communications fell apart and panic spread both up and down the chain of command:

As soon as telegraphic and telephone communications with Brigades ceased to exist, Divisional Headquarters in many cases became paralysed. They had become so welded to a set-piece type of warfare, that when open warfare occurred, they failed to appreciate the situation, and were unable to function independent of a fixed headquarters.

British staff officer.

The ferocity of the fighting is recorded in the War Diaries of each of the battalions taking part. The one for 2/6th Battalion, South Staffordshire Regiment is typical. This battalion was part of 59th North Midland Division, one of six Territorial Divisions involved in the first day's fighting. They were Second-Liners, which meant that most of their original volunteers had been sent to the First-Line battalions and their numbers then replaced by conscripts. By the time they arrived in France they were probably the least experienced part of the British line. Their reputation was not particularly high and little was expected of them. It is said that one Army Commander declared 'God save me from the New Army and Second Line Territorials.'

> We weren't taken very seriously. If they wanted anything special doing they didn't send for us.

During the battle the Division bore the brunt of the German attack in their sector and the casualties of the 59th Division were the heaviest of the day. Only one officer from the three Staffordshire battalions engaged, managed to return to report to Brigade headquarters. Despite maintaining a desperate defence and severely disrupting and delaying the German advance, some attacking units began to break through the Staffordshire line and assault the flank of the 34th Division on their left.

The 2/6th Battalion was hit particularly hard, first of all by the shelling with a mixture of high explosive and gas and then by the attack itself. Within just a few hours they recorded that most of the Company Commanders, the junior Platoon Officers and 600 men had been posted as missing, including the Commanding Officer and the Doctor. As a fighting unit they had more or less ceased to exist. When news reached Major Curtis in the Reserve Line he hurriedly put together a tiny force of the last two officers, 2nd Lieuts. Maitland and Bradbury, and 50 men including members of the battalion band, transport drivers, and newly arrived and bewildered reinforcements. This motley group moved towards the fighting and held a section of the front line of the Third System of Defence east of Mory for the remainder of the 21st and the whole of the following day under heavy shelling and repeated attacks. Only when their flanks had been turned and they were in danger of being surrounded did they fall back to a ridge line covering the village of Ervillers where they were eventually relieved by the Suffolks.

The Battalion War Diary, written up during the actions it describes gives some idea of the scale of the disaster and the bravery of the men involved:

**20th**   Situation normal. No casualties

**21st** Heavy enemy shelling of back areas commenced between 2 & 3am, also heavy bombardment by enemy of Front and Support Line with H.E. and Gas Shells from 4am - 8am. Enemy attacked in mass formation at 9am and succeeded in capturing the Front Line and also effected a flank move and got through to Railway Reserve and Battalion Headquarters.

23 Officers and about 600 O.R.s are missing, including Lt.Col. J. Stuart Wortley, Capt. C.E.L. Whitehouse (Adjutant), Capt. W.A. Adam, Capt. W.A. Jordan, Capt. T.L. Asbury & Capt. W.S. Lines (Company Commanders). The following Officers are missing:- Lieut. Butler, Lieut.R.G. Boycott, Lieut. L.J. Shelton, 2/Lieut. H.P. Bunn, 2/Lieut. H.E. Shipton, 2/Lieut. H.W. Gregory, 2/Lieut. J.A. Leyton, 2/Lieut. Baxter, 2/Lieut. Spibey, 2/Lieut. Howarth, 2/Lieut. Hickman, 2/Lieut. Gough, 2/Lieut. Yates, 2/Lieut. Bonahor, 2/Lieut. Rigby, 2/Lieut. Jones & Capt. W.M. Christie R.A.M.C. Major H.M.C. Curtis proceeded to the line with details from the Transport Lines, a party of 2 Officers ( 2/ Lieut. Maitland & 2/ Lieut. Bradbury) & 50 O.R.s including Band and specialists under training and held a portion of the front line of the Third System of Defence, east of Mory, until relieved at 4am., 22nd.

**22nd.** 4am. Major Curtis and party took up a position on the Army Line 500 yards N.E. of Mory and held this position all day in spite of heavy enemy shelling and attacks. Owing to the enemy having driven back the Divisions on our flanks, we received orders to move back at 1am to CITY TRENCH and defences at HAVRINCOURT. Leaving two Coys. under Maj. Wilkes of HUMBLE to act as outpost line in JERMYN ST., & LONDON T. At 10am enemy made repeated attacks on our bombing stop in LONDON T: each time he was driven back without making any headway leaving many dead in the trench. At 4pm information was received that the 50th Brigade on our left had withdrawn leaving our left flank in the air. Our outpost line was therefore obliged to withdraw to CLARGES AVENUE & KNIGHTSBRIDGE. At 6pm information was received from HUMBLE  that they were being heavily attacked. A great concentration of fire was directed against the oncoming enemy by our rifles and L.G.s (Lewis Guns) and the enemy's attack was successfully broken up without reaching our line.

**23rd** At 2am orders were received to withdraw to YORKSHIRE SLAG HEAP where Batt was in support to HUNT & HUMBLE. At 8.30am accompanied by intense bombardment the enemy made a determined attack on HERMIES, a great hand-to-hand struggle took place & the enemy was successfully driven off leaving hundreds of dead in front of the wire.

War Diary

One of the 600 men who were missing on the 22nd was Private **Alfred Beckett**, 2/6th Battalion South Staffordshire Regiment. Reported missing, presumed killed on March 21, 1918, aged 19. No known grave and commemorated on the Arras Memorial to the Missing. Lived in Holmbridge on Yew Tree Lane and was a member of the choir at Holmbridge Parish Church.

Alfred Beckett

Other local men involved in the fighting on March 21st were members of the 9th Battalion Duke of Wellington's Regiment. These were the men who had volunteered in 1914 in St. George's Square and in Halifax in response to Lord Kitchener's appeal - 'Your Country Needs You'. These 'New Army' men were probably the most idealistic and patriotic in the British Army, having enlisted in that first flush of enthusiasm in 1914. Their first experience of war had come in 1915 at the Battle of Loos but it was on the Somme in 1916 that they were really put to the test, and there they had suffered terrible casualties. By then the supply of volunteers had largely dried up so the replacements were made up of conscripts and the very local character of the battalions was somewhat diluted. Nevertheless, there remained many ties back to the West Riding.

The 9th 'Dukes' were part of 17th Division holding the northern part of the Flesquieres Salient with 51st Highland Division on their left and 63rd Naval Division on their right. On the 16th March they relieved the 2nd Lincolns and took up positions in London Trench and Yorkshire Slag Heap in the Forward Zone. When the bombardment started they moved forward to occupy the first line of outposts but by 10.30am had been forced out of Hughes Trench when the Germans burst in on a frontage of 200 yards. Over the next few days they were attacked continuously.

Later that morning, and working in conjunction with the Divisions on their flanks, what was left of the battalion withdrew to Rocquiney to be part of the Reserve Force. Even then, despite being utterly exhausted and hungry - they hadn't slept or received rations since the battle began - they manned the trenches.

# The Third Army

General Byng's Third Army, to the north of the Fifth Army, was responsible for 28 miles of the Front Line, most of it covering the Flesquieres Salient, a prominent bulge in the German line. The British had been in residence in the northern part of the Salient for over a year and had ample time to strengthen the defences and complete the Battle Zone, but the southern part of their sector was a different matter. Here there was plentiful barbed wire but an incomplete trench system and the Battle Zone was nowhere near ready. Neither were there enough troops to fully man the line.

Once the battle began, what troops there were on that sector had either been killed or, more likely, taken prisoner. In fact the losses on both Army fronts - Third and Fifth - were a disaster - forty-seven infantry battalions had been severely mauled by mid-morning. These were the forces holding the Forward Zone, few of whom managed to make it back to the Battle Zone. The situation was particularly serious for General Gough who had lost thirty percent of his troops in the first hour and a half of a battle that was to last for sixteen days.

The only real success on this first day for the British was that the Flesquieres Salient held out. It had been heavily bombarded with gas and attacked in several places but all German penetrations of the Front Line had been repulsed and evicted. Defenders congratulated themselves on repelling the enemy.

In fact, the Germans had no intention of attacking it in any great strength and had no wish to encourage the defenders to fall back. They were happy for the British to stay exactly where they were. The German plan was to encircle the eleven miles of British trenches and positions in the first twenty-four hours of the battle and then to destroy or capture three full divisions and elements of two others. It didn't work.

Third Army defences held out until they were later ordered to withdraw while the Fifth Army collapsed. By the evening of March 21st General Gough's men were in complete disarray and he ordered a retreat behind the Somme and the Crozat Canal. Gaps now began to open up between the Third Army and the Fifth Army and the Stormtroopers poured through.

The German Eighteenth Army advanced over 12 miles in two days of fighting and tore a fifty mile gap in Gough's line but at considerable cost to themselves - 56,000 casualties. It wasn't a complete walkover for the attacking Germans and there were numerous places where they failed to advance more than a short distance into British lines. The distance between the Forward Zone and the Battle Zone was nearly two miles in places and the Battle Zone itself was almost as deep. Fierce resistance from many of the redoubts slowed the German advance considerably and despite the day being a disastrous one for the British, it hadn't been the unqualified triumph the Germans had hoped for and desperately needed. Less than a quarter of their first day's objectives had been achieved, and those at great cost with a rapidly growing casualty list. A casualty list, moreover, comprised of the German Army's finest. In addition, the unexpected success of the German Eighteenth Army in the south led Ludendorff down a blind alley. Ever the opportunist, and true to his belief in 'seizing opportunities', he abandoned the plan of moving north-west and instead reinforced this southern thrust into the empty Somme countryside where there was nothing of any tactical, strategic or operational importance until, and if, the Germans could reach Paris.

On March 23rd, the Germans found themselves close enough to Paris to bombard the city with three specially made guns from Krupp. It took each shell four minutes to cover the distance and on that day the Germans fired more than twenty, killing 256 Parisians. The Kaiser was delighted and declared '…the battle won, the English utterly defeated.'

He ordered schools in Germany to close and the children directed to celebrate the great victory. He presented Hindenburg with the Iron Cross with golden rays, the highest medal he could offer. The last previous recipient was Marshall Blucher for his battles against Napoleon.

An advance in the south meant that the German drive threatened to drive a wedge between the British and the French and despite five French divisions being sent north to help their allies the retreat continued.

On March 25th the Germans broke through and split the British forces, capturing Bapaume and Noyen and threatening the absolutely vital city of Amiens. A scratch force of 3,000 men was somehow found to hold the line, including 500 American railway engineers. In London, there was talk of retreating to the Channel ports. The urgency of the military situation forced an emergency conference of generals and politicians at Doullens which resulted in the appointment of the French Marshal Foch with overall charge of all Allied forces. It was an inspired move and it created a command structure which was able to resist what was becoming more and more like an unstoppable German advance, a re-run of 1914.

# 'Dukes' to the rescue.

The newly re-organised and re-named 5th Battalion, Duke of Wellington's Regiment, the Holmfirth and Huddersfield men, entered the battle at this point. In the early hours of the 25th they marched from their reserve area to Achiet-le-Petit, a five hour march that placed them directly in the path of the advancing German forces. They set out in Fighting Order - haversack on back, full water bottles at their side, steel helmets with covers, their box respirator in the alert position and wearing greatcoats.

It was a difficult march on crowded roads - crowded with artillery and guns moving rearwards in the opposite direction to the one the 'Dukes' were taking - but they eventually took up positions facing south-east and guarding the railway. For company they had 2/7th 'Dukes' on their left and 2/4th 'Dukes' behind them acting as Brigade reserve. There were no organised troops on their right flank, instead there was a constant flow of frightened men from 41st, 19th, 25th, 42nd and 51st Divisions moving through their lines in mixed and confused units and retreating from the enemy just behind them.

Before dusk the Germans were spotted on the skyline in front of the hurriedly dug outpost holes. The only artillery support available, 3 guns, were suddenly ordered to withdraw at 11pm, no-one knew why, leaving the 'Dukes' on their own to face the night attacks. In the darkness the Germans attacked directly from the front but also from the direction of Miraumont.

At 3.30am after beating off numerous assaults, they were ordered to retreat to a line hastily drawn on a map between Pussieux and Bucquoy, a few miles behind them. By the time they were organised it was daylight and the enemy followed them in large numbers. One Yorkshire unit ran into a German cyclist patrol, about 40 strong, who were armed with the new sub-machine guns, but managed to drive them off with their own Lewis guns. On the way to their new positions they passed an abandoned British ammunition dump and, after replenishing their own stocks, blew the whole lot up.

They formed a defensive line about 300 yards in front of the main road and positioned their Lewis gun teams in front of it. Three companies formed the line (about 300 - 400 men) and each company placed three platoons in front and one in reserve. By pushing to their right they discovered and eventually linked up with the 9th Durham Light Infantry, just in time as the enemy attacked in force round about 10am. While they were fighting off these attacks they got news that German cavalry had entered the fight on the right flank necessitating a transfer of troops under fire from their own left. The Brigade reserve, 2/4th Battalion, was thrown in to help the defence, and contact with the 2/7th on the left was lost until the following day. Towards the afternoon, eleven British tanks appeared and acted in support.

The intense attacks continued throughout the next day, the 27th, as the Germans became more and more determined to take the position, and they finally began to succeed during the evening when bombing parties wiped out units of the Durhams, forcing the Dukes' right flank. Somehow the line was reorganised and held.

On the 28th the Germans made a decision to shell the defenders before attacking in major force and a devastating barrage caused chaos in the lines held by the 5th, the 2/4th and the 2/7th Battalions. At 10.30am the German elite 2nd Reserve Guards Regiment attacked along the whole front held by the 'Dukes'. One particularly strong enemy bombing force east of Rossignol Wood managed to isolate a whole platoon of 'D' Company under the command of 2nd Lieut. Cawthra. A message got back to the rest of the battalion at 1.05pm that they were still holding out but when, after several attempts to mount a rescue, units managed to reach that part of the line they found that the platoon and their officer had been overwhelmed and none were left alive.

The following day the enemy brought up trench mortars to add to the constant artillery fire before massing towards evening for yet another assault. Again they were frustrated, losing yet more men, and the 'Dukes' held the line.

During the following night, the 30th, and still under constant gunfire, survivors of the 5th Battalion were relieved by the 8th and the 2/5th West Yorkshires and went back into support.

It had been a trying five days and nights. They had lost two officers and thirty soldiers killed; six officers and 126 men wounded and one officer and fifty men missing. A total of 215 casualties, nearly a third of the battalion.

Near Noyon, on the 27th, French forces finally halted the German advance in the south. They were just fifty miles from Paris. Three days later it was the turn of the British and Dominion troops to take the offensive when an attack by a combined force of Canadian, Australian and British troops retook Moreuil Wood, just eleven miles east of Amiens.

It was as far as the Germans got with Operation Michael. The Allied line had bent but it hadn't ruptured. In just a few days battle the British had suffered 200,000 casualties, with 90,000 men taken prisoner and the loss of 1,300 artillery pieces.

General Gough was sacked on the 28th and returned home the next day. Public opinion, encouraged by Lloyd-George, blamed him, somewhat unfairly, for the retreat and the loss of territory.

The Germans too sustained huge numbers of casualties - 239,000 dead and wounded. The numbers included Ludendorff's youngest stepson, a pilot, shot down over the battlefield.

Ernst Junger gave his own classic account of the battle from the German side in his autobiographical book *Storm of Steel*. He had been taking up positions ready for the attack on British lines when accurate artillery shell fire wiped out half of his company. Junger survived and led what was left of his men on a successful advance but was wounded twice, once in the chest and a less serious wound on his head. When he returned to his regiment some three months later he found despondency and widespread acceptance that victory was impossible and that Germany had lost the war. In August he was wounded again for the seventh time since joining the army in 1914. Desperate to avoid being captured by the advancing British he managed to stand and began to make his way back despite pouring with blood as his lung drained from yet another chest wound. He managed to reach a machine-gun post where the doctor helped to get him evacuated. As he was being carried in a tarpaulin to the rear the doctor was shot and killed and some of the stretcher bearers wounded. One soldier picked him up and carried Ernst on his shoulders until he too was shot and killed. Another soldier took his place.

The first that Holmfirth knew officially about the enemy onslaught (rumours had been circulating for days) came via the local newspapers on March 28th.

# TESTING TIME IN THE WEST

Last weekend the long-expected German offensive was launched in the West. It had been boomed and advertised by the enemy as though there were no question as to its immediate and complete success. By the accession of men and guns brought from the Russian Front, the Germans calculated on sweeping everything before them and bringing the war to a victorious end. From their standpoint they have accomplished a good deal, but the cost has been out of all proportion to the gains of territory. The predominant fact seems to be that they haven't won yet as they expected they would do. They have not broken through our lines or inflicted a crushing defeat on the British and French Armies, and if they fail to do that and do it pretty quickly they have not only not won the war, they have lost it. If they fail this time after the gambler's mad act of throwing everything into the final plunge they will never accomplish their ambition of world domination. Without appearing to minimise the gravity of the situation, it would appear as if our forces had the measure of their opponents and despite the superior numbers of the enemy at certain points the British line has held. It is easy to understand the havoc such sheer weight of men and guns would have on the badly-equipped and ill-disciplined Russian Army, but our men are made of different stuff. The remarkable thing about this titanic struggle is that while we at home have been holding our breath in suspense and apprehension, those in and near the battle are confident in our ability to hold the enemy, and having held him, to wait until he has exhausted his mad bull rush, and then turn again upon him and take full toll of his ambitious folly.

Colne Valley Guardian, March 29th, 1918

It was quite a prescient article and it predicted fairly accurately what would eventually happen.

The great gamble hadn't yet run its course, and Ludendorff next attacked in Flanders on April 4. The Germans still held considerable forces on the Western Front and this time the plan was to cross the River Lys, capture the southern part of the Ypres Salient and push the British all the way back to Calais and Dunkirk in an operation named 'Georgette'. It was originally named 'George' but the losses sustained during 'Michael' meant that the assault had to be substantially reduced in size. Nonetheless, it was to be a major attack.

After another Bruchmuller bombardment, which included 40,000 gas shells on Armentieres, the German Fourth and Sixth Armies with twelve

123

TO - 5th. Duke of Wellington's (W.R.) Regt.

Divisional Commander wires aaa Men are doing splendidly aaa
Congratulations aaa I know how tired they are but we have got to
stick it aaa ANZAC Division are now joined up to 5th. Australian
Bde Fort COLINCAMP to S. of HEBUTERNE aaa.

(sd)............Capt.
186th. Infantry Brigade.

27.3.18.

---

attack divisions in the first wave and another fifteen behind them advanced on a twenty mile front. This time they employed 2,208 guns and 492 aircraft but used lower quality troops.

They were faced by six British divisions (five of whom had been involved in the recent 'Michael' fighting and had been transferred to a quieter sector where they could begin the process of replacing losses, re-equipping and recovering) and two Portuguese. The main focus of the attack, involving four German divisions, hit one of the Portuguese divisions head on and it immediately collapsed and their troops fled. The 1st Bavarian Reserve Regiment who attacked the sector held by the Portuguese wrote in their war diary 'The trench garrisons surrendered after only feeble resistance.'

The Germans took 6,000 prisoners and opened a three-and-a-half mile gap in the lines. At the same time they fired 2,000 tons of mustard gas, phosgene and diphenylchlorasine on the British, incapacitating 8,000 men, blinding many and killing thirty.

The British retreated yet again and on April 11th, faced with a deadly serious situation, General Haigh issued his Special Order of the Day:

There is no other course open to us but to fight it out. Every position must be held to the last man: there must be no retirement.

With our backs to the wall and believing in the justice of our cause each one must fight on to the end. The safety of our homes and the freedom of mankind alike depend upon the conduct of each one of us at this critical moment.

All the gains made at enormous cost the previous year at Passchendaele by the British were lost. Messines and Mount Kemmel fell on the 25th and the British retreated to the very gates of Ypres. The German advance was finally stopped, with the help of the French, on April 29th, and yet again they had failed to reach any of their objectives.

Ludendorff called 'Georgette' off. The German offensives had cost them nearly 350,000 casualties; the British Expeditionary Force had lost 240,000 men, half of them Prisoners-of-war and the French had 92,000 killed, wounded, missing and taken prisoner.

It wasn't simply in numbers of casualties that the Germans had lost the battles - the fighting had decimated their front-line storm troops, the specially selected fit, enthusiastic and experienced young men who had been specially trained to carry all before them. They were irreplaceable.

There was a significant pause while the Germans rested and retrained. Prisoners-of-war returning from Russia were transferred to the Western Front and, using experience gained in the recent fighting, units were re-equipped with more light machine-guns, rifle-grenades, and anti-tank rifles. Tactics were refined and practised.

This time the target would be the French. Code-named 'Blucher', the attack on the Chemin-des-Dames ridge, north of the River Aisle between Reims and Soissons began in the early hours of the morning of May 27th. Bruchmuller excelled himself. For this battle he employed 5,263 guns against the 1,422 of the French and British. They fired almost 2,000,000 shells in just a few hours, before attacking with fifteen divisions and another twenty-five following them. Again they were lucky with the weather, fog covered the battlefield, and the French were very unprepared.

The defence consisted of a mixture of French and British divisions, seven in the front line and nine in reserve. The five British divisions held the eastern part of the sector and, yet again, consisted of troops that had been sent there to rest after being mauled in previous battles. Their intelligence people predicted the attack but the French, under Dechene, refused to believe the evidence. To make matters worse, General Dechene ignored orders to hold the front line with a minimum of troops and mass his forces in the second, rear, position. Instead, in what was considered a very old-fashioned way by this stage of the war, he packed the front line with the bulk of his troops with the result that they were decimated by Bruchmuller's barrage and, when the attack began, the survivors simply melted away.

The Germans crossed the marshes, scaled a 300-foot ridge, found the bridges intact over the River Aisne, and advanced some thirteen miles into Allied territory. It was even better than the very first day of 'Michael' on March 21st. Four French divisions were wiped out. At the small village of La-Ville-aux-Bois-les-Pontaverts, a British artillery battery of field guns - 5th Battery, 45th Brigade - and what was left of a battalion of infantry, the 2nd Devons, refused to withdraw despite facing overwhelming odds. They continued to resist and fire the guns until every man was either a casualty or a prisoner. After the war the French awarded the whole battery the Croix de Guerre. In a testament to the fierceness of the fighting and the destruction of the battlefield, of the 540 graves in the Commonwealth War Graves Cemetery at Ville-aux-Bois 413 of them are unidentified British soldiers and 'Known unto God'.

By May 29th the Germans had reached the Marne - echoes of 1914 - and were once again within fifty-six road miles of Paris. A sense of panic reached the very top of political and military circles. The British Cabinet discussed evacuating the Army. A million people fled Paris and the French Government considered leaving the capital and moving south. But gradually, French troops, with increasing American assistance, began to stabilise the line around the River Marne and the German advance began to slow down. A counter-attack by twenty-five French and two American divisions finally halted it on June 2nd. The American troops carried chewing gum as a thirst quencher.

A famous casualty on the British Front was General Freyberg who was seriously wounded for the ninth time on June 3rd:

> I was wounded by a big shell during a minor operation. I was very shaken for a bit; it threw me several yards and wounded me in the leg and head. I had the bits out at the casualty cleaning station. It was rather an ordeal.

The man standing next to him had lost both legs and an arm.

# SPECIAL ORDER OF THE DAY
## By FIELD-MARSHAL SIR DOUGLAS HAIG
### K.T., G.C.B., G.C.V.O., K.C.I.E
#### Commander-in-Chief, British Armies in France.

To ALL RANKS OF THE BRITISH ARMY IN FRANCE AND FLANDERS.

Three weeks ago to-day the enemy began his terrific attacks against us on a fifty-mile front. His objects are to separate us from the French, to take the Channel Ports and destroy the British Army.

In spite of throwing already 106 Divisions into the battle and enduring the most reckless sacrifice of human life, he has as yet made little progress towards his goals.

We owe this to the determined fighting and self-sacrifice of our troops. Words fail me to express the admiration which I feel for the splendid resistance offered by all ranks of our Army under the most trying circumstances.

Many amongst us now are tired. To those I would say that Victory will belong to the side which holds out the longest. The French Army is moving rapidly and in great force to our support.

There is no other course open to us but to fight it out. Every position must be held to the last man: there must be no retirement. With our backs to the wall and believing in the justice of our cause each one of us must fight on to the end. The safety of our homes and the Freedom of mankind alike depend upon the conduct of each one of us at this critical moment.

*D. Haig. F.M.*

General Headquarters,
Thursday, April 11th, 1918.

*Commander-in-Chief,*
*British Armies in France*

There were still more German attacks to come over the next few months but essentially Ludendorff's gamble had failed. The German offensive had won them nearly ten times the amount of territory the Allies had taken during the whole of 1917 but at the cost of nearly one million casualties.His insistence that strategy would take care of itself so long as he had his tactics right was shown to be nonsense. His belief that Britain was the main enemy of Germany and that once she was defeated,

France would capitulate within days, took little notice of the quality of the troops he was facing. Once the British learned to deal with the increasingly predictable methods of infiltration in the initial stages of the battle they quickly found ways to counter it.

Though the Front Line bent, it never broke and the British troops manning it, though battered, remained unbowed and confident that they could match the best the German Army could throw at them.

But the battles had cost Holmfirth dearly.

# Those killed in March 1918

UPPER THONG SOLDIER DOES HIS 'BIT

Walter Thewlis

**Walter Thewlis** Gunner No.152658. 'A' Battery, 71st Brigade, Royal Field Artillery. 71st Brigade was part of the second of Kitchener's New Armies and was attached to 15th Scottish Division. Killed in action on March 22nd aged 28. His body was never recovered and his name is inscribed on the Arras Memorial to the Missing.

He was born in Thongsbridge and lived in Wooldale with his wife, Ada and his two-year old daughter, Amy. He sang in Wooldale Methodist Chapel choir and played football for Wooldale, cricket for Thurstonland and was a keen athlete. Before enlisting in August 1916 he worked as a scourer for Messrs. Lancaster & Sons at Mytholmbridge.

It is with the deepest regret that I have to inform you that your husband Gunner Thewlis of this Battery was killed in action on the 22nd of this month. He was hit by several pieces of shell while out mending telephone wires and you will be glad to hear that he was killed instantaneously and suffered no pain. Your husband is a very great loss to the Battery as he was good at any work he was given to do. He was an excellent gunner and when he began to learn signalling about four months ago he picked it up very quickly, so much so that after three months he was qualified as a first class signaller. In addition he was a most gallant soldier and I shall find it most difficult to replace him in the Battery. His body will be buried in a British military cemetery, the location of which will be sent to you in due course. In conclusion I can only assure you that no man ever did his duty in a better and more gallant manner than your husband.

Major Willett. 71st Brigade R.F.A.

**James Stead** Rifleman. No. S/26067. 8th Battalion The Rifle Brigade. This was a Kitchener New Army unit and was attached to 14th Division. He died of severe wounds to the head received on March 23rd, aged 28. He is buried at Noyon British Cemetery, south-east of Amiens. James was born in Meltham but moved to No. 3 Lane End, Holmfirth when he married. He played in the Meltham Brass Band and Hinchliffe Mill Brass Band.

James Stead

He was quite unconscious and although he was immediately attended to by very skilful surgeons and nurses he never rallied at all and passed away quite peacefully shortly afterwards.

Dressing Station Chaplain.

Harry Leece

**Harry Leece**. Gunner. No. 154366. 297th Siege Battery, Royal Garrison Artillery. Died of his wounds at No. 8 Casualty Clearing Station on March 26 aged 28, and he is buried at Duisans British Cemetery, just west of Arras.

He was originally a Staffordshire man from a small village outside Stoke-on-Trent but served as a Policeman in Holmfirth for many years and was well known. He had enlisted in April 1917 and married Miss Annie Armitage at Holmfirth Methodist Church before his transfer to France in July.

By now the intensity of the fighting in France was abundantly clear to everyone in the West Riding and so was the contribution made by local men and boys. Local papers made constant reference to the gravity of the struggle and called it the most momentous period of the war. Photographs and obituaries came to dominate the pages.

OFFICER'S TRIBUTE TO A BRAVE LAD.

**John (Jack) Brooke**. Driver. No. 222994. 17th Divisional Ammunition Column. R.F.A. Killed in action on March 25, aged 28. His body was never recovered from the battlefield and his name is recorded on the Arras Memorial to the Missing.

He was a Holmfirth man, married to Mary, and worked at Albion Mills in Thongsbridge.

He, with two others were killed in _____ on the afternoon on the 25th March taking up ammunition to the infantry during the retirement. Your husband was only with the section a few weeks but he will be greatly missed, for during his brief stay he proved himself a good soldier, and I am deeply grieved at his loss.

John (Jack) Brooke

A Lieutenant who was also on the limber had a narrow escape. The shell explosion that killed Driver Brooke blew him off his feet and a piece of shrapnel hit and smashed his revolver rather than his hip, while a separate piece wounded him in the arm.

**Joseph Garside**. Private. No. 16434. 2/5th Battalion, Duke of Wellington's Regiment. Joseph was posted missing, presumed killed on March 25. He has no known grave and is commemorated on the Arras Memorial to the Missing.

Born and lived in New Mill.

Joseph Garside

Norman Bruce

**Norman Bruce**. Gunner. No. 231391. 108th Brigade HQ, R.F.A. Killed by shrapnel when a shell burst quite close to him. He 'died instantly' according to a friend on March 27 aged 25. No known grave, his name is recorded on the Pozieres Memorial to the Missing.

Norman had married Louie the year before in Holmfirth and they lived in South Lane. He had worked at Rock Mills for a time before becoming a clerk in Wakefield. His brother Robert was killed in April 1917, the day Norman was married.

**James Heap**. Private. No. 241715. 9th Battalion, Duke of Wellington's Regiment. Died of wounds on March 24, aged 21 and is buried at Doullens Communal Cemetery Extension.

He had enlisted under the Derby Scheme on his 19th birthday and was posted to France the following year.

He lived in Ward Place, Holmfirth and worked at Lower Mills. Played cricket for Cartworth Moor.

Private J. A. Heap

HOLMFIRTH SOLDIER MISSING:
NEWS WANTED.

**Bertram Higginson**. Private. No 201251. 1st Battalion The Royal Scots Fusiliers. Reported missing on March 28 and has no known grave. His name is recorded on the Arras Memorial to the Missing.

He was from Burnlee and worked at Digley Mills before enlisting in February 1916.

Bertram Higginson

**Walter Booth Bray**. Private. No 23585 2/7th Battalion Duke of Wellington's Regiment. Killed in action on March 27 and buried at Pommier Communal Cemetery. He was married and lived in Thongsbridge, worked at Deanhouse Mills. A keen cricketer - he was day cricket professional for Emley Cricket Club - and football player.

AN ATHLETE'S ARDOUR.

Walter Booth Bray

**Willie Earnshaw**. Private. No. 240891. 2/5th Duke of Wellington's Regiment. Killed in action on March 27th. He has no known grave and his name is remembered on the Arras Memorial to the Missing.

Willie was brought up in Cinderhills and worked as a weaver at Butterworth's, Lower Mills in Holmfirth. He was a keen footballer, playing for both Holmbridge and Underbank.

> I am sorry to say I have lost some pals this last time in, as Bill and Frank of Holmfirth, were killed and Jimmy was wounded...Bill's death was a shock to me, as he was always so cheerful and confident of being one of them to return, but it has been ruled otherwise - another good lad has given his all and we have lost a real chum.

Willie Earnshaw

# Those killed in April 1918

**James McMath**. Private. No. 14237. 2nd Battalion Duke of Wellington's Regiment. Killed in action on April 18th. His body was never found and he is mentioned on the Loos Memorial to the Missing. He lived with his wife and two children at No. 60 Station Road, Holmfirth and worked at Albert Mill, just down the road.

The 2nd Battalion were known for their aggressiveness when in the trenches and James, who had volunteered at the very beginning of the war, had already taken part in fourteen trench raids.

FATEFUL MESSAGE TO ING HEAD.

[Driver Harry Bray]

**Harry Bray.** Driver. No. 223380. 24th Battery, 38th Brigade Royal Field Artillery. Taken ill on March 5th while in France, he died of pleurisy and pneumonia at 10am on April 16th, and is buried at Etaples Military Cemetery, aged 30. After a particularly bad attack he appeared to rally for a few days before relapsing and never regained consciousness.

He was born and brought up at Cinderhills, Holmfirth, but on marrying he moved to Ing Head and, before enlisting, was the manager of the Holmfirth Cooperative Store.

**Thomas Howard.** Corporal. No. 203745. 1/6th Battalion, Duke of Wellington's Regiment. Killed in action by shell fire on April 14th aged 24. He has no known grave and his name is commemorated on the Tyne Cot Memorial to the Missing.

Thomas was one of the first to enlist in 1914 and had recently been transferred from the 1/5th Battalion 'Dukes' as part of the army reorganisation. He was married to Hilda and had a four year old daughter, Phyllis. They lived at Dam Head in Hinchliffe Mill and Thomas worked as a weaver at Digley Mills.

FRIEND'S TELLING MESSAGE.
HOW A HINCHLIFFE MILL SOLDIER FELL

Thomas Howard

I am very sorry to be the bearer of bad news to you and very much regret to tell you that Thomas lost his life about five days ago. From enquiries I have made, it appears that he was in the market place of a certain town when an enemy shell exploded near him, killing two and wounding two. Lads from his section tell me that he had been slightly wounded previously in the

134

hand but did not go away with it and they speak very highly of his conduct. Later on I may be able to give you more particulars. I know what a terrible blow this will be to you. I pray that God may be with you in this terrible hour of trial. As a friend I mourn his loss very deeply. We were always good pals.

**Joe Woodhead**. Private. No. 46769. 'D' Company, 12/13th Battalion Northumberland Fusiliers. Reported missing and later found to have been killed in action on April 18th aged 34 years old. His body was never found and his name is recorded on the Tyne Cot Memorial to the Missing.

His family in Station Road, Holmfirth, received a field post card from him the day before he was killed telling them that all was well. He was a painter and decorator before he enlisted working for Mr. Quarmby and was an active member of Lane Chapel singing in the choir and acting as secretary for the Sunday School.

Joe Woodhead

Henry Hirst

**Henry Hirst**. Sergeant. No. 307747. 1/7th Battalion Duke of Wellington's Regiment. Killed in action on April 28th and is commemorated on the Tyne Cot Memorial to the Missing. He was aged 28. Sgt. Hirst lived on Woodhead Road, Hinchliffe Mill and was one of those young men in the Drill Hall in Holmfirth who marched off to war in August 1914.

When the Germans attacked their position just south of Ypres, Sergeant Hirst and his officer decided to move forward to meet the assault head on. The officer survived but Henry was killed by machine-gun fire and 'died instantaneously without the least suffering', one of about one hundred casualties suffered by the battalion in one hour's desperate fighting.

He was my platoon sergeant and was the most respected and best liked man in the Company, and his death creates a gap amongst us which can never be filled - a gap of sentiment, for he was almost idolised by officers and men alike.

CINDERHILLS FAMILY'S RECORD

Wilfred Charlesworth

**Wilfred Charlesworth.** Private. No. 242836. 1/6th Battalion Duke of Wellington's Regiment. Killed in action on April 14th aged 29. His name is commemorated on the Tyne Cot Memorial to the Missing. Wilfred lived with his family at 33 Cinderhills Road and worked at Rock Mills, Holmfirth as well as playing rugby for Underbank, Hinchliffe Mill and Netherthong. He was killed during an enemy attack that had managed to break through the Duke's lines and was threatening Battalion Headquarters. The 1/6th suffered 488 casualties in just a few days fighting. Of Wilfred's two brothers, one, Robert, had recently been reported as missing and the other, Harold, had just been awarded the Meritorious Service Medal.

**George Herbert Booth**. Private. No. 301950. 2/7th Battalion Durham Light Infantry. Killed in action on April 2nd. He has no known grave and his name is recorded on the Pozieres Memorial to the Missing. George was married with two children and lived at Liphill Bank, Holmfirth and worked at Clarence Mill in Holmbridge. A friend of his wrote (rather insensitively) to his wife:

> I saw him just before he went into action and shook hands with him. He was quite cheerful. We knew we were in for a hot time but I did not think it would be the last time I should ever see him. The news that he had been killed was a great shock to me because he was the only pal I had out here whom I knew. Of course I have some good pals in the Regiment. Well I am glad to tell you we have got out of it and I think I am a lucky chap.

George Herbert Booth

ONE OF THE FIRST TO GO.
ANXIOUS TO GET TO THE FRONT.

Harry O'Melia

**Harry O'Melia**. Lance Corporal. No. 267884. 1/6th Battalion Duke of Wellington's Regiment. Died of his wounds on April 23rd aged 21 while having his leg amputated and is buried at Etaples Military Cemetery.

Harry was part of a well-known Irish family in Holmfirth and lived in Norridge Bottom working just round the corner at Albert Mills. He was yet another of the original Territorials who marched out of the Drill Hall in Holmfirth in 1914.

**Harold Swallow**. Lance Corporal. No. 26393. 4th Battalion Grenadier Guards. Killed in action on April 13th aged 22. He has no known grave and is commemorated on the Ploegsteert Memorial to the Missing. Harold lived at Longley, Holmfirth and worked at Washpit Mills. A keen athlete and cricketer he also attended Choppards Sunday School and was a member of the singing class.

> Your son was killed whilst taking part in heavy fighting against great odds and died gallantly upholding the name of the great Regiment to which we have the honour to belong.

Lieut. Colonel Pilcher.

GREAT REGIMENT'S HONOUR.
LONGLEY CORPORAL MAINTAINS TRADITION.

Harold Swallow

The 4th Battalion Grenadier Guards were engaged in a last ditch defence of the British line on April 12 and 13 and at one point, when their ammunition ran out, were reduced to mounting bayonet charges on the attacking German troops. Their casualties for the two days fighting amounted to 31 officers and men killed, 136 wounded and a staggering 362 men missing.

Fred Howarth

**Fred Howarth.** Sapper. No 251954. 33rd Light Railway Operating Company, Royal Engineers. Died of his wounds at No 44 Casualty Clearing Station, Poperinghe, Belgium on April 25 aged 35. He is buried at Nine Elms British Cemetery.

Fred was married to Lucy and they lived at 28 Holt Lane, Holmfirth. He was a weaver at Kaye and Stewarts Mill in Lockwood.

Lucy received the news of his death on the fourth birthday of their only child.

The chaplain of the military hospital wrote to Lucy:

…He was interred in the adjoining cemetery along with three of his comrades who had made similar sacrifices…he was killed instantaneously and did not suffer any pain. My own son was killed early in the war so I can sympathise with others who are bereaved.

Robert Bruce Tucker

**Robert Bruce Tucker**. Private. No 242947. 1/7th Battalion Duke of Wellington's Regiment. Killed in action on April 29 and buried at Klein-Vierstraat British Cemetery.

Married with three children, the youngest two years old, Robert lived in Hinchliffe Mill and worked at Greenwoods, Digley Mills.

He was killed by a German artillery shell which hit him directly in the back.

One wonders what they found to bury.

**Harry Roebuck.** Private. No 28433. 25th (Tyneside Irish) Battalion Northumberland Fusiliers. Killed in action on April 17 aged 22 and buried at Mont Noir Military Cemetery. He was one of five men killed by the explosion of a single German shell. Harry lived at Cliffe, Holmfirth and worked at a number of local mills. He played for Underbank as a centre or wing three-quarter.

An officer wrote to Harry's father:

> He was one of the bravest fellows I have ever met…By his bravery and utter disregard of danger during the heavy fighting from the 21st to 23rd March, he was responsible for saving over fifty men of his Company from being completely surrounded by the enemy.

Harry Roebuck

**James Albert Senior**. Private. No. 44679, 2nd Platoon, 'A' Company, 12th/13th Battalion Northumberland Fusiliers. James was from Muslin Hall, Holmfirth and worked as a presser at John Crowther's mills before he joined the army in 1916. He was reported missing on April 18, 1918 aged 27. His name is on the Tyne Cot Memorial to the Missing.

James Albert Senior

**Lewis Booth.** Private, No. 38160, 17th Battalion, West Yorkshire Regiment. Lewis was a Wooldale man and the husband of Ann. He worked as a stoker at Cooper and Liversedge at Honley and was taken prisoner by the Germans on the 21st of August, 1917.

He contracted pneumonia a few months later in his prison camp and died at Cassel, Germany on April 21st, 1918. Buried at the isolated and peaceful cemetery of Niederzwehren, Cassel, Germany.

Lewis Booth

**Harry Hirst.** Private, No. 33513. 185th Company, Machine-Gun Corps (formerly No 4606 Duke of Wellington's Regiment). Harry grew up in

Lane End, Holmfirth and played cricket for Cartworth Moor. He had been a motor driver for Victoria Mill in Lockwood before joining up. He caught dysentery at Secunderabad, India and wrote home that his doctor was from Holmfirth, his ward orderly was from Lindley and his nurse was from Oughtibridge. He died onboard his hospital ship on Sunday April 28th, 1918 and was buried at Pieta Military Cemetery, Malta.

Your son Harry was brought on board with very little chance of getting through but still there was a chance that he might get home in time to see you all which he was very anxious to do. However this was not to be and in spite of all the doctors, Sister and Orderlies did he passed peacefully away on the evening

Harry Hirst

of the 28th April. He was just as well off for comfort on board as on land and he did not suffer you will be glad to know. He simply was tired out and wearying to go. He sent his love to you all and asked me to tell you he was quite ready to go 'home'. He was buried with full military honours at Malta as we happened to call there.

Rev. Arthur Outram, Chaplain to the Forces.

**Harry Singleton**. Private. No 45290. 13th Battalion York and Lancaster Regiment (formely No 59384 West Yorkshire Regiment). Harry was raised in Burnlee, Holmfirth and worked at Clarence Mills in Holmbridge. He joined the army in September 1917 and arrived in France in April 1918. He was reported missing just eleven days after arriving for trench duty on April 12th aged 18. He is buried in Le Grand Beaumart British Cemetery, Steenwerck.

Harry Singleton

**Harry Beever**. Private. No 45028. 2nd Battalion York and Lancaster Regiment.

Harry was captured by the Germans after being shot in the arm and left on the battlefield. He was posted missing on March 22 but managed to get a postcard home to his wife in Flowery Field, Hade Edge, a month later telling her that he was a prisoner and that he had lost his right arm but she was not to worry and 'I shall come home and we shall be re-united.' At the beginning of July his wife received notice that he had died on April 20. He was 29 years old and is buried at Cologne Southern Cemetery in Germany. (His brother John had died of wounds just a year earlier.)

Harry Beever

PTE MELLIN SWAINE

**Mellin Swaine**. Private. No 21/715. 1/5th Battalion West Yorkshire Regiment. Mellin grew up at Wall Nook in Cumberworth and worked at Senior and Sons, the brewers. He was reported missing, presumed killed, on April 25 aged 22. His body was originally buried in a small battlefield cemetery but was later re-interred in the much larger, concentration cemetery of Sanctuary Wood.

Also killed in action during this time:

**Willie Ishmael Addy.**Private. No 30/346 12/13th Battalion Northumberland Fusiliers. Killed in action on March 28. His body was never recovered from the battlefield and his name is recorded on the Pozieres Memorial to the Missing. He was born and brought up at No 20, Townend Terrace (now renamed Flush House Lane), Holmbridge.

**Ernest Sanderson**. Private. No 77893 15th Battalion Durham Light Infantry. Killed in action on March 31. No known grave, his name is carved on the Pozieres Memorial to the Missing. Ernest was the son of Fred Sanderson of Far Cliffe, Holmfirth.

**Walter Shaw Rodgers**. Private. No 30394 11th Battalion East Yorkshire Regiment (Hull Tradesmen). Walter grew up at 197 Woodhead Road in Holmbridge and attended Hinchliffe Mill Wesleyan School. Before his enlistment in May 1917 he was employed as a motor-man at Henry Mitchell and Sons. He left for France just three days before his 19th birthday and was killed in the Battle of Hazebrouck two weeks later. He has no known grave and his name is on the Ploegsteert Memorial to the Missing.

**Herbert Moorhouse**. Private. No 36047 'B' Company, 1st Battalion Loyal North Lancashire Regiment (formerly No 174493 Royal Field Artillery). Herbert and his wife Mary lived in Holme village and he was posted missing, presumed killed on April 18th, 1918 aged 33. His body was never recovered and his name is on the Loos Memorial to the Missing.

**Reginald Marsden Kinder**. Private. No 44510, 8th Battalion Lincolnshire Regiment. Reginald was originally from New Mill but grew up at Mount Pleasant, Hade Edge, and worked at Washpit Mills. He enlisted in February 1918, was sent to France in March 1918 and was killed in action in April 1918 aged 19. He was buried at Gommecourt British Cemetery No 2.

**Tom France**. Corporal. No 27716. 2nd Battalion West Yorkshire Regiment. Tom lived in Marsden at Bank Bottom Farm but, unusually, his name is on the war memorial in Holmfirth. He enlisted at the very beginning of the war and went to France in 1917 where he was killed in action on April 24th, 1918. He has no known grave and is commemorated on the Pozieres Memorial to the Missing.

**Fred Watson England**. Private. No 29041. 2nd Battalion Duke of Wellington's Regiment. Fred (one of two Fred Englands on the Holmfirth Memorial) grew up in Hepworth and worked for the Prudential Insurance Company. He was killed in action on April 15th aged 33 and is buried in Point-du-Hem Military Cemetery.

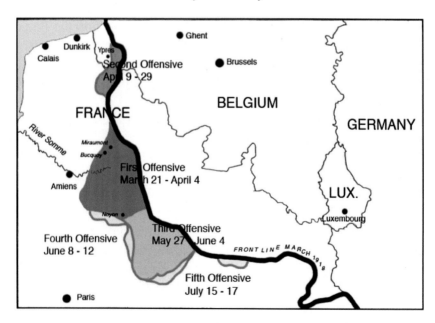

# Meanwhile....

Admiralty press release.

On April 23rd, St George's Day, British naval forces attacked Bruges canal at its entrance into the harbour at Zeebrugge. It was a daring and courageous attempt to stop, or at least severely curtail, the ability of German shipping and U-boats to move into the open sea where they could sink British craft in the English Channel and the southern North Sea. As the U-boats' 1918 campaign began to be more successful and Allied losses at sea mounted, the need for the Admiralty to do 'something' became acute.

The plan called for a night attack and involved some 75 ships and over 1,700 men. At one minute after midnight, HMS Vindictive and two Liverpool ferries - the Daffodil and Iris II - were to land 200 sailors and a battalion of Royal Marines on the mile-long mole guarding the harbour. Their diversionary task was to destroy German gun positions which might threaten the main attack on the canal entrance. At the same time and to prevent the enemy from reinforcing their troops on the mole, two British submarines packed with explosive and each crewed by one officer and four seamen (all volunteers) were to aim their boats at the iron bridge which connected the mole to the shore. Before abandoning their

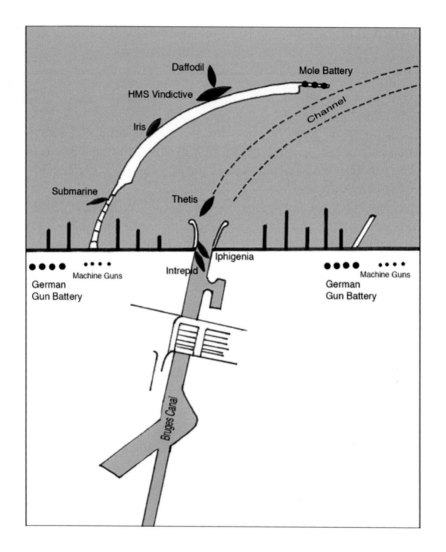

The naval attack at Zeebrugge.

craft they were to engage an automatic steering system and then transfer to waiting boats in order to escape the explosion which, it was hoped, would destroy the only means of getting on to the mole.

While all this was going on, the main thrust of the attack involved sailing three old cruisers, filled with concrete into the mouth of the Zeebrugge canal and scuttle them, thereby blocking the U-boat exit.

145

Like most complicated plans, things went wrong from the beginning. A sudden wind change blew away the smokescreen and exposed Vindictive to heavy German fire, killing many of the sailors and marines. Worse still, Vindictive was forced to land in the wrong position, depriving the troops that had managed to get onto the mole of vital heavy gun support. Both Daffodil and Iris, because of their size, were unable to land troops directly and their task was to push Vindictive up against the mole and then discharge their own troops onto Vindictive and then onto the mole itself.

One of the two British submarines had already been delayed and would eventually arrive too late to take any active part in the operation, but the second one, commanded by Lieutenant Sandford - who was later awarded the Victoria Cross - successfully wedged itself between the iron pillars of the bridge and, after the fuses had been set and the crew rescued by launches, blew up the viaduct and prevented any German reinforcement.

The failure of the sailors and marines to destroy German guns on the mole meant that the full force of enemy gunfire could now concentrate on the three concrete filled blockships - HMS Thetis, Intrepid and Iphigenia - as they attempted to sail into the narrow canal entrance. Under heavy, point-blank fire, Thetis hit an obstruction and was knocked off course. She was scuttled prematurely. The other two managed somehow to reach the canal opening and were deliberately sunk in the narrowest part between 12.15 and 12.45.

The whole operation had taken just 45 minutes. Eight Victoria Crosses were awarded, most to officers but also to Sergeant Norman Augustus Finch, a Royal Marine, and to Able Seaman Albert McKenzie. British casualties were 583 and the Germans lost 24.

Within a few days of the attack, the Germans had created an opening on the West side of the canal by removing two piers and dredging a new channel near the sterns of the block ships. Three days after the attack, traffic was back to normal.

# HOME NEWS 2

Despite everything, there was no loss of morale or spirit among the Huddersfield / Holmfirth / Colne Valley soldiers. If anything, there was a new and real belief, unseen since 1916, that not only did they have the measure of the Germans, they were beating them. Some began to think about when it would be all over.

> We are still all happy and smiling and I have been with many of the local lads during the last few weeks and they all looked well and cheery. We still keep going ahead and I hope we shall not be long before we are able to return to our homes once more a glorious and notorious army. I often wonder what it will be like when the boys do come home.

Yet it seemed that things had to get worse before they could get better. Huge casualties during the fighting in March and the following months needed to be replaced, and entailed yet another 'comb-out' of available men at home. Lloyd-George proposed a number of new conditions in his speech on the Manpower Bill.

The age limit for conscription was to be raised to 50 and it was expected that some 7% of that age group would still be fit enough to serve (for some categories - doctors for instance - the limit was raised to 55). This created a paradox. Many members of the Military Tribunals, who decided which appeals against conscription were either accepted or rejected, were now liable for conscription themselves. It was suggested that their places should be taken by discharged soldiers meaning that a situation could arise where an ex-soldier sat in judgement on the man who sent him into the army in the first place. Sons, serving abroad, were already writing to their fathers with tips and advice on how to cope with camp life, training and sergeant-majors.

Every fit man under the age of 25 was now to be conscripted - no exemptions. This had an acute effect on local trades - all foremen, overlookers and loom tuners under the age of 30 went. Other workers were directly targeted - blend shade getters, woollen scribbling engineers, wool scourers, wool driers, cloth scourers, cloth millers or fullers, card fettlers, woollen mule spinners, woollen mule piecers, worsted warp dressers, blanket raisers, cloth raisers, beamers, weftmen, yarnmen, carters, and lurrymen, whether they drove horses or motor vehicles. Local tribunals were to be more carefully regulated to prevent them from being too 'kind' to applicants for exemption. The period of calling-up notice was to be reduced from 14 days to 7. Ministers of Religion were now liable to be called up for non-combatant service.

A further 50,000 men were to be conscripted from the mining industries. Another 100,000 men from munitions work. Many more from transport and the Civil Service.

For the first time in a while Holmfirth Cattle Market - held on Hollowgate in those days - was packed. Messrs. Sykes and Son offered 68 beasts at prices which would have been unthinkable a few years previously. Calving cows sold for £47 10s; newly calved cows £46 10s; lying off cows £45 2s 6d; lying off heifers £37 10s and store heifers £26 2s 6d. Dairy cows would usually fetch from £40 to £46, sheep ranged from 52s 6d to £7 each and clipped sheep were sold by weight - 9s to 9s 6d per stone.

Under government rationing regulations, fourteen 'fat beasts' were graded and allocated to Holmfirth butchers. The queues outside the shops were already forming. More meat on the market forced a change in the rationing laws. The Meat Cards for children below the age of ten specified half of the adult amount but from May onwards any child over the age of six was allowed a full portion.

RETURNED CAPTIVE'S SAD DEATH.

Irvine Brook

There was excitement in Holmfirth at the expected return of **Irvine Brook.** Irvine was a Muslin Hall boy and a member of the 2/5th Duke's who had been severely wounded in the jaw and captured by the Germans on his birthday the previous May, 1917. After a year in a prisoner-of-war camp where his wounds were only partially treated he was one of a number of badly wounded and permanently disabled British prisoners who were exchanged for equally wounded Germans. He returned to Britain to a hospital in London and his family visited him frequently. He had had quite an exciting time in the trenches. On one occasion he was hit by a piece of shrapnel which bounced off the body armour he happened to be wearing and seriously wounded the soldier standing next to him. On another occasion a German bullet which undoubtably would have killed him was deflected by a metal shaving mirror he had in his breast pocket.

He was a returning hero. Unfortunately, after undergoing yet another operation to repair his shattered face - this time relatively successfully - he died. His mother had been with him after the operation and had left him in good spirits, but before she could board the train home she received a telegram saying that he had passed away.

Alonzo Drake

Holmfirth Cricket Club got the season off to a flying start, bowling Golcar out in less than twenty overs. Admittedly, Holmfirth had the famous Alonzo Drake playing for them and he, and fellow bowler Potter, dismissed Golcar's openers and their No. 3 in their first two overs and six players in total for 13 runs. Alonzo Robson Drake was one of those sportsmen who appear only once in a generation. He had started his sporting life as a footballer playing for Doncaster Rovers before moving to football's top flight and Sheffield United, who, after a couple of seasons, sold him for the then startling sum of £700 to Birmingham. Queen's Park Rangers followed, then five years with Huddersfield Town and finally Rotherham Town before retiring from football in 1914 in order to concentrate on cricket. He had already played 157 matches for

Yorkshire before the beginning of the war as a devastating bowler (in the 1911 season he took 79 wickets at 22.40) and was also a more than useful left-handed batsman. He is one of only three bowlers to have taken all ten wickets in an innings for Yorkshire. Surprisingly when he tried to enlist, at the outbreak of war, he was rejected by the army twice. Known for being a heavy smoker the doctors recognised symptoms of disease and he was in ill-health for the rest of his life. He died, aged just 34, in February 1919 a few months after helping Holmfirth defeat Golcar. He's buried in Honley.

# The Special War Bond Week.

## Holmfirth's Soliloquy

To buy, or not to buy,
That is the question —
Whether 'tis better to buy
War Bonds now
Or hesitate;
And the Germans leave you
With nothing but your eyes
To weep with.

Holmfirth Express, May 4, 1918

Governments sold War Bonds as a way of financing wars. In essence, instead of borrowing vast sums from private financiers - as was the original practice - modern governments print and pour money into general circulation but then encourage citizens to pay that money back to the government as a means of controlling inflation. One method of paying that money back is for the people to buy War Bonds, usually accompanied by appeals to patriotism flavoured with a little self-interest. National War Bonds were issued in 1917 and paid 5% interest (or 4% tax-free for 25 years), a rate even Lloyd-George described as 'penal' - penal, that is, for the Government. Anyone who already held a War Bond, Treasury Bill or War Expenditure Certificate, could convert them to this new, much more generous, issue (these existing government debts already covered the 1711 collapse of the 'bubble' of the South Sea Company; the bonds issued to fight the Napoleonic and Crimean Wars; the compensation paid out after the Slavery Abolition Act and the Irish Distress Loan of 1847). The 1918 issue raised £2.08 billion.

On December 3rd, 2014, George Osborne, speaking for the Treasury, announced that Her Majesty's Government would finally redeem the outstanding bonds on March 9th, 2015. If your grandparent / great grandparent had decided to buy £10 worth of War Bonds in 1918, Mr. Osborne would have handed you (by my amateur calculations) £1,315 and one penny just 97 years later.

In a country committed to total war, leisure time was limited. When not actually at work, the population of Holmfirth was busy organising, volunteering, raising or giving money to help the continuation of the struggle against Germany. In May, as part of a rolling national campaign aimed at persuading local communities to buy War Bonds, Holmfirth was given a target to pay for the construction of nine military aeroplanes. The town was given one week to raise the sum of £22,500, and when people gasped at that unlikely prospect it was pointed out that the people of Ilkley (of all people!) had raised double their allotted quota just a few weeks previously. As an incentive, Holmfirth was promised a visit by a number of flying machines all the way from Tadcaster on the following Tuesday.

The whole town turned out for the occasion but fog and high winds spoilt the day. When telephone communication was finally made with the aeroplane headquarters, the voice on the other end confirmed that the weather in Tadcaster was too foggy for the journey to be attempted. The same was true the following evening, and again the following day. No aeroplanes ever landed in Holmfirth.

Despite this setback, the people threw themselves into the task of raising this huge sum. Astonishingly, the target was reached by Tuesday morning; by that evening it had been exceeded; by Thursday it had more than doubled. When the investments were counted on Friday night the amount was £45,268 18s. The following day, Saturday, a further £2,151 10s arrived, making a grand total for the week of £47,420 8s.

This was a staggering sum of money (equivalent to £1,849,380 today) raised by a small Yorkshire town with a population (if outlying districts are included) of perhaps 20,000 to 30,000 in 1918. It equates to over £61 for every man, woman and child in the district - four months' wages in 1918 (according to Bank of England statistics). It's likely, of course, that local textile, engineering and other firms, who were doing well out of the war, would have made substantial purchases of the Bonds, but even so it was a stunning achievement.

It's notoriously difficult to make a direct comparison between the wages earned and expenditure of 1918 and today - every economist disagrees on what variables should be taken into account - but here's one (very unscientific method):- a pint of beer in 1918 cost an average of about 3p, or 80 pints for a pound (£1 = 20s or 240 pence). At my local, 80 pints of bitter today at £3.10 would cost me £248!

Again, using Bank of England figures, the average annual wage for a male manual worker in 1913 was £106 and the cost of living was £108. By 1918 inflation meant that the gap was considerably wider with earnings at £185- £191 and the cost of living at £216 (British Social Trends since 1900). Figures for female workers in 1922 show annual wages of between £50 and £103.

The 'average' family (if such a thing exists) spent their income in 1918 as follows: 38.7% on food; 7.1% on alcoholic drink; tobacco 2.9%; rent 7.5%; fuel 4.1%; clothing 11.1%; household durables 4.3% ; transport 4.7%. Leaving 20% for other goods or savings, or the purchase of War Bonds.

A quick reminder of pre-decimal currency:

12 pennies (d) = 1 shilling
20 shillings (s) = 1 pound (240 pennies)
1 guinea (gn) = 1 pound and 1 shilling (21 shillings/ 252 pennies)

Examples of inflation:

|  | 1914 | 1918 |
| --- | --- | --- |
| Women's dresses | 8s | 15s 11d |
| Women's underwear | 3s 2d | 6s |
| Boots | 11s 6d | 22s 4d |

Huddersfield, of course, had already donated one brand new flying machine to the Canadian Air Force way back in February in a ceremony on the high ground at Greenhead Park. The machine, a Sopwith Camel, was described as 'of perfect construction, and a thing of beauty'. Even the Guard of Honour, furnished by 9th Battalion West Riding Volunteer Regiment, was 'one of the finest ever seen'. Before a crowd of thousands, Mrs Brook broke a bottle of champagne on the plane and named it 'Huddersfield'. A small bronze medallion reading 'Heaven's Light Our Guide' was fixed to the fuselage and everyone stepped back and waited for the inaugural flight over the town. Unfortunately, the heavens opened and the much anticipated flight was cancelled.

Huddersfield was a generous place.

**PUT IT INTO**

**NATIONAL WAR BONDS**

'Tank Week' arrived in the town at the beginning of the year in February and citizens were implored to buy War Bonds. A tank which had arrived during the night from York trundled from its resting place in Station Yard to St. George's Square. The tank on view in the square was the 'Nelson', one of the newer, smaller Mark IV's, though still weighing some forty tons. Marsden, typically, had decided to make its own tank of wood and canvas built around a motor-car. Though it delighted the people of Marsden (over £5,000 was raised), all the attention was on Huddersfield. Monday found the square packed with thousands of visitors and every window and balcony was filled with people. Large numbers of itinerant tradesmen did a roaring trade in miniature models of the tank, photographs and crude drawings printed on every available kind of material from serviettes to table cloths. The Volunteer Band played until the Mayor arrived in full regalia, accompanied by the mace bearer and the Town Clerk in wig and gown, to open the proceedings.

A jaw-dropping £1,079,952 0s 6d was raised on the first day of the campaign. On Saturday, the final day, the queues waiting to buy the Bonds were so long that an extra office was opened in the large stockroom at the George Hotel and the post office staff had to be augmented by volunteer local bank officials.

| Monday | — | — | — | £1,079,952 |
| Tuesday | — | — | — | £193,727 |
| Wednesday | — | — | — | £214,280 |
| Thursday | — | — | — | £303,456 |
| Friday | — | — | — | £371,701 |
| Saturday | — | — | — | £517,783 |

By the end of the week the total raised was £2,680,899, a sum beaten only by the far larger city of Glasgow and working out at £24 17s 3d per head of population (West Hartlepool held the record of £37 per head).

Some of the individual sums subscribed were impressive. Mr. S. W. Copley (chairman of the Western Australian Insurance Company) gave £50,000. Messrs Dawson and Beaumont £15,000. Mr. Beaumont and Mrs. Lucy Beaumont from Slaithwaite each gave £2,500.

# Those killed in May 1918

BOMBARDIER FRED ENGLAND
ROYAL FIELD ARTILLERY

**Fred England**. Lance Bombardier. No. 35516 'A' Battery, 38th Brigade, Royal Field Artillery. Fred was wounded in the head during the April fighting and evacuated to No 14 General Hospital, Boulogne where he died on May 9th at the age of 27. Buried at Boulogne Eastern Cemetery.

He lived with his parents at Sycamore Cottage, New Mill, and enlisted at the beginning of the war with his brother Percy. They trained together and were sent to France together but Percy was wounded in 1916 and after spending months in hospital was eventually discharged. Before the war Fred worked as a dyer at Beaumonts in Honley.

SEAMAN ARTHUR ROODHOUSE
HMS SILVERY HARVEST

**Arthur Roodhouse**, deck hand on the converted trawler HMS Silvery Harvest was drowned when his boat was involved in a collision off Berry Head on the 16th May. Berry Head is a coastal headland off Torbay in Devon. The UK Royal Navy and Royal Marines Graves Roll records his death as 'Killed or died through means other than disease, accident or enemy action.'

Another ex-pupil of New Mill National School and described by friends as a 'fine, tall, well behaved young man, altogether a smart young fellow', he had worked at Moorbrook Mills before enlisting. His brother, Dyson Roodhouse, had only just returned to France after recovering from wounds. His mother, Ida, was a widow and the family lived at 31 Sude Hill, New Mill. Arthur was thirty three years old. His body was never recovered for burial and his name is recorded on the Plymouth Naval Memorial.

**Joe Lockwood**. Rifleman. No 242342. 2/7th Battalion, West Yorkshire Regiment, attached 185th Trench Mortar Battery. Joe was from Austonley, 169 Woodhead Road and worked at the Bridge Foundry in Holmfirth. A keen cricketer who played for Holmbridge First Eleven. He was killed alongside his friend Fred Bray whose parents ran the 'Boot and Shoe Inn' at Scholes. Killed in action on May 24th, 1918 and buried in Gommecourt British Cemetery.

OFFICER'S TRIBUTE TO A PRIVATE.

[PTE. J. LOCKWOOD.]

**Arthur Mettrick**. Private. No 270061. 2nd Battalion West Yorkshire Regiment. Arthur was married and lived at 38 Brownhill Lane, Holmbridge. Before enlisting in April 1917 he had worked as a weaver at Clarence Mills with his brother Frank who had died of wounds the previous September. Two younger brothers were still serving - Lewis in France and Percy, recovering from being gassed, in Ireland. His wife received official intimation from the Infantry Record Office that Arthur had been killed in action on May 27th, 1918 aged 31. He is buried in Sissonne British Cemetery.

HOLME BRIDGE FAMILY'S DEVOTED SERVICE.

[PTE. A. METTRICK.]

[Sergt John Whitehead Atkinson.]

**John Whitehead Atkinson**. Sergeant. No 20264. 2nd Battalion Yorkshire Regiment. John's father was the butcher in New Mill and he himself worked in the trade for Taylor's in Crosland Moor. He had served in France for over three years before being killed by shellfire on May 26th at 5.50 in the afternoon. His younger brother Randall had been killed the previous year.
Buried at St. Patrick's Cemetery, Loos.

HADE EDGE SOLDIER'S CAREER.

Herbert Kaye

**Herbert Kaye**. Private. No 241370. 1/4th Battalion Duke of Wellington's Regiment. Herbert was born and raised at Folly Farm, Hade Edge and worked locally at Washpit Mills. He had enlisted in 1915 and arrived in France just in time for the bitter fighting on the Somme. Eventually brought out of the trenches suffering from trench feet but returned after just a few weeks. He was gassed in the fighting in September 1916 and invalided home with Enteric Fever in 1918. Returning to his regiment in April he was shot in the neck a fortnight later and died in hospital on May 1st, 1918. Buried at Boulogne Eastern Cemetery in a plot not far from Fred England.

**John Brownhill Ashton**. Driver. Royal Field Artillery. John lived in Thongsbridge and was a farmhand working for a number of local farmers before enlisting at the beginning of the war in 1914. After three years in France and Belgium he was discharged in 1918 and took up employment in Glasgow. Whilst there he contracted pneumonia and died at the Glasgow Royal Infirmary in May 1918 aged 28.

**Gerald Daniel**. Private. No 250761. 1/6th Battalion Durham Light Infantry (Formerly No 3416 Duke of Wellington's Regiment). Gerald had been born in Halifax but lived in Holme Village before enlisting. He was killed in action on May 21, 1918 and has no known grave. His name is carved on the Soissons Memorial to the Missing.

# Those killed in June 1918

**Wilson Turton**. Private. No 5424. 22nd Battalion, Australian Imperial Forces. Originally from Cinderhills, Holmfirth, Wilson had emigrated to Australia, married and had three children, before volunteering for the army on hearing that his brother Fred had been killed in France.

He died on June 15, 1918, aged 37 and is buried at Mericourt-L'Abbe Communal Cemetery Extension.

[Ptr. Wilson Turton.]

**William Bertram Coldwell**. Private. No 53387. 'A' Company, 15th/17th Battalion West Yorkshire Regiment. William was born and raised in Quarry Mount, Holmfirth and attended Holmfirth Secondary School. He enlisted in May 1917 and was killed in action just over a year later in June 1918 aged nineteen. Buried at Cinq Rues British Cemetery.

[Able Seaman A. Chaplin.]

**Alfred Chaplin**. Able Seaman. No J/40505. Royal Navy, HMS Saumarez. Alfred was from Hinchliffe Mill and had grown up at Glen Royd. He was a talented musician and played with Hinchliffe Mill Brass Band and Holme Brass Band and worked in the twisting department of Digley Mills. He had enlisted at the very outbreak of war in 1914 in the Duke of Wellington's Regiment but was discharged during training because of rheumatism. Later he tried to enlist in the Holme Valley Battery, Royal Field Artillery but was turned down on medical grounds. He was finally accepted into the Navy in 1915 but was accidentally drowned when his boat capsized in June 1918. Despite divers making numerous attempts to find him, his body was never recovered and his name is written on the Plymouth Naval Memorial to the Missing. He was aged 26.

RIFLEMAN PASSES AWAY AT HOME.

[Rifleman Herbert Battye.]

**Herbert Battye**. Rifleman. No C/7662. 3rd Battalion King's Royal Rifle Corps. Another Hinchliffe Mill man from Lower Water Side. He worked at Whiteley and Greens Mill before enlisting in November 1915. He served in Salonica where he was wounded and contracted malaria, eventually being invalided home where he was expected to make a full recovery. Unfortunately he died suddenly on June 6, 1918, just a week after his arrival aged 24. Buried at Holy Trinity Burial Ground, Holmfirth, his funeral was attended by wounded soldiers from the Holmfirth Auxiliary Hospital.

**Herbert Farrand Hogley**. Private. No 29304. 2nd Battalion Duke of Wellington's Regiment. Herbert had grown up in Spring Grove, Thongsbridge before marrying Florence. He worked in his father's painting and decorating business of Messrs. Lawson and Hogley before enlisting in 1916. Wounded twice, he was killed in action by shell fire on June 23, 1918, aged 34. Buried Le Vertannoy British Cemetery, Hinges.

HOLMFIRTH SOLDIER KILLED AT HIS POST.

[Private H. F. Hogley.]

**Jack Bamforth**. Private. 2/5th Marine Battalion American Marines. Jack was born in Prickleden in Holmfirth and was six when his parents, Mr. and Mrs. Harry Bamforth emigrated to the United States. Before enlisting in 1917 (at the age of 17) he had worked in the postcard business with his father in New York. The telegram announcement of his death in action arrived at his parent's house on Jack's nineteenth birthday. Died June 15, 1918. His body was taken back to America and he is buried close to the Hudson River, just north of New York - Hillside Cemetery, Courtland Manor.

A WORTHY SON OF HOLMFIRTH.

[Pte. Jack Bamforth.]

# The Yanks Are Here

American troops were beginning to arrive in substantial numbers at last. There were just 200,000 Americans in France in January 1918. Five months later their numbers had reached 873,691, rising to 1,867,623 by the end of October, more than the British Army had in the field in that theatre of war at that point.

The Germans hadn't really believed that the Americans could arrive in sufficient strength or in time to influence their own grand strategy but a combination of the Royal Navy - who carried over 51% of the total force - and, ironically, German ships that had been impounded by the Americans, managed an extraordinary feat of organisation by delivering an army from one continent to another in a few short months.

The American Expeditionary Force was commanded in France by Major General John J. Pershing, the most junior of the seven major generals in the American Army (but it helped if your father-in-law was Chairman of the Senate Armed Services Committee). Earlier on in his career he had fought alongside Theodore Roosevelt in Cuba and so impressed the future president that he was promoted from Captain to Brigadier General over the heads of 882 more senior officers. Given the painfully slow promotion process in the American Army at the time, his startling rise in rank would not have made him especially popular with colleagues.

During 1916 he was based on the Mexican border where he suffered personal tragedy when his wife and three daughters were burned to death in an accident at their married quarters. His only son survived.

Nonetheless, despite his personal grief, he arrived in France with his senior staff in June 1917 to the wild delight of the French who pointedly reminded him that it was France that had led America towards liberty, freedom and democracy (conveniently ignoring the fact that never under the Bourbons, the Revolutionaries or Napoleon had France herself ever been liberal, free or democratic). They whisked him off to visit the tomb of Lafayette who had been so influential during the American War of Independence and he was widely credited in the media for declaring 'Lafayette, nous sommes voici'. In truth, the phrase was actually uttered by an officer on Pershing's staff, but, no matter, it went down very well with the public.

For all their enthusiasm the American volunteers were untrained and inexperienced in trench warfare and the French, struggling to contain a whiff of mutiny and a tidal wave of discontent in their forces after the horrendous losses of 1917, were desperate to have the American soldiers incorporated into their own army, something Pershing was determined to avoid. The British suggested a more pragmatic approach to training the newly arrived soldiers. American battalions should form part of British brigades; when these battalions were sufficiently able to perform on their own they should form brigades which would serve with British divisions; American brigades would then form divisions which would serve with British corps, and finally American corps with British armies. At that point, the by now trained and experienced Americans would form their own independent army. It made sound military sense. But not to the Americans who would have viewed such a move as almost reverting to the colonial status they had broken away from. Though largely forgotten in Britain, it was only a hundred years since the British had burnt down the President's official residence in Washington, resulting in it having to be rebuilt and repainted - hence the White House.

Britain, in common with most other European armies, was historically familiar with serving as part of a coalition, but the Americans have always been reluctant to serve under another country's flag. They still are. Pershing refused the offer and he was right to do so. There was no mistaking his orders from the President which were that there was to be no involvement in the fighting until the American Army was ready in its own right, and certainly not under the direction or control of any other body (though Pershing bent the rules on a number of occasions and allowed his troops to take part in actions). And the General himself needed time to shape the Army's High Command. Again, he made few friends with his insistence in dismissing the 'too old, too fat or too deficient' senior officers under his command. One of the first to be sent home was Major General William L. Sibert. Pershing wrote his assessment to the Secretary of War, Newton D. Baker:

> Sibert. Slow of speech and thought…slovenly in dress, has an eye to his personal interests. Without any ability as a soldier. Utterly hopeless as an instructor or as a tactician. Fails to appreciate soldierly qualities having none himself. Loyal as far as it suits his purpose. Opinionated withal and difficult to teach. Has a very high opinion of his own worth.

One early tongue-lashing was delivered to American army doctors who somehow believed that  they were still civilian practitioners but practising abroad. After one unannounced inspection by General Pershing they were ordered to wear uniform, stand to attention and salute and would be inspected the following day.

Part of the problem for the Americans - echoing the ones faced by the British in 1914 - was the lack of just about every piece of modern equipment and arms - from steel helmets to artillery pieces. In the end they made use of French aircraft and guns, British trench mortars, grenades and helmets, French machine-guns (the American designed Lewis gun used by the British was a far better weapon but it had been rejected by the American military before the war). British rifles were rebored to take American ammunition. There were no boots available so troops were issued with shoes. Horses were far too few because America had hoped to buy them from Spain, but Spain, still angry because the Americans had refused to sell them cotton - which would have found its way to Germany - wouldn't sell them any. The British reduced their own artillery gun teams from six horses to four so that the Americans could have at least some to pull their French guns.

British army staff courses were expanded to accommodate American officers and French and British instructors worked with the troops. It wasn't something that Pershing was particularly happy with. He felt that the French were too war-weary and over-emphasised the defensive, whereas the British were much more aggressive in their attitude  and more in tune with the American approach.

The Americans had become disillusioned with their major partner, France, quite soon after their arrival. The French continually pressed Pershing to amalgamate his units with their own but this approach only served to make the American General even more determined to form a purely American force.

The French army of 1918 was exhausted and riven with mutiny, desperate to have some 'stiffening' of American troops.
At the height of the German offensive on the British in March, Pershing was presented by his intelligence staff with an assessment of his two allies:

> The morale of the British officer and man is just what could be expected of the British soldier. They do not have the attitude of a

year ago, but they do show that they are full of fight. One gains the impression that they are out to stay with it to the last, regardless of cost and that they expect to be able to hold the Germans... There is no air of gloom, and in watching the soldiers moving to the Front they seem to be taking it all in a day's work...Their spirit is admirable.

The French, on the other hand.

> ...there are two factions among the higher French officers and staff officers. One faction has never abandoned the idea of drafting Americans into French units - the other realises the necessity of forming larger American units but considers the morale of the French is so poor at present as to necessitate the dispersion of American units so as to bolster up failing French morale...We are also face to face with another fact - many of our officers...and, it is believed, soldiers, are distinctly disgusted with French tutelage... The French methods are not suited to our troops and we should not delay longer in telling the French in very plain language.

> The United States Army in the World War 1917-1919, Volume 5

Joint Anglo-American training generally worked well. The American rank and file preferred British rations to their own, despite the lack of coffee, and were enthusiastic fans of the rum issue. They were equally fond of brandy. The US 2nd Division, comprising one regular army brigade and one Marine Corps brigade, were in support of the French during the fighting in May and were billeted in the town of La Ferte for one night. The Marines discovered a brandy distillery down a side-street in the town and, in a spirit of brotherly comradeship, shared it with the army. The entire division went on to loot the abandoned town and marched away the following morning replete with trussed chickens and with half of them wearing ladies' hats.

Gradually American units took over parts of the French line and became fully involved in the fighting including the attack on Belleau Wood on June 5th. The previous day had seen French troops retreat from the German offensive and pour through the American lines. French aircraft had mistakenly reported that the Americans were falling back and frantic telephone calls were made to the officer commanding the Marine Corps Brigade demanding to know why his men were retreating. Colonel Neville's reply was typical, 'Retreat? Hell - we only just got here!'

Many years after the war, a visiting American Marine officer was amazed to find the Mayor of Bouresches, near Belleau Wood, driving around in an old Dodge pick-up truck sporting Marine Corps markings. When asked where he had obtained the truck the Mayor replied that he had been sold it by a Marine during the fighting of June 1918.

By August there were over a million soldiers of the United States in France and General Pershing formed the First US Army. They were given their own sector of the Front Line - a forty mile section around the Saint-Mihiel Salient, held by the Germans since the opening days of the war and, up until now, regarded as a quiet sector.

Pershing decided to 'blood' his forces in an attack on the Salient. He would attack the ten German divisions based there with nine American and four French divisions totalling 450,000 Americans and 110,000 French soldiers. He asked General Haig for the loan of 750 heavy tanks but the British were already involved in their own successful offensive and, instead, he used 267 light tanks supplied by the French. The force was to be commanded by Brigadier General Samuel D. Rockenback whose Chief of Staff was a certain Colonel George S. Patton, already magnificent in his cavalry breeches with pearl-handled revolvers on both hips. The air component of the attacking plan was drawn up and led by Colonel Billy Mitchell, probably the best known American in Europe, who went on to become the 'father' of the emerging American Air Force. He organised over 1,500 British, French and Italian aircraft - fighters and bombers - during the battle. The artillery support comprised 3,020 guns, loaned by the French and mainly manned by Americans.

The battle was to begin on September 12, Pershing's fifty-seventh birthday. There was a cunning deception plan. The American High Command had recently demoted one of its divisional commanders for incompetence but hadn't yet announced it publicly. With much fanfare this officer, Colonel Bundy, was sent to a very comfortable hotel in the rear with instructions to prepare plans for an American attack through the Belfort Gap, close to the Swiss border and well away from Saint Mihiel. Pershing gambled on the fact that German secret agents would quickly learn of this plan by studying Bundy's wastepaper bin and decide that the Americans would attack up the Rhine Valley.

The attack began in a heavy drizzle and thick mist at 5.00am after a four hour artillery bombardment which caught some units of the Germans already in the middle of withdrawing from their positions. The Americans had devised a novel way of dealing with the defensive barbed-wire in front of enemy machine-gun posts. This was to cut the wire wherever they could using long-handled cutters left over from the Spanish-American War and then throw rolls of chicken wire over the barbed entanglements to make a crossable roadway for infantry. The French were fascinated but decided that it was only suitable for the Americans as they all had long legs and big feet.

The battle lasted six days before the Germans retreated to their Hindenburg Line and the Americans claimed victory - even though they weren't allowed to capture the town of Saint Mihiel itself - that had to be liberated by French troops. All objectives had been taken with about 16,000 prisoners and 450 guns. American losses totalled 7,000 casualties with some 1,500 dead.

By the end of the war that number had reached 204,000 wounded, missing and prisoners-of-war and 53,000 American soldiers killed in action.

# Hard Times

In these Hard Times.
You've got to put up with anything
In these hard times.

Oh, if you live to be ninety-four
And carry on to the end of the war
You may get leave, but not before,
In these hard times.

You may get more or you may get less,
But apple and plum's your best I guess,
For the strawberry jam's for the sergeants' mess,
In these hard times.

Soldier's version of a popular song of 1918

At the time, only a fool would have predicted a British victory and an end to the war in 1918. For the previous four years the Home Front had been repeatedly told of Germany's imminent collapse as she tottered on the brink of defeat. And yet suddenly, seemingly out of nowhere, there had come a massive German counterattack in March that threatened to finish the conflict in Germany's favour. It was unthinkable.

By the middle of the year when the panic was mostly over and the enemy advance halted, the politicians and the generals indulged themselves in an orgy of blame. Haig blamed Lloyd-George for troop shortages and the Prime Minister poured scorn on the conduct of the war by the High Command. The Germans, everyone supposed, would go back on the defensive; pause, rest and refit; replenish their forces with the 1919 intake and resume fighting. The British Cabinet, in the meantime, made war plans for 1919 and 1920.

The Wipers Times was in possession of a master-plan to win the war:

We will take first of all the effect of war on the male population of Germany. Firstly, let us take our figures of 12,000,000 as the total fighting population of Germany. Of these, 8,000,000 are killed or being killed, hence we have 4,000,000 remaining. Of these, 1,000,000 are non-combatants, being in the Navy. Of the

3,000,000 remaining, we can write off 2,500,000 as temperamentally unsuitable for fighting, owing to obesity and the ailments engendered by a gross mode of living. This leaves us 500,000 as the full strength. Of these, 497,240 are known to be suffering from incurable diseases; of the remaining 600, 584 are Generals and Staff. Thus we find that there are 16 men on the Western Front. This number, I maintain, is not enough to give them even a fair chance of resisting four more big pushes, and hence the collapse of the Western Campaign.

For people at home, suffering from years of increasing austerity, 1918 was set to be even worse. By now the State controlled most aspects of people's lives - where you worked, what you earned, what you ate and drank, what you read and saw and, particularly, what you said. There were shortages of most of life's basic necessities - coal, newspapers, food and soap. Personal hygiene suffered and bodies stank. Individual freedoms became more and more limited. Travel became difficult if not impossible. Despite the fact that rationing made a fairer distribution of food possible, it didn't eliminate queueing and long lines of waiting people grew ever longer as the year went on. The Defence of the Realm Act (DORA) became even more intrusive in people's lives. It became a criminal offence for a woman with Venereal Disease to have sex with a serving soldier, which made it difficult for those women married to soldiers who had, most probably, been infected by their husbands in the first place. DORA was no empty threat; nearly a million people were prosecuted under its various rulings during the war years; some were executed.

The streets of most towns and cities were full of wounded soldiers in their distinctive uniform of blue jacket, white shirt and red tie. Most had limbs missing or walked with sticks or crutches. Those unable to walk were pushed around in carriages that resembled prams. Some - and these had often been soldiers on sentry duty, who were the only members of the trench line who were ordered to stick their heads above the parapet - were hideously facially deformed, lacking noses, jaws, temples. Most of the population was constantly tired, some were exhausted, by the demands of employment, queueing for food and necessities and the anxiety caused by the absence of loved ones. Too many homes had already received the brown envelope from the telegram boy on his blood-red bicycle and there were too many front rooms with photographs turned to the wall.

The Times of London lectured its readers on how to conduct themselves in these trying times:

> Be cheerful, face facts and work; attend volunteer drills regularly; cultivate your allotment; don't listen to idle rumours and don't think you know better than Haig.

Despite all the anxieties, the sorrows, the shortages and the general war-weariness there was no breaking of the national spirit. People looked forward to the end of the war but it would be an end on their terms, a victorious end. The enthusiasm and excited belligerence of 1914 had given way to a stubbornness and a determination to carry on and see it through to the end. And the people in the little town of Holmfirth were no exception.

One, two, what shall we do?
Three, four, go to the war...
......
......
Seventeen, Eighteen, War abating
1920 PEACE AND PLENTY.

Nina MacDonald, War-Time Nursery Rhymes

If only.

The frequent mention of Amiens in the news during March and April made many residents of Holmfirth look anew at the ancient monument in Towngate which held a plaque stating that the pillar had been erected to commemorate the 'Short lived peace of Amiens'. They knew it as 'Th'owd Genn', built on the site of the old village stocks, and presumably named after the village constable of the time, James Genn of Longley.

Others in the town were still struggling to come to terms with the change in diet brought on by rationing and the Express felt obliged to tell people how to eat cheese. Before the war when cheese was cheap, it was considered 'indigestible' for anyone with a 'weak digestion'. Now that it was expensive but plentiful it was important for as many people as possible to eat it. The secret, according to the Express, was to grate it and spread it on potatoes, salads, and most kinds of vegetables to make a 'solid, well-balanced and easily digested meal'.

Thank goodness for Dr. Cassell's Instant Relief Tablets.

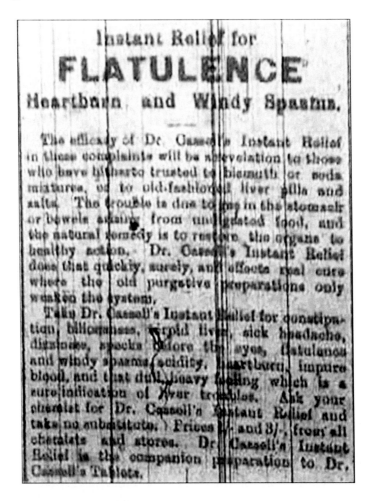

Keen followers of the war had been intrigued by the story of the guns used to bombard Paris. These specially made guns were capable of firing a 10 inch shell for a distance of 75 miles and, understandably, caused great consternation in the French capital. When the bombardment first began the French Government decided that life should go on as normal and trains, buses and trams, as well as the Metro should continue as usual. Warning was given to the populace by policemen banging drums or blowing whistles. This casual approach (and a rising casualty list) lasted no more than a day before Parisians took to their cellars whenever the alarm was sounded. They calculated that each discharged shell would cost 2,000 francs (£80). Twenty-four shells had been fired onto the city by Sunday, at the rate of one every 20 minutes, and the total cost was £1,920.

The consensus of opinion in Holmfirth for this Jules Verne creation was mixed. There were those that argued, without ever explaining how or why, that the science-fiction gun was an altogether new way of using centrifugal force. Others were convinced that the shell being fired was, in fact, made in two parts. The first part, fired normally from the gun, somehow divided in two during flight, say after twenty miles, releasing a new projectile with a propellor that continued to its destination. The argument persisted until someone pointed out that the solution was more likely to be that the Germans were simply using a more powerful propellant.

During the recent fighting, it was reported that German troops often halted their advance in order to loot and consume captured or abandoned supplies and this was given as a reason as to why they often failed to reach their objectives. Badly fed for years and with worn-out uniforms German soldiers were amazed at the sheer quantity and variety of supplies available to the ordinary British soldier.

A German Lieutenant described the areas behind the English front lines as 'a land flowing with milk and honey' and after one particularly fruitful day's finds wrote that:

> …our men are hardly to be distinguished from English soldiers. Everyone wears at least a leather jerkin, a waterproof either long or short. English boots or some other beautiful thing…there is no doubt the army is looting with some zest.

> Rudolph Binding

By this stage of the attack German soldiers were advancing with chickens under their arms, some were driving cattle ahead of them. The discovery of a wine-filled cellar would often result in a complete halt while men got drunk. But, despite their own privations, the soldiers in the German Army were better off and better nourished than the general population back home in Germany.

By mid-1918 the German civilian diet was appalling and the Huddersfield Examiner never missed a chance to point out to everyone the difference between consumption here and what the enemy on their Home Front were forced to eat. Bread was a constant topic for discussion. German bread was adulterated to a far greater extent than in Holmfirth and would include quartz, sand, chalk and sawdust. It was, as the Examiner described it, an acquired taste; a bit like Bombay Duck.

> When cut, the bread emits a peculiar smell, which is at first almost fruity, and not exactly disagreeable, but afterwards grows sharper and finally becomes overpowering and offensive. The crumb of such breads is at first somewhat moist, then becomes sticky, more or less yellow-brown in colour and when cut or broken hangs together in long, sticky, tough threads.

> German newspaper article.

Tea and coffee substitutes had been common in Germany since the early years of the British blockade on her trade routes, but by now the list had grown to include just about every leaf and root available - not the fruit, mind you, that was far too valuable - blackberry, raspberry, strawberry, birch, coltsfoot, hazel, chestnut, pansy herb, St. John's Wort, polygony, knot grass, dead nettle blossoms and very well dried blossoms and roots. Pressed and roasted grape skins were a familiar 'coffee' variety and were joined at the beginning of 1918 with the cultivation of the roots of reeds.

Soup had been a staple meal for years but soup substitutes were often passed off as the real thing until laws were passed making it illegal. Substitutes were not required to contain any meat extract, or vegetables, fat, or seasoning. There was supposed to be a minimum of 2 per cent nitrates and not more than 7.5 per cent salt. Apart from that, anything that wouldn't actually kill you could be used - and was.

The final indignity for a German man was the extensive use of beer substitutes. One Berlin newspaper described the new 'officially censored beer, of uniform colour and gravity'. It was coloured bright blue, as blue as a cornflower.

Local Holmfirth and District papers would publish any number of articles about how bad things were for the enemy in order to muffle complaints about poor conditions or shortages here. Stirring tales of soldiers enduring suffering while people back home complained about trivialities always went down well.

The Colne Valley Guardian published a piece about a group of Milnsbridge men, part of 9th Battalion Duke of Wellington's Regiment (Kitchener's Army) who had been engaged in the recent fighting. These men, desperately tired after spending two days and nights in the trenches under enemy gunfire were positioned in adjacent shell-holes that had been eloquently named No. 4 Post. When the British battalion on their left attempted a counter-attack against the advancing enemy the Germans opened up a tremendous barrage against the whole of the British line.

> But what is a post in the army? Two shell-holes, roughly covered with wood and ground sheets had been connected together and termed No. 4 Post. One sergeant, one lance-corporal and seven privates made up the party who manned this post, the sergeant and four privates in one shell-hole, and the lance-corporal, with the remaining three, in the other. They made themselves as comfortable as possible under the circumstances and settled down, when daylight came, to snatch what rest they could after a weary night of watching and waiting. At noon the burst of the shells, which had been quite near enough in the morning, began to creep nearer to this small band of men and caused them to look at each other in an apprehensive manner.
> At 2.15 pm the half-expected happened. A shell dropped straight amongst the sergeant and his men in No. 1 shell-hole, killing one outright, seriously wounding another, slightly injuring a third, and giving to the fourth that terrible brain-snap which is called "shell-shock", the sergeant alone escaping.
> Before the men in shell-hole No. 2 had time to gather together their scattering wits, down came another shell right into their midst, but this was a 'dud' and apart from shock and a premature burial the four escaped unhurt. What was to be done? There were no means of communicating to Headquarters what had happened. All that could be done was to lay low and await as best they could the arrival of night-time, so that the dead might be buried, the wounded carried away and relief brought for the survivors of that horrible day.

> Colne Valley Guardian, March 1918

It took a brave civilian to complain about a lack of sausages after reading this, and for those workers who might be tempted by the thought of taking a day off work.

There was no shortage of employment. The new blue cloth for the men and women of the recently created Royal Air Force was being manufactured in large quantities in local worsted mills and the American market was still buoyant. These same mills were already producing half-a-mil lion yards of flannel goods for the military, standard tweeds for the home market and more and more cheap cloth for suits for discharged soldiers. There was so much work on order but fewer and fewer workers to actually operate the machines - the recent and latest 'combing-out' of yet more men from the industry to send to the Army meant that the whole industry was beginning to creak. At this point the unions decided on a show of strength and the General Union of Textile Workers supported by the National Association of Textile Workers demanded a 48-hour working week with no reduction in wages. It was a bit of a bombshell.

Tram and 'bus workers, many of them women by this stage of the war, had already threatened to strike if they weren't paid the same rates as the men they had replaced. The threat was quickly settled with a 4/-s rise and the promise of £1 per week over pre-war rates.

To everyone's surprise, it was announced that South America was now involved in the war. Argentina, though expressing its wholehearted support for the Allies had decided to remain neutral for the time being, but Brazil had declared war on Germany. The large Brazilian steamship

Parana, loaded with coffee and making its way to Britain, had been torpedoed by a German U-boat and three Brazilian sailors had been killed. The news provoked riots and mass demonstrations throughout Brazil and German shops and businesses were burnt and sacked. Pro-German politicians were forced to resign. But with an army of only a few thousand men, Brazil's involvement in the war was always going to be fairly minimal. After arranging loans from American banks (which would be repaid with Brazil's share of reparations from a defeated Germany at the end of the war) and with much fanfare and cheering crowds, the Government dispatched twenty officers and a few sergeants to join French forces in Europe. Luckily for them, the war ended a few weeks after they arrived.

As the battles in the Somme region continued there was considerable concern in Holmfirth about the likely outcome. One Colne Valley soldier, who had recently re-joined his unit after leave in Milnsbridge, wrote:

> Now when I was at home there was a tremendous amount of 'wind up' - a fearful amount. That was in the initial days of the German advance and nearly everyone was asking 'Is it possible that they can break through?' As the Commander-in-Chief says 'We have our backs to the wall'. We are alright so long as the wall lasts. English workers constitute the wall. We have no ' wind up' here, but it is annoying when one is 'up against it' to hear of dissension at home. If the wall stands we are alright.

The Holmfirth Military Tribunal under Councillor Brooke was as busy as ever. The casualty list produced by the latest fighting had created even more pressure to find recruits for the army.

A youth of eighteen was represented by his father who complained to the panel that two of his four sons had enlisted at the beginning of the war and a third had been called up and was now serving in the trenches. His youngest son had been medically examined twelve months previously and classed as B2. He had now been examined again and this time passed as Grade 1, but, said his father 'I don't see how they could pass him in Class A when he can only see with one eye'. But this was 1918 and by now the medical criteria for enlistment had been considerably diluted. It was pointed out to the panel by Mr. Tinker, the Military Representative, that when recruits had defective eyesight they were trained as bombers and not marksmen. The young man's application  was dismissed. A local farmer applied for exemption on the grounds that he was fully employed working his sixteen acres. The panel allowed him to stay but ordered him to buy and raise not less than half-a-dozen pigs in addition to his existing livestock.

If the Military Tribunals were busy, so were the police courts. Harry Nichols of Cumberworth was charged with shooting his neighbour Edward Benson with a revolver. Mr. Benson was a farmer and Mr. Nichols lived in a cottage close to the farmer's land. A dispute over access to a fresh water well had arisen over time and there was bad blood between the two. On May 8th farmer Benson was confronted by Nichols who shouted 'I want to live and I'm going to live. Tha's never let me have any peace sin' I came to t' place.' He then called him a rather insulting name and pulled a revolver from his trouser pocket aiming it at Mr. Benson, who promptly dropped the bucket he was carrying, grabbed a spade and held it in front of his head for protection. Nichols fired three shots, two of which hit the spade and the third hit Benson in the thigh. Satisfied, Nichols put the revolver back in his pocket and went back into his cottage. It was too big a case for the Holmfirth Police Court and Mr. Nichols was committed to the Assizes.

During an argument at work, Willie Mountain punched Joe Booth in the mouth, knocking out four of his upper teeth and loosening five of his lower ones. Mr. Booth was seeking damages of £3 10s to pay for the dentist and £7 for the suffering he had endured. Mr. Mountain had offered to pay £2 but was eventually ordered to pay £5 5s to Joe at the rate of 10s per month.

Mrs. Hepworth sought a separation order from the courts alleging cruelty by her husband. Mr. Hepworth had shaken and struck her and slapped her across her mouth when she refused to clean the horse's harness. Moreover he only allowed her 23s per week, out of which she had to buy food, clothing for themselves and the children, and pay the gas and rates. It was impossible "to make do', she said, and she had left him and taken the children. The Bench didn't agree that this was cruelty and dismissed the case.

In an age when belief in Spiritualism was common (even General Haig had attended seances and was a firm believer) there was an unusual charge of fortune-telling at the Huddersfield Police Court in March. Two women were being prosecuted and the first, a young, married woman named Florence Hall, was charged with unlawfully pretending to tell fortunes with intent to deceive. She had been visited by a Miss Hoyle (who was in fact an undercover lady police officer) who handed her a pair of gloves. Florence took the gloves, rolled them in her hands, closed her eyes and said:

> "You have had an anxious time this last month, and have been worried, but the next four months will be brighter. If you will only follow the thoughts and impressions which you have at night, the last thing before going to bed, you will not go far wrong. I can see a child with forget-me-nots all around her, which has passed into the spirit world. I can see an elderly lady with her hand on your shoulder and she is always with you. I see you in a country garden, and the lady would pass away at the age of about 60. I see standing behind you a broad-set man wearing khaki. He will be about 30 years of age. He is wounded, but will get well again. There are also friends in khaki over the water, but all will be well with them. There is a fair man in khaki over the water, and he will pass away over the next few months. An elderly gentleman will pass away and you will benefit from the will. The spirit friends will answer you two questions."

(I'm unsure which is the more remarkable - the extent of Florence's spiritual knowledge or Miss Hoyle's word-perfect memory).

Florence charged her two shillings. In her defence, Florence claimed that she had seen spirit forms for the past seventeen years, since she was twelve years old. She had practised for about nine years and trusted her spirit friend. She had a son serving in France and had not heard from him in a fortnight but the spirit had confirmed that he was well. In fact, she said, her spirit had already told her before Christmas that the police would be coming to cause trouble but not what the outcome of the case would be. The Bench dismissed the charge against her.

The next defendant was Emma Knight who had also been visited by the lady police officer, Miss Hoyle. Emma declared that she had been a member of the Spiritualist body for twenty-nine years and believed it to be the "truest religion God Almighty had created". Once she had ascertained that Miss Hoyle was single she gave a more gloomy forecast:

> "There is a medium man in hospital and he will die. We tell you all that the spirits tell us, good or bad. There are tears for you, and a coffin…You will benefit by his death and have money… You will have an offer of marriage, which will be a good one financially…

(I see) a tall, dark person suffering from cancer who would pass away suddenly and quite unexpectedly. Take notice of these things as they will come true".

She was found guilty of deceit and fined £2.

Poor Lizzie Maynard, married to a soldier serving in France, and depressed by illness was prosecuted for attempted suicide. She had thrown herself into the canal by Slaithwaite Bridge but was rescued by Joe Sykes who was passing by at the time and heard the splash. She was discharged with a warning as to her future conduct.

Three brothers aged 16, 11 and 10 stole Mr. Grainger's tricycle worth an estimated 5/-. Superintendent McDowell stated in court that the boys lived in an isolated part of the moors and their behaviour had got completely out of hand - they needed stricter supervision. Their father, who had been summoned to court to explain the boys' actions, expressed sorrow for the shortcomings of his offspring and regretted the occurrence. They were each bound over for twelve months in the sum of £5 and ordered to pay costs of 17s 6d.

Huddersfield Temperance Hall (courtesy of the Huddersfield Daily Examiner).

The calls for total abstinence, even in Holmfirth, had never subsided and Canada led the way in 1918 by going 'dry'. Legislation was introduced which prohibited the manufacture of intoxicating liquor, and it became illegal to transport alcohol across provisional borders. (Prohibition lasted until 1920 in most provinces before being repealed). In West Yorkshire the Huddersfield branch of the Women's Total Abstinence Union held their annual meeting at the VictoriaTemperance Hall in New Street where the President, Mrs. Mossop, declared that the crisis at the Front could only be solved by the universal adoption of abstinence. The same message was hammered home by General Bramwell Booth in an article for the Daily Chronicle. Bramwell had succeeded his father William as head of the Salvation Army and was a stern advocate of prohibition, believing that the power of the Established Church was more than enough to enforce a total ban on the evils of drink:

General Bramwell Booth

Let the Churches resolve that from a given date they will admit to their fellowship no more of those who traffic in and profit by the drink. If the Churches would resolve it and would act up to their resolution, they could do away with the sale of intoxicants within a week....
The moral force of the whole movement against intemperance and its related vices would be enormously increased. Drink destroys the whole conception of liberty, equality, and fraternity; they are inconsistent with its bondages.

Huddersfield Town was having an 'up and down' season, playing well one week and then losing badly the following game. They were unlucky against Sheffield and should have won after opening the scoring with a penalty but their defence wilted in the second half and Glennon scored a hat-trick. The following week Town played Leeds City in front of a crowd of 3,000 Huddersfield supporters. Sandy Mutch, Town's regular goalkeeper and a Scottish international, made an early mistake resulting in a fairly easy goal for Leeds scored by Knee, and Leeds' forwards dominated the first thirty minutes of the game. Dominated, that is, until Hall equalised and then scored a second to take the lead. Frank Mann, an England international, scored a third - three goals in ten minutes. Leeds scored again and by now the game had become littered with fouls and feelings were running high, both in the crowd and on the pitch. Hall settled the matter with a beautifully taken penalty kick, putting the ball way beyond the goalkeeper's reach.

(The following season 1919-1920 could well have been Huddersfield Town's final one in the League after just twelve years when plans were unveiled to amalgamate the club with the new team of Leeds United, following the demise of Leeds City. There was uproar in the town and fans flocked to buy shares in the club in an attempt to keep it as a going concern. £30,000 was raised and the club survived. Not only did it survive but it thrived. The shock of possibly losing the club somehow sparked a revival of fortunes and that season saw a run of one defeat in 25 games resulting in promotion to the First Division and their first ever appearance in the FA Cup Final against Aston Villa - losing finally to Billy Kirton's goal in extra time.)

Men of the 2nd Battalion Duke of Wellington's Regiment who had been wounded in the recent fighting and were now recuperating put on a show which raised £40. The performers, led by Lieutenant Hirst from Aspley, included Private Norman Sanderson of Berry Brow who sang the tenor piece 'Let me like a soldier fall'. It brought the house down.

# 'Tout-de-suite, and the tooter the sweeter'

## The 5th 'Dukes' back in action - The Battle of Tardenois.

And the war went on. Chief Quartermaster General Ludendorff, by now running the country as well as the war effort, was under attack with a concerted assault by the British, French and Americans. His initial success in the fighting against the French line in May had resulted in the formation of a salient in Allied territory stretching from Rheims towards Paris and embracing the Plains of Tardenois. In July the Germans made another attempt to widen the breach. Their attacks, starting on the 15th, quickly smashed through an Italian division that was holding the line with the Italians losing 9,334 soldiers out of a total force of less than 24,000. General Berthelot immediately pushed two recently arrived British divisions, the 51st Highland and the 62nd West Riding, down the Adre Valley and on to the Tardenois Plain to halt the German advance. After some bitter fighting they managed to hold the Germans who then began to retreat. On August 1 the Allies continued the attack and advanced another five miles. It was a major victory and a bloody defeat for the Germans who lost 29,367 men as prisoners, 793 guns, 3,000 machine-guns and a calculated total of 168,000 casualties. Soldiers in the West Riding division said that they had never seen so many dead enemy soldiers as they found in the woods after the battle.

This defeat marked the end of a string of successful German attacks and the beginning of a series of victories for the Allies that, in the next one hundred days, would bring Germany to her knees.

The soldiers of the 5th Battalion 'Dukes' had played a vital part in the battle on the Tardenois Plains and had suffered accordingly.

A typical British army battalion of the Great War might only spend 5-10 days a year actually in battle, but, given the intensity of the fighting, those few days might involve 50% casualties. They would also spend 60-100 days in front line trenches, often suffering heavy casualties through enemy shelling or enemy raids. The remainder of their time was spent in reserve lines or at 'rest', both places involving constant labour on fatigues or intensive training.

But the Yorkshiremen of 62nd Division had had a relatively quiet time for the previous few weeks. The 5th Battalion had been given an opportunity to go swimming in the local pool at Germaine and the regimental band had played a concert in the town square during the evening.

At 8pm that evening an order was received detailing a major attack on German lines for the next morning. They were to be part of a three-division assault - themselves forming part of 62nd West Riding Division, the Scots of 51st Division and (because they were in a French part of the line) the 22nd French Colonial Division.

They left their billets at midnight on July 19th and marched to their attacking positions on the western edge of the Foret de la Montagne, just east of the Chateau at Courtagnon. The roads were crowded with French troops and transport and it took them until 4am. The Scottish 51st Division was on their left and zero hour was 8am, July 20.

The 62nd Division were attacking on a two brigade front - 187th Brigade on the right of the assault and 185th Brigade on the left - some 5,000 men forming a line stretching roughly two and a half miles.

Their objective was the village of Sarcy, just less than eight miles away, a pleasant three hour walk in peacetime. In the end it took them five days to get to Cuitron, just halfway to their objective, and until the 28th to fight their way into Bligny.

The nature of the terrain, woods and undergrowth, favoured the German defenders and progress was slow and casualties heavy in all units. The British were advancing over the open country of the Ardre valley with wooded ridges on the flanks whose spurs contained a myriad of German defences. The corn which covered most of the ground stood two feet high and hindered reconnaissance while the carefully sited and hidden machine-gun nests were difficult to spot and eliminate.

One part of the advance would be held up, then another, while the attackers worked their way round the flanks, or crept close and bombed the posts.

The Holmfirth / Huddersfield men of the 5th Battalion were part of 186th Brigade and they would form the second line of the attack, following 4,000 yards behind the other brigades and leapfrogging through them to seize Tramery, a couple of miles further on. There was no reserve - just about every fighting man in the battalion was part of the assault - somewhere between 500 / 600 officers and men.

When the whistles blew they moved forward pushing and dragging their Lewis Gun limbers and their ammunition and bomb carts on a front of about 700 yards. The German shelling was intense and caused casualties from the outset. - 'A' and 'D' companies reported 25% wounded and killed by the time they reached the edge of the Bois de Bourcy.

In front of them the situation was unclear and the advance had been held up. They stayed where they were until the evening when they received orders to attack and take the villages of Marfaux and Cuitron where German troops were threatening to cut off a number of men of different attacking regiments who had taken shelter in shell holes and were isolated.

Battalion Headquarters received the orders to attack at 6.30pm with zero hour and an artillery barrage set for 8pm - an impossibly short timescale, particularly so, as given the intensity of the fighting contact had already been lost with 'A' and 'D' companies. Nonetheless, officers frantically made attempts to reconnoitre the attacking ground and found that the men would have to cross 800 yards of open fields that were covered by German machine-gun posts from the front and from a machine-gun nest in the woods to their left. With no cover for the infantry the attack would have been an act of suicide and Battalion Headquarters staff made frantic efforts to contact Divisional Command and explain the difficulties. With minutes to spare before they were due to set off, they managed to get a message through and the attack was cancelled.

The men dug in for the night and spent the following day reorganising the four companies - 'A', 'B', 'C' and 'D' - to compensate for the casualties of the previous day.

On the 22nd they were ordered to capture the Bois du Petit Champ which was heavily defended by the Germans. Officers came up with a clever plan - 'A' and 'D' Companies were to skirt the edge of the northern section of the wood while 'B' and 'C' companies did the same on the southern part.

Every 300 yards, a platoon of fifty or so men would detach themselves from the rear of each advancing company and form a strongpoint. From those strongpoints small groups of soldiers would enter the wood and search for German positions which they would then attack and destroy.

Zero hour was 12.15pm and the attack began with a murderous artillery barrage falling just 250 yards in front of the battalion. This barrage remained stationary for the first ten minutes and then moved forward 100 yards at a time. Machine-guns, both British and French, saturated likely German positions in the wood.

They quickly discovered that the undergrowth in most places was as thick as that found in a tropical jungle and the hidden German machine-gun teams had been trained to fire in the direction of sound. Attacks needed to be made at close range and casualties increased as the range shortened. At a critical point in the assault, two companies of the 5th Devons were sent in support.

'A' Company captured ten machine-guns and took about 40 prisoners within the first 500/600 yards, though at the cost of heavy casualties of their own. The two companies covering the southern sector were even more successful, taking over 20 machine-guns and 80 prisoners, before 'C' Company were counter-attacked by a strong German force and surrounded. The Germans killed everyone in the outposts before launching a bayonet charge on the main position which was eventually beaten off with the one remaining Lewis gun. The Germans then attacked with bombing parties using stick grenades and forced the last few defenders to retreat to a shell hole on the wood's perimeter where a shellburst killed the gun crew and put the Lewis gun out of action. By this stage,'C' Company of some 200 men had been reduced to 2 officers and six men who managed to escape to 'B' Company's positions.

Nonetheless, the remaining three companies - 'A', 'B' and 'D' - slowly managed to link up their positions in the woods and form a line which pushed the Germans back. The 53rd Prussian Regiment facing them mounted desperate counter-attacks throughout the day but each one was repulsed and the 'lads' held the line. They also captured two officers and 206 men, and forty-one machine-guns.

On the 23rd, another battalion of the West Riding Division,the 8th West Yorkshires, was given the task of clearing the wood completely. Their attack was only partially successful but it was the final straw for the Germans and they abandoned the Bois du Petit Champs during the night.

The 5th 'Dukes' were now re-organised and took up a position outside the hamlet of Cuitron in support of the 2/4th 'Dukes' as they advanced towards Bligny. There were great hopes for this attack and the Corps cavalry were ordered to the front but were brought to a halt with heavy casualties before they could reach the village which wasn't cleared until

July 28th when it was attacked and captured by the 2/4th and the 5th battalions.

That night the men were relieved at 3.30am by the 2/4th Kings Own Yorkshire Light Infantry and moved to a line about 500 yards in front of Marfaux to act as Divisional Reserve force. They were absolutely exhausted after eight days and nights of continuous hard fighting in difficult terrain but their most urgent task was to determine the casualty list. It made for depressing reading - thirteen officers and 400 other ranks had been killed, wounded or were missing.

The survivors numbered just 130 fighting men. The Division as a whole had lost 136 officers and 3,990 other ranks. (Figures taken from 'The West Riding Territorials in the Great War')

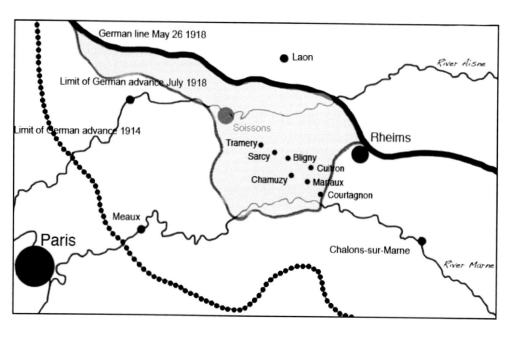

# Those killed in July 1918

**Fred Green**. Private. No 242029. 1/5th Battalion Duke of Wellington's Regiment.
Fred lived at Bank Top, Holmbridge and worked as a weaver at Clarence Mills, Holmbridge. Keen footballer, he played regularly for Holmbridge Football Club. He was shot badly in the leg on the 23rd and evacuated to No. 12 General Hospital but died two days later on July 25, 1918 aged 24. He is buried at St. Sever Cemetery Extension, Rouen.

The hospital chaplain wrote to his parents:

> Private Green wishes me to tell you that he has been wounded and he is now in this hospital. I feel bound to tell you that his condition is serious, though he is a little better than at first. Naturally everything is being done for him to ensure his recovery and give him comfort.

**Harold Hampshire**. Private. No 38748. 7th Battalion York and Lancashire Regiment.
Harold lived at Greenhill Bank Road, New Mill, and was a keen athlete running for the Holmfirth Harriers and playing football for New Mill A.F.C. He worked as a pattern weaver in Kirkbridge Mills.

He was quite badly wounded in the chest in 1917 and was brought home to a hospital in Reading to recuperate, returning to his regiment as soon as he was well.

Killed in action when a German shell exploded in the trench where he was working. Aged 20.

Buried in Harponville Communal Extension Cemetery.

Harold Hampshire

PTE J. MELLOR.

**Joseph Mellor**. Private. No 22237. 2/4th Battalion Duke of Wellington's Regiment. Joseph lodged with Mrs. P. Lee in Underbank Old Road, Holmfirth after his parents died and worked as a millhand at Albion Mills in Thongsbridge.

He enlisted in April 1917 and arrived in France the following January. Killed in action near Rheims on July 20 aged 19. Buried at Marfaux British Cemetery.

[PTE JAS WM O'MELIA.]

**James William O'Melia**. Private. No 203160. 2/6th Battalion West Yorkshire Regiment. James was the cousin of Harry O'Melia who had died of wounds in April and was part of the extended O'Melia family who lived in Norridge Bottom, Holmfirth. He was killed in the same fighting as Joseph Mellor, see above, on the same day and buried just a few rows away in the same cemetery - Marfaux British Cemetery near Rheims.

**Fred Tinker**. Private. No 32104. 'D' Company, 2/5th Battalion Duke of Wellington's Regiment. Fred was a farmer's boy from Howood Farm, Holmbridge and worked as a porter on Holmfirth railway station. He had enlisted in 1915 and arrived in France in August 1917. He was killed by shrapnel from an exploding shell in the same fighting as the above soldiers on July 22 near Rheims aged 25. His body was never found after the battle and his name is recorded on the Soissons Memorial to the Missing.

THE RALLY OF THE HILLS.

[PTE. FRED TINKER.]

**Arthur Whiteley**. Private. No 42060. 6th Battalion King's Own Scottish Borderers.
Arthur grew up at Carr Green, Holmfirth and went to Netherthong National School. He was employed in the receiving and delivery department of Bottom Mills and was a keen cyclist. He had been in France just five weeks when he was killed by a shellburst in the section of trench where he was on duty. Two other men in the trench also died. Killed in action July 26, 1918, aged 30.
Buried at La Kreule Military Cemetery.

CARR GREEN SOLDIER'S INSTANT DEATH.

[PTE. A. WHITELEY.]

Also remembered

**Arthur Kaye**. Private. No 39396, 5th Platoon, 'D' Company, 2/4th Battalion King's Own Yorkshire Light Infantry. (Formerly No 6520 Duke of Wellington's Regiment). He had been born in Hepworth, but lived with his wife, Mary, at 24 Underbank Old Road, Holmfirth and worked at Lower Mill. He was taken ill a few months after arriving in France and came home to recover. He returned to the trenches in March 1918 and was involved in the fighting around Rheims in July. He was reported missing on July 20, 1918 and was presumed killed on that date. His remains were found later and he is buried at Bodily Crossroads Military Cemetery.

**Turner Thorpe**. Private. No 24793. 1/7th Battalion Duke of Wellington's Regiment. Turner enlisted on the outbreak of war in 1914 and in the succeeding four years was wounded twice before being captured by the Germans in April 1918. His wife, Edith, received news that he had died of 'intestinal catarrh' on July 16, 1918. He was 29.

# Drawing to an end
# August and September 1918

It had been just one year since the battles at Passchendaele and the newspapers were full of 'In Memoriam' notices, remembering the husbands, brothers, sons and fathers who had fallen in the fighting twelve months before. One hundred and three names on the Holmfirth Memorial are the names of the men and boys killed in 1917, a total that surpasses, but only just, the number killed in this final year of the war.

**BAILEY** - In loving remembrance of my dear husband, Gunner James Bailey, who was killed in action the 15th of August, 1917, and was interred at Menin Road Cemetery, Ypres.

> We have lost, heaven hath gained
> One of the best the world contained.

- From his loving Wife, 42 St. George's Road, Scholes, Thongsbridge

**BETTS** - In loving memory of my dear husband, Gunner Talbot Betts, R.G.A., who was killed in action on August 11th, 1917 and was interred at Dickebusch Military Cemetery, near Ypres.

> A faithful husband so true and kind,
> No one on earth like him I'll find;
> One year has gone and none can tell
> The loss of one I love so well

- From his loving Wife and Child.

**HILTON** - In ever loving memory of our dear son, Harry Hilton, who was killed in action in France on August 16th, 1917

> He laid down his life that we might live.

- From his sorrowing Father and Mother, Sude Hill, New Mill

**SWALLOW** - In loving memory of my dear friend, Private Frank
Swallow, killed in action August 14th, 1917

He did not stop to reason,
When first the war began,
He went and did his duty
Like a soldier and a man.
His King and country called him,
That call was not in vain,
In Britain's roll of honour
You'll find my dear friend's name.

- Giles St., Netherthong

Mr and Mrs Beardsell of Hightown received news that their son had
been wounded for the second time - this time in the face - and was in a
military base hospital. Victor Lindley of Hade Edge had been shot in the
left hand and was in hospital in Southampton along with Herbert Lockwood from Scholes who had been hit by shrapnel in the foot.

Mr. and Mrs. Whiteley's son, Arthur, had been killed.

More Holmfirth men had been taken prisoner by the Germans - Harry
Jakeman, formerly of Stubbin, Hinchliffe Mill, Private Harry Brook and
Brook Turner of Deanhouse, Wilfred Smith, Albert Battye of Brownhill
Lane, Holmbridge, Lewis Bailey whose parents lived in Scholes.

By August 1918 there were 414 local men who were prisoners-of-war
and funds were raised to provide them with bread and parcels of food.
Messrs. Watkinson & Sons gave £7 10s each month - enough for two
prisoners; the Holmfirth Parish Church Mothers' Union raised 15s and
Mrs. Tinker gave £5. Captain Sykes in the trench line in France donated
£5.The cost of each parcel sent was £3 7s 6d and the Fund needed over
£1000 each month.

Soldiers in the Front Line wrote home regularly and the mood was
generally upbeat:

I saw a good lot of Holmfirth lads the day we came out of the
line. They were going up as we were coming down. First one was
shouting and then another. They seemed a cheerful lot.

Some people seem to think the war will finish before this year
goes out. I am confident we have the Germans beat. It is only national suicide for them to carry on any longer. I think something
very dramatic in our favour will happen before long.

What do you think of the situation now? I think the tide is in our favour. Fritz said the Yanks wouldn't make much difference. I think he will have altered his opinion now. They're a smart lot of men are the Americans and I guess they've come to win the war for us.

It is extremely good of the Holmfirth ladies to take care of the local lads who have gone to do their bit. I am sure they appreciate the gifts they receive and it cheers us up to think that so many kind ladies are looking after our needs...The papers have had good news lately. That's the stuff to give' em, eh! Old Jerry has got to be beat, and I don't think he has a leg to stand on.

Lieutenant-Colonel Walker who commanded the local 5th Battalion, Duke of Wellington's Regiment wrote to Councillor Brook who was Chairman of the Holmfirth District Council concerning the recent, heavy fighting:

In the recent fighting in the second battle of the Marne, the local Territorial Battalion had the honour of taking a share and were able on one of the days to storm a strongly-fortified German position, capturing 207 prisoners, 41 machine-guns and two trench mortars. We have asked that four of these machine-guns should be presented to Holmfirth by the Battalion as a memento of their share in this great battle. The Authorities have allowed our request and at some future period the guns will arrive for your disposal. Unless you have a more fitting place, I suggest that the guns be sent to the local Drill Hall of your Company where they could be kept.

An unnamed officer of the Battalion wrote to the Holmfirth Express:

The Battalion has recently taken a very distinguished part in the second Battle of the Marne and had gained for itself an even bigger reputation than it had before. We are all very proud to serve in our local Battalion. We were in the battle for ten days, and in one day's fight alone the Battalion took over 200 prisoners and over 40 machine guns and two trench mortars.

Even the French Commander was delighted:

Thanks to the heroic courage and proverbial tenacity of the British, the continued efforts of this great army corps have not been in vain.

And life went on.

For weeks now, people had been urged by the War Office to save and collect fruit stones and the shells of nuts and it was finally revealed why - they were to be converted into charcoal for use in gas-masks. Scientists had discovered that charcoal made from nuts and stones had absorption properties far superior to other forms and hundreds of tons were needed. 'Stone and Shell Clubs' had already been set up and every town, village, hotel and institution was implored to join in the project.

There was a national shortage of jam and in New Mill the members of the Food Control Committee were already making plans to harvest the local blackberry crop. Schools were being asked to take their children into the countryside to pick the fruit. Each child would need to provide their own basket and, unusually, there was a system of payment - 3d for every pound of fruit collected. The Girl Guides and the Boy Scouts had already enrolled. A prominent member of the committee was Annie Ballantyne, Headmistress of the National School in New Mill, and it would be her pupils who would be doing the work. (Annie's officer son, Phillip who had enlisted in 1914, would be killed the following month in October, just two weeks before the end of the war)

On Saturday, August 3rd, the Holmfirth Branch of the National Association of Discharged Soldiers and Sailors held a Forget-Me-Not-Day where all the ladies of the branch paraded through Holmfirth with bunches of Forget-me-not flowers which they sold to passers-by to raise funds. It was a successful day - £51 6s 10d. - notwithstanding the rain which poured down throughout the afternoon and caused the planned cricket match between wounded soldiers of the Holmfirth Auxiliary Hospital and discharged Holmfirth soldiers to be abandoned. Instead, the Hinchliffe Mill Brass Band played during the evening concert at the Drill Hall where the star turns were R.H. Jackson, the well known Yorkshire ventriloquist and his dolls, and Lance-Corporal MacVee who delighted everyone with his mimics and whistling.

The Matron of the Holmfirth hospital was Mrs. A. H. Roberts - in fact it was she who had suggested in 1915 that the town should create and support a local hospital that would accommodate six wounded soldiers. Since then she had been the mainstay of the place and in August 1918 she was awarded the Royal Red Cross, a military decoration for exceptional services in military nursing. The first ever recipient of the award from Queen Victoria was Florence Nightingale.

Textile workers, represented by their General Union, were awarded an increase in their war bonus of between 7% and 9%, giving male workers an extra 24s 6d in their wage packets.

It was needed. Things weren't just in short supply, they were also expensive. Manpower demands from the army had resulted in another fifty thousand miners being conscripted as well as thirty-five thousand young agricultural workers and cuts in the supply of coal and limits on the supply of electricity were expected for the coming winter. Mr. Wilfred Whiteley, prospective Labour candidate for Holmfirth and District spoke at an open-air meeting at Upper Bridge, arguing that too much was expected of the working-classes:

> One day there was a call for more men for the Army, another it was for silver bullets, then for the victory war loan, another for the consumption of less bread, another for the production of more ships and on another day for the production of high explosive shells. Now we had come to the point when we were told we were having to face drastic reductions, which would affect the poorer classes to a greater degree than any other class.

# How to use less COAL

Be prepared. Buy fire bricks now.

Do not start fires until it is really cold.

Indulge less in the luxury of a hot bath. A cold bath in the morning, for those who can stand it, is more healthy and keeps you warm longer.

**Remember—the more careful you are at the beginning of the winter the less will be your difficulty at the end. Make a good start, so as to have something in hand.**

His speech wasn't particularly well received, and there were a number of interruptions:

> You want to go into Germany and see if they want a member or two there. We are not going to have any pacifism - I will tell you that straight. If you want to be a German, go onto Germany.

Now that people could begin to dare to imagine war's end, the Holmfirth Express had great fun in re-printing many of the German Kaiser's speeches:

> Remember that you are the chosen people!
> The spirit of the Lord has descended on me because I am the Emperor of the Germans! I am the instrument of the Almighty. I am His sword, His agent. Woe and death to all those who oppose my will! Woe and death to those who do not believe in my mission! Woe and death to the cowards! Let them perish, all the enemies of the German people! God demands their destruction; God, who by my mouth, bids ye do His will !
> Exterminate first the treacherous English, and walk over General French's contemptible little army.

> August 19, 1914

> America had better look out after the war. I shall stand no nonsense from the Americans.

> October 22, 1915

> Germany is invincible, in spite of the superior number of our enemies, and every day confirms this anew. Germany knows her strength and she relies on God's help.

> July 31, 1916

> England is particularly the enemy to be struck down, however difficult it may be.

> August 23, 1917

> Our victorious armies have not yet succeeded in entirely breaking our enemies' will to destruction but Germany's sons with unshakeable confidence are rallying round their supreme War Lord to win for the Fatherland life, happiness and freedom.

> July 11, 1918

The hour is grave, but trusting in your strength and God's gracious help we feel ourselves strong enough to defend our beloved Fatherland.

October 27, 1918

With Germany and its armed forces in utter turmoil, the Kaiser abdicated in November 1918.

The British Army of 1918 had transformed itself from the one that had fought just a few years previously. It was no longer the army of 1916 - that army with its idealistic enthusiasm and utter self-belief, but which was only just beginning to experiment with military technology and had yet to master the notoriously difficult art of controlled and accurate artillery fire. That relatively untried army, bursting with confidence, had found itself unprepared for the sheer savagery and scale of modern mass warfare.

Since then it had learned - sometimes lessons learned through terrible cost - and the army of 1918 was now a formidable military machine as good as the German Army and in many respects better.

Artillery was a case in point. At the beginning of the war a gun was fired, gunners watched where the shell landed and made adjustments, fired again and adjusted height and bearing until they were on target. There was no doubt that shellfire could certainly solve the problems posed by trench warfare. Trenches and dugouts could be destroyed, defenders killed and barbed wire cut if enough guns could be brought to bear on the designated target. And therein lay the problem. In the early part of the war and up until 1917, guns were inaccurate, shells were often unstable in flight and frequently failed to explode at all, and shrapnel was, at times, ineffective against thick belts of barbed-wire - high explosive was more efficient but in short supply. Enemy gun batteries were notoriously difficult to locate, being small and mobile.

It took years to provide solutions. New factories were developed and built; scientists and engineers were tasked with coming up with new types of propellant, explosives, shells and the means of delivering them. A Ministry of Munitions was formed that greatly increased the amount of firepower available to the army. Heavy guns that had been in particularly short supply in 1914 were now plentiful. There was almost an unlimited quantity of shells for gunners to fire. Scientists devised ways to locate enemy guns through the techniques of 'sound ranging' and 'flash spotting'. Sound ranging involved a line of microphones that recorded the sound of passing enemy shells which then provided enough data to work out where the shells originated. Flash spotting used forward observers to watch for the muzzle flash of German guns and then use a complicated system of triangulation to work out their position. Highly accurate maps of all the fighting areas were now commonplace.

And the gunners themselves now had the technical skills to match. Artillery officers took measurements of wind and air pressure before firing; detailed records were kept of each gun, particularly the number of rounds fired, so that officers could compensate for wear and tear on the gun's barrel; weight, type and particular propellant would all be taken into account when choosing which shell would most effectively destroy the target.

The excitement of being bound up in war was long gone. Now the mood was much more sober and it was 'a job to be done', not one to take pleasure in. From the top down - through the whole command structure - there was a core of professionalism running throughout the army.

After two years of high command Haig and his generals began to grasp the secret of battlefield success, of when to move and when to hold back. The machine they controlled had mastered the science of production and logistics - the ability to provide unlimited war materials, from guns to ammunition to tanks, and the means to ensure that those materials were always in the right place and time. No private soldier ever went hungry, no artillery formation ever went without shells or guns. And the men were good at what they did - which, no matter how many different ways it was phrased, came down to one essential aim - killing the enemy in greater numbers than you yourself were losing. (Many generals on all sides of the conflict were convinced that by 1918 the war had become one of attrition i.e. last man standing wins). In this respect it helped if the enemy was attacking (as the Germans did between March and July) and you were behind sound defences and from where you could inflict heavy losses as they exposed themselves. But even when the tide turned after July 28 and the British attacked and forced the Germans into retreat it was a carefully considered and clever campaign by men, at all levels, who were able to read the battle, switch the focus and keep the enemy confused, surprised and off balance.

The period from the end of July 1918 to November 11 and the armistice was one of unrelenting pressure from the British, advances unseen since the invasions of 1914, and the complete collapse of the enemy's armies.

> A great series of battles, in which, throughout three months of continuous fighting, the British Armies advanced without a check from one victory to another.

> Despatches, page 257

From July 28 onwards the Germans were in retreat. The French had stopped the advance on Paris on July 18; in the north the British had re-captured Meteren; and the Americans and the French moved on Soissons.

Just a few weeks before, with Paris at their mercy, the Germans had been confidently expecting peace overtures from the defeated Allies. The German Chancellor, Georg von Hertling, later wrote:

> That was on the 15th. On the 18th even the most optimistic among us knew that all was lost. The history of the world was played out in three days.

Ludendorff had lost his great gamble. Haigh knew it; Hindenburg knew it; the French and British War Cabinets knew it; most of the German Army knew it. People at home suspected it. Commander-in-Chief of Allied Forces, General Foch, issued an Order of the Day to his French army:

> Four years of effort aided by our faithful Allies, four years of trial stoically accepted, commence to bear their fruit...Today I say to you: Tenacity, Boldness, and Victory must be yours.

On July 22nd the Kaiser arrived at General Hindenburg's advanced headquarters at Avesnes in France to be given a full report on the failed offensives and the successful Allied counter attacks. Deeply depressed he described himself to companions as '...a defeated War Lord'.

As early as January of that year a British intelligence report to General Haig's headquarters had stated:

> The German accession of morale is not of a permanent character and is not likely to stand the strain of an unsuccessful attack with consequent losses...If Germany attacks and fails she will be ruined.

She had attacked, she had failed and from this moment on Germany was lost. Ludendorff was winning battles but going nowhere. Some German generals (General von Lossberg and others) advocated evacuating France completely and reforming on the German border as a way of saving the army. Both Hindenburg and Ludendorff, after pushing aside the Kaiser and his more moderate advisors, blamed others for the failure. Hindenburg wrote to his wife that it wouldn't be his fault if Germany lost the war:

> That fault would lie with the homeland which had not succeeded in imparting the necessary spiritual strength to the fighting front.

Starvation throughout the homeland was no excuse, he said. Ludendorff also blamed the German people for the collapse:

> In Berlin they only felt their own impotence in face of the enemy's spirit; they lost the hope of victory, and drifted. The desire for peace became stronger than the will to fight for victory.

The Allies, recognising Germany's weaknesses, continued to apply pressure and General Haig planned for the next major offensive - an attack in August, eastwards from Amiens, through the Somme valley.

On July 25th the recently renamed Royal Air Force dropped 300 tons of bombs behind the German lines near Amiens. As the 5th Battalion 'Dukes' were capturing Bligny on July 28th, major American forces on their left were attacking the German-held villages of Seringes and Sergy. It was desperate fighting against the elite Prussian Guards and the Americans later built a cemetery there covering more than thirty-six acres and holding 6,000 headstones for their dead.

The first ever airborne supply drop to advancing troops took place in June when 100,000 rounds of ammunition were dropped to Australian machine-gunners as they attacked and captured Hamel on the Somme.

There were Italian successes against the Austrians along the Piave delta and 3,000 Austrians were taken prisoner. One of the Americans wounded during the fighting was an eighteen year old volunteer ambulance driver named Ernest Hemingway. He was hit by shrapnel from an Austrian mortar shell as he was handing out chocolate to Italian soldiers and was later awarded the Italian Silver Medal of Military Valour.

Near Soissons a young German corporal was part of the general retreat and distinguished himself by his courage and conduct. Unusually for a corporal, he was awarded the Iron Cross, First Class for his 'personal bravery and general merit'. Corporal Hitler wore it for the rest of his life. The officer who recommended him for the award, Captain Hugo Guttman, was Jewish.

Meanwhile in Russia battles were still raging and the situation became even more complicated. The Red Army was fighting the White Army while the Black Anarchist Army fought everyone. Somewhere a Green Army was rampaging through the vast Russian landscape. The Germans were in control of the Baltic region and Ukraine; German troops were in Finland and Germany had created the independent Georgian Republic. The British War Cabinet, anxious to protect huge military stores in Murmansk and Archangel which had been donated to the Russian Army, sent forces to guard and keep them from the Bolsheviks. They also offered to train and arm the hundreds of thousands of anti-Bolshevik Russians.

There was already one foreign force fighting the Bolsheviks in Russia. This was the 60,000 strong Czech Legion in Siberia formed from prisoners-of-war who had been liberated by the Treaty of Brest-Litovsk and who were keen to fight the Bolsheviks as part of their efforts to secure an independent Czechoslovakia. They even tried to fight their way through Russia to Europe to join the Allies in their fight against Germany, even though they had spent the war fighting on behalf of the Germans. (I said it was complicated!)

At the end of June, the Czech Legion reached the port of Vladivostok, defeated the Red Army units stationed there and took control of the port. President Wilson suggested that the Japanese should immediately send 12,000 troops to 'rescue' the Czechs. The British declared that they would be sending a regiment from Hong Kong. In the end the Americans went.

One week later in Yekaterinburg on the night of 16-17 July, 1918, in an orgy of violence that had become the norm, Bolshevik troops shot, bayoneted and clubbed to death Tsar Nicholas II, his wife Tsarina Alexandra and their five children Olga, Tatiana, Maria, Anastasia, and Alexei and all those who had made a decision to accompany them into imprisonment - Eugene Botkin, Anna Demidova, Alexei Trupp and Ivan

Kharitonov. All of their bodies were then stripped, mutilated, burned and disposed of in a field called Porosenkov Log in the Koptyaki forest.

Despite their reputation for extreme violence against opponents, the Bolsheviks were struggling to maintain their power base in Moscow. The Socialist Revolutionary Group, who were happy to continue the war against Germany, attacked and wounded Lenin and killed two of his closest colleagues. Lenin sent Stalin to the Volga city of Tsaritsyn to carry out reprisals which he typically conducted on a ferocious scale, describing his actions in a telegram to Moscow as 'Systematic mass terror against the bourgeoisie and its agents'. They later renamed Tsaritsyn as Stalingrad.

# The 'Black Day' of the German Army
# 'A tres bon stunt.'

By the beginning of August the British Army had largely recovered from its weaknesses in manpower dating from the earlier part of the year and, despite losses incurred in the recent German attacks, was in a position to undertake a major offensive. The French found themselves in the same position the British had been in months earlier - heavy losses during the recent battles coupled with an existing manpower shortage meant that they could no longer be the leaders in any planned offensive. From now on until the end of the war they could only act in a support role as junior partners.

Haig wanted to build on his successes during the fighting throughout July and he was now commanding an army that was probably the best trained, most experienced and fully professional force the country had ever seen.

His plan was to use the Fourth Army commanded by General Rawlinson and the Fourth Army packed quite a punch. It already contained British III Corps comprising five British divisions (one of which also included an American regiment - 131st Infantry), and the Australian Corps, made up of six crack divisions. To these he added three Cavalry divisions and the Canadian Corps of five elite divisions. The Canadians had taken no part in the recent fighting and they were fresh, intact and eager to fight. He also allocated to Rawlinson the biggest number of tanks to be assembled for one battle during the whole war.

Haig's aim was ambitious and not just about capturing territory. He wanted the complete destruction and demoralisation of the German Army. To support the attack Haig also took command of the French First Army on his right flank.

Secrecy during the extensive preparations was vital and the British had learned important lessons from the way the Germans had assembled their armies in the March offensives. Fourth Army areas were saturated with signposts reading 'KEEP YOUR MOUTH SHUT'. The same message was posted in every soldier's pay book. Instructions to officers included:

> Nothing attracts attention to an offensive more than a large number of officers with maps looking over the parapet and visiting Observation posts.

Accordingly, reconnaissance of German lines was severely restricted. All movement of troops or transport towards British lines was forbidden in daylight. Groups were organised to march away from their own lines in order to fool the watching Germans.

To screen and disguise the arrival of the Canadians, the Australians edged to their right of the line and III Corps moved to the left. This apparent 'thinning out' of the Allied positions deceived the Germans completely and Haig finally decided that the attack would commence on August 8.

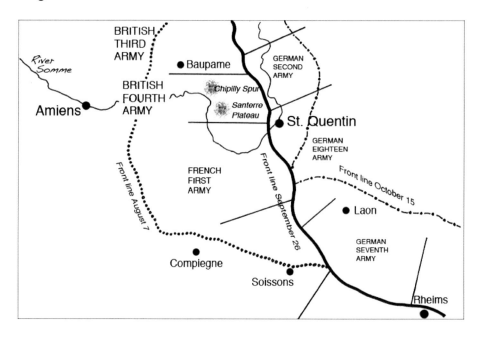

Zero hour was set for 4.20am for the Fourth Army and forty five minutes later for the French who wouldn't be using tanks and would need a short preliminary bombardment of the opposing trench lines. Rawlinson had decided to dispense with artillery to open the battle and was relying on the 342 heavy Mark V and 72 medium Mark A tanks - the Whippets. (The title 'Whippet' was something of a misnomer. Each tank weighed fourteen tons, carried a crew of three and four Hotchkiss machine-guns; maximum road speed was 8.3 mph, a little slower than a horse at a steady gallop). There was also a number of the new Mark V Star model; these were extra long, extended tanks, invaluable for crossing wide trenches and anti-tank ditches and also capable of carrying twenty to twenty-five fighting men. Unfortunately, a design fault inside the tank caused carbon monoxide poisoning after a few hours so that, having reached the destination, crew and passengers were close to collapse and needed considerable recovery time before they were capable of functioning again.

The air above the battle was to be controlled by over 800 aircraft, 376 of them fighter planes and, in a sign of what was to come in the next war, one squadron was tasked to work exclusively with the tanks - a particular tactic noted and recorded by the Germans who, a generation later, developed the idea into Blitzkreig - lightning war. Even this number was dwarfed by the French contribution on the right whose total air strength was 1,104 - a combined number of nearly two thousand Allied planes. The Germans scraped together 365 aircraft.

Rawlinson had amassed 2,070 guns and howitzers for the initial assault and as they prepared to open fire at 4.20am observers could see that ground mist had formed in the valleys and was spreading to the higher ground. This may have hampered the waiting aircraft but it was a definite bonus to the attacking infantry, as it had been for the Germans on March 21.

As the barrage opened and the tanks and troops set off, Haig and the High Command waited anxiously until the mist began to clear mid-morning and the scale of the success of the attack became obvious. There was a hold-up on the British III Corps Front but nowhere else had the advance been halted or even delayed. All forward movement had been completed on time and without problems; the supporting troops had passed through the front divisions according to plan as though it were a training exercise. The Australians reached their first objective by 7am; their second by 10.30am and by 11am the Canadians were alongside. By 1.30pm it was all over.

Apart from some delays on their extreme flanks caused by the French and the British, the Australians had taken all their planned objectives and the Canadians had advanced almost eight miles.

> ...the whole Santerre plateau seen from the air was dotted with parties of infantry, field artillery and tanks moving forward. Staff officers were galloping about, many riding horses in battle for the first time...No enemy guns appeared to be firing and no co-ordinated defence was apparent.

Official History 1918

German prisoners-of-war.

The Australians captured 183 German officers, 7,742 soldiers and 173 guns for a loss to themselves of about 3,000 casualties; the Canadians took 114 officers, 4,919 other ranks, 161 guns and too many machine-guns and mortars to count. Their casualty list was 3,500.

Several years after the war, the Commander of the Canadian forces, General Sir Arthur Currie, commented:

> The success of the Australians and Canadians on August 8th was so startling...that in my opinion G.H.Q. had no definite ideas what to do...I also know that senior staff officers hurried up from G.H.Q. to see me and to ask what I thought should be done. They indicated quite plainly that our success had gone far beyond expectations and that no-one seemed to know what to do. I replied in the Canadian vernacular: ' The going seems good: lets go on.'

Only on the flanks was there a problem. The Germans opposite III Corps had shelled the British lines throughout the night, drenching the area in gas and preventing any kind of co-ordinated attack. The defensive lines were particularly strong here and there was parity in numbers between attackers and defenders. The steep, wooded terrain made life difficult for tanks and, consequently, far fewer had been deployed here than elsewhere. The British 58th Division failed to take the Chipilly Spur where the high ground dominated the left of the Australian advance leaving them exposed to intense machine-gun fire. This is where they suffered most of their casualties. Even further to the left of the attacking line, the British 18th Division was unable to move beyond its first objectives.

The reasons for these failures weren't too difficult to spot. Both these British divisions had been heavily involved in the German offensive a few months earlier and had been badly mauled. They were 'casualty' divisions, lacking experienced officers and N.C.O.'s and with ranks filled with the latest recruits from England. Expecting them to be able to prepare for a major attack in the dark and wet and under heavy shelling and then fight a well entrenched and determined enemy was a step too far.

Conditions in the French First Army to the right of the attack were just as disappointing even though the going was much easier for them. Despite orders to achieve 'the greatest rapidity…it is forbidden to wait for neighbouring divisions…the attacks will be pushed on and continued until night' they ended up five hours behind the Canadians. The French General in command was found almost in tears because three battalions of his Colonial Infantry had fled in panic when they encountered a single German machine-gun.

The armoured component of the attack had gone well. The tanks took care of enemy machine-gun posts and defence lines but proved vulnerable to brave German gunners who refused to leave their guns, often shooting at almost point-blank range. Nine out of ten tanks in one sector were hit and set on fire by field guns at seventy yards. Twelve tanks were attacked at a range of half a mile as they exposed themselves at the top of a ridge and six were hit immediately and another three within a few hundred yards.

The Whippets did everything expected of them. They captured artillery batteries from the rear, shot up retreating columns of German troops and helped in the mopping-up operation.

But despite their successes of the first day it would be another generation before tanks became the war-winning machines they were designed
to be. Firstly, the problem of reliability needed to be solved. Of the 414
tanks that trundled into battle on August 8 only 145 were still in action
the following day; by the 10th this number had fallen to 85; just thirty-eight tanks were available on the 11th and a meagre six on the 12th.
Conditions for the crews inside the tanks were simply appalling.

> It is very often not realised what is meant by the exhaustion of the
> crews; this in the case of tanks does not merely mean bodily fa-
> tigue. The crews of one battalion after some hard fighting became
> absolutely exhausted and most of them physically ill. The pulses
> of one crew were taken immediately they got out of their tank; the
> beat averaged 130 to the minute or just twice as fast as they should
> have been. Two men of one crew temporarily lost their reason and
> had to be restrained by force, and one tank commander became de-
> lirious. In some cases where infantry were carried in the tank, they
> fainted within three-quarters of an hour of the start. At the time the
> physical strain on crews accentuated by the extreme heat was not
> fully appreciated by commanders of some formations.

R.A.C. Papers, 'Short Report on Tank Corps Operations'.

In the air, August 8 was a day of mixed fortunes. Low flying aircraft disrupted German movement, attacked staff-cars and shot-up machine-gun
posts, but towards the afternoon reports began to pour in to Headquarters that the roads leading to the bridges over the Somme were packed
with retreating German troops and horse-drawn transport. If the bridges
could be bombed and destroyed the effect could result in total disaster
for the German Second Army who would have no means of escape. But
German pilots, recognising the importance of the bridges, fought desperately throughout the day against the waves of British bombers and
shot down forty-five RAF planes and badly damaged another fifty-two.
The bridges, and the Second Army, survived.

One of the German pilots that day had recently taken over command of
the famous 'Richthofen circus' and flew numerous sorties; his name was
Hauptmann Hermann Goering.

The second day of the battle, August 9, was crucial for the Allied advance but in the end proved a disappointing day. No German support
troops had yet moved into place and, to all intents and purposes, the
Canadians and the Australians were faced with a gap in the German line.

The Chipilly Spur had at last been taken by the British 58th Division (with the help of the American 131st Regiment) and, back at Headquarters, the road ahead seemed clear. But somehow it never really got going. The furthest advance of the day was the three miles covered by the Canadians. The problem was that no-one on the British side, whether in high or divisional command, had any real experience of open warfare and found themselves at a loss when given freedom of space. After four years of static trench warfare they had forgotten how to conduct a war of movement. Staff officers had become over-reliant on a complicated and intricate trench telephone communications system and were reluctant to move forward and possibly lose control over advancing units. There was also the fear of the expected German counter-attack and the need to quickly create some kind of defensive position. No-one quite appreciated how demoralised the German Army was.

As each day passed the attacking troops became more exhausted and as enemy resistance stiffened the advance slowed. Up ahead lay the desolation of the old 1916 Somme battlefield, a place of abandoned and collapsing trenches and shell holes, covered with rusting barbed wire. It was not a pleasant prospect.

For the German Army though, there was no disguising the catastrophe that had occurred on the opening day:

> As the sun set on August 8th on the battlefield the greatest defeat which the German Army had suffered since the beginning of the war was an accomplished fact. The position divisions between the Avre and the Somme which had been struck by the enemy attack were nearly completely annihilated. The troops in the front line north of the Somme had also suffered seriously, as also the reserve divisions thrown into the battle in the course of the day. The total loss of the formations employed in the Second Army area is estimated at 650 to 700 officers and 26,000 to 27,000 other ranks. More than 400 guns, besides a huge number of machine-guns, trench mortars, and other war material had been lost.

German monograph: Die Catastrophe des 8 August 1918

Ludendorff, who by now was de facto ruler of Germany (even Hindenburg had been reduced to little more than a figurehead) was called to a conference at Spa in Belgium on August 13 - ironically enough in the Hotel Britannique - where, it was assumed, he could inform everyone that the war was lost.

# Those killed in August 1918

[PTE. DONALD BEARDSELL.]

**Donald Beardsell**. Private. No. 241842. 12th Battalion Highland Light Infantry. Born and raised in Holme Village and worked at Whiteley and Green's mill in the valley bottom. Enlisted in 1916 but was returned home suffering from some disease. He was treated in a number of hospitals, including Holmfirth Auxiliary Hospital and was then posted to duties in Ireland and Scotland before returning to France. He died of wounds received on August 9, 1918. Buried at Arneke British Cemetery.

[PTE. J. W. CHAPMAN.]

**John William Chapman**. Private. No 152793, 6th Dragoons (Inniskilling). Before enlisting in 1915 John had lived in Woodhouse, Holmbridge and worked as a teamer delivering provisions for Henry Mitchell and Sons. He died of wounds on August 9, 1918. No known grave but his name is carved on the Vis-en-Artois Memorial to the Missing.

**Harold Farrar**. Rifleman. No C/7226. 18th Battalion King's Royal Rifle Corps. Harold was yet another employee of Washpit Mills. He had been raised in Underbank but, before enlisting in 1915, lived with his wife in Church Terrace, Holmfirth. After three years serving in France he managed to get home leave but was wounded and died of his wounds just four weeks after rejoining his regiment on August 24th, 1918, aged 23. He is buried at Lijssenthoek Military Cemetery.

Harold Farrar

**James Haigh**. Private. No 29310. 10th Battalion West Yorkshire Regiment. (Despite the rank of Lance-Corporal given in the newspaper, James' rank in Huddersfield's Roll of Honour is given as 'Private').

James was from New Town, Holmfirth and worked with his brothers as a plasterer. He enlisted in 1915 and was killed in action on August 27th, 1918, aged 22. Buried at Bulls Road Cemetery, Flers.

LANCE-CORPORAL J. HAIGH.

**Albert Battye**. Private. No 48004. 13th Battalion The Royal Inniskilling Fusiliers (formerley 38142 West Yorkshire Regiment). Albert was born and raised in Hinchliffe Mill, Holmfirth and played football for Hinchliffe Mill AFC. He was a strong Wesleyan, singing with his local church choir and being a member of the bible class. Married with one little daughter, he enlisted in 1916. Suffered from a severe attack of trench feet during the summer of 1917 and was killed in action on August 27th, 1918. He was buried in Nieppe-Bois (Rue De Bois) British Cemetery, Vieux-Berquin.

**Kenneth Hinchliffe**. Private. No 29318. 8th Battalion King's Own (Royal Lancaster Regiment).

Kenneth grew up in Holmfirth and worked at Albion Mills in Thongsbridge before enlisting. He graduated from his army training as a first class Lewis gunner but was killed in action a few weeks after arriving in France on August 23. The Regimental chaplain explained to his mother in a letter that Kenneth had been killed instantly by either a bullet or shell fire. He was 18 years old.

Buried at Douchy-les-Ayette British Cemetery.

# 96 DAYS

From August 8th to November 11th and the end of the war was just 96 days. Somehow, without anyone really realising it (apart from General Haig, Commander-in-Chief of the British Army) - not the British Government, certainly not the French or the Americans and perhaps not even fully accepted by the Germans - the war was almost over.

Ludendorff, as head of the German Army, wanted the fighting to stop, but only so that he could negotiate a successful peace treaty, one that allowed Germany to retain large parts of occupied Belgium and France. If that proved impossible then the fighting would begin again (his army had other ideas). On August 9th he told an army colleague 'We cannot win this war any more, but we must not lose it.'

One of the most senior German army commanders, Crown Prince Rupprecht of Bavaria wrote on the 10th 'Our military situation has deteriorated so rapidly that I no longer believe we can hold out over the winter; it is even possible that a catastrophe will come earlier.'

When seven fresh German divisions arrived to take their place in the Front Line they were greeted by drunken German soldiers shouting 'What do you war-prolongers want?'

On August 12th, Ludendorff informed the newly appointed Chief of the Naval Staff, Admiral Scheer, that only German submarines could now win the war 'There is no more hope for the offensive. The generals have lost their foothold.'

The senior military advisor to King-Emperor Charles told the Kaiser that Austria-Hungary 'could only continue the war until December.'

Yet when the Kaiser summoned his principal military advisors and allies to a meeting on August 13th Ludendorff failed to present a fully realistic appraisal of the war situation and instead vacillated between unfounded optimism and blaming the Home Front for defeatism. There was concern over his mental health. A psychologist advised him to rest and to sing German folk songs every morning.

There was talk at the meeting of seeking an intermediary to open peace negotiations but only on the condition that Germany retained Belgium and Alsace-Lorraine. This was self-delusion on a grand scale. The more the politicians and generals talked it seemed, the more they disregarded reality and the more optimistic about the outcome of the war they became. After a week of intense discussion the Kaiser's Foreign Minister - Otto von Hintze - told the assembled leaders that the army believed that '… there is no reason to doubt ultimate victory. We shall be vanquished only when we doubt that we shall win.'

At the same time in London Winston Churchill was informing Lloyd-George that, given the number of tanks in current production, the Tank Corps would need to be increased to 100,000 men by June 1919. Lloyd-George himself had already written his memorandum to the Dominion Prime Ministers arguing for a decisive Western Front offensive in 1920.

General Foch, representing the French Army, had asked for the 1920 conscripts to be called up a year early so that he could have fresh troops for the fight in 1919. He was outvoted by military and political opinion that wanted the British and Americans to take the lead in any attack. The French would merely act in a supporting role from now on.

On August 14th, the newly created Inter-Allied Munitions Council met in Paris to discuss the particular needs of the soon-to-be massive American Army in France. It was decided that the Americans would be equipped with a mixture of British and French weapons and that a tank factory would be built specially for them.

Churchill pointed out that the Germans possessed:

> …far the larger supplies of the irritant mustard gas, but our outputs were broadening daily. Although the accidentally burned and blistered at the factories exceeded 100% of the staff every three months, volunteers were never lacking.

What was clear to everyone was that the British offensive starting on August 8th around Amiens had been a resounding success. The combined Australian, Canadian and British assault on the German Second Army had been a masterpiece of planning, deception, surprise and operational excellence. On the Somme in 1916, the British had attacked in battalions numbering a thousand men equipped with four Lewis light machine-guns and one or two light trench mortars. At Amiens in 1918, the numbers of attacking soldiers in each battalion had been reduced to just 500 men but they had with them thirty Lewis guns, eight trench mortars, sixteen rifle grenadiers, air support and six tanks. The British had learned their lessons.

Of the 27,000 German soldiers lost in that one day, over 18,000 of them had surrendered. This worried the German High Command more than anything else - the collapse in fighting spirit and the willingness of German soldiers to surrender at the first opportunity. German units moving into the line were jeered as 'strikebreakers'. The British Fourth Army War Diary records that the Germans 'surrendered freely and in large numbers without any serious fighting.'

A young British Second Lieutenant, Alfred Duff-Cooper (later to become First Lord of the Admiralty) was in action for the first time, ahead of his men and attacking a railway cutting:

> Looking down I saw one man running away up the other side of the cutting. I had a shot at him with my revolver. Presently I saw two men moving cautiously below me. I called to them in what German I could at the moment remember to surrender and throw up their hands. They did so immediately. They obviously did not realise that I was alone. They came up the cutting with their hands up, followed, to my surprise, by others. There were eighteen or nineteen in all. If they had rushed me then they would have been perfectly safe, for I can never hit a haystack with a revolver and my own men were eighty yards away. However they came back with me like lambs, I crawling most of the way to avoid fire from the other side of the railway.

British forces attacking yet again on the Somme on August 21st advanced a further two miles and took 2,000 Germans prisoner. On the 24th the British captured Thiepval Ridge; Mametz Wood on the 25th; Delville Wood on August 27th. Before August was out the Germans had abandoned all the towns and villages of Flanders that they had won at enormous cost just four months earlier. During August alone the Allies had captured 150,000 German soldiers, 2,000 guns and 13,000 machine guns.

For the first time General Haig voiced his belief that the war could be won in 1918. After Amiens his one and only preoccupation was to end the war in the shortest possible time. When Churchill arrived to talk about Munitions policy for the following June, Haig told him he intended to get complete victory in the next few months. He told Churchill:

> We are engaged in a 'wearing-out' battle - - and are outlasting and beating the enemy. If we allow the enemy a period of quiet, he will recover, and the 'wearing-out' process must be recommenced. In reply. I was told that the General Staff in London calculate that the decisive period of the war cannot arrive until next July.

He had already read a copy of the latest 33-page Memorandum from the War Office General Staff and had written in the margins 'Words! Words! Words! Lots of words and little else. Theoretical rubbish! Whoever drafted this stuff could never win any campaign.'

In his orders to Army Commanders he emphasised how much and how quickly things had changed and encouraged them to pursue this new British approach to making war. Twenty one years later the Germans would call it Blitzkrieg and use it to conquer most of Europe:

> Risks which a month ago would have been criminal to incur, ought now to be incurred as a duty. It is no longer necessary to advance in regular lines and step by step. On the contrary, each division should be given a distant objective which must be reached independently of its neighbour, and even if one's flank is thereby exposed for the time being. Reinforcements must be directed on the points where our troops are gaining ground, not where they are checked…

For the Germans the attacks on them were relentless. While the British Third Army under General Byng was forcing them back across the Somme Valley the French attacked east of Soissons and pushed them back over the River Aisne. The same day the Americans captured Juvigny, five miles north of Soissons and two days later the Australians entered Peronne.

Even though many of them were new to the fighting, these American troops were by now giving a very good account of themselves. There were over 800,000 in France, including the Black 369th Infantry Division and when this unit was sent to work as stevedores they protested vehemently and demanded to be sent to the Front. It was pointed out to them that it was actually illegal under American Law for them to serve alongside white American soldiers and they were sent instead to fight alongside the French. The American Marine Brigade had been heavily involved in recent fighting and had lost nearly 50% of its fighting force, including a young Jack Bamforth, member of the Bamforth family and born in Holmfirth. General Pershing visited some of the wounded in hospital and his biographer records a moment when he spoke to a young soldier who had lost his right arm. The boy had been operated on the previous day and, lying in bed, said apologetically 'I cannot salute you sir'. Pershing replied 'No son, it's I that should salute you.'

American soldiers had certainly impressed the civilian population. Vera Brittain, serving as a nurse in France wrote in her diary after seeing a group of marching soldiers:

> They were swinging rapidly towards Camiers and though the sight of soldiers marching was now too familiar to arouse curiosity, an unusual quality of bold vigour in their stride caused me to stare at them with puzzled interest. They looked larger than ordinary men; their tall straight figures were in contrast to the undersized armies of pale recruits to which we were grown accustomed. At first I thought their nice, clean uniforms were officers, yet obviously they could not be officers, for there were too many of them; they seemed, as it were, Tommies in heaven. Had yet another regiment been conjured out of our depleted Dominions? I wondered, watching them move with such rhythm, such dignity, such serene consciousness of self-respect. But I knew the colonial troops so well, and these were different; they were assured where the Australians were aggressive; self-possessed where the New Zealanders were turbulent".
>
> Suddenly she hears a cry from behind her - Look! Look! Its the Americans.

On September 3rd, General Foch, Supreme Commander of all the Allied Forces on the Western Front, gave the order for continual attacks along the whole length of the line and the French and Americans finalised their plans for a massive, joint attack on the St Mihiel Salient. They had brought together more than 3,000 guns and 40,000 tons of ammunition. The British had promised the American Commander, General Pershing, three hundred tanks, but because of the fast moving advances in their own line they couldn't be spared. The French had promised 500 tanks but only delivered 267. Fifteen miles of road, leading to the attack point had been specially constructed while sixty-five evacuation trains had been positioned in railway sidings to take the estimated and expected 21,000 wounded to hospital.

On September 12th, in the pouring rain, 200,000 American troops, supported by 48,000 French attacked on a twelve-mile front. Two days later French troops entered St Mihiel. In addition to the more 'normal' high-explosive shells, American gunners fired 100,000 phosgene ones; in the air, under American command, the largest ever air armada was in action with American, French, Italian, Belgian, Portuguese and Brazilian planes.

Lieutenant-Colonel George S. Patton informed the men under his command 'American tanks do not surrender so long as one tank is able to go forward. Its presence will save the lives of hundreds of infantry and kill many Germans.'

Colonel William Donovan of the Rainbow Division ordered his men to 'Get forward there. What do you think this is, a wake?'

In two days of fighting the Americans captured 13,000 German soldiers and two hundred guns. The Germans surrendered in droves. One American sergeant, armed only with an empty revolver, brought back three hundred prisoners. When the waiting Americans first saw this column approaching they assumed it was a counter-attack.

It was a major success for the Americans. St Mihiel had been held by the Germans for over four years and had previously resisted several large French attacks. Ironically, Hindenburg had already given orders to evacuate the salient. The Americans attacked as the Germans were about to abandon the position having already withdrawn most of their heavy guns.

Elsewhere in the world the war continued its miserable progress and crawled slowly to a close. In the Embassy at Petrograd the British Naval Attache, Captain Cromie, was murdered by the Bolsheviks who had been alarmed by reports that various counter-revolutionary groups had links with the British through the Embassy (it was probably true, and Captain Cromie was, in fact, the head of British Intelligence in Northern Russia). On August 31st, the Embassy was invaded by an armed group of Bolshevik secret police who proceeded to rampage through the building, searching and shooting. Captain Cromie who was in a meeting drinking tea according to Foreign Office accounts, grabbed his revolver and killed three of the enemy before being shot himself on the grand staircase. His body was looted and mutilated. All of the remaining Embassy staff were arrested and detained.

Back in Britain there was outrage and the representative of the Bolsheviks in London, Maxim Litvinov, and his staff were placed in 'protective custody' in Brixton Prison until all of His Majesty's Embassy staff in Petrograd were set free.

On the morning of September 2nd the Bolsheviks announced the birth of the institution of Red Terror and promptly executed 512 of their opponents. British troops were advancing against the Red Army near Murmansk and the Americans landed 4,500 soldiers at Archangel. The situation was 'fluid'.

Elsewhere on September 14th, the Allies launched yet another assault on Bulgarian positions on the Salonica Front. The Serbians, fighting alongside French and Senegalese troops, made a bayonet charge against Bulgarian machine-gunners. Two days later, the French used flamethrowers and drove the defenders from three mountain peaks which had dominated and blunted Allied attacks for the last three years. The Commander of the Bulgarian Second Army attempted to persuade the King, Tsar Ferdinand, to listen to peace overtures. The Tsar ordered him to go back to the front line and get himself killed. Nonetheless, two Bulgarian regiments mutinied and refused to fight.

A few days later the South Wales Borderers and elements of the Greek Army attacked towards Lake Doiran. After some tenacious fighting they reached the important summit of the Grand Couronne but were forced back by intense Bulgarian machine-gun fire only to find, as they ran back down the hill, that the British had mistakenly released a gas cloud behind them.

The Bulgarians started to retreat on September 20th and declared a Republic one week later. The British arrived on September 25th at about the same time as the French were entering Macedonia, forcing the Germans into headlong retreat. The southern approaches to both Germany and Austria were now wide open.

In Palestine, on the same day, British infantrymen had broken the Turkish lines and Allenby's cavalry raced northward along the coastal plain. The Turks, accompanied by German units, fled. At Megiddo - the original biblical Armageddon - where they had been ordered to make a stand, only the Germans fought and the Turks retreated. British cavalrymen reached Nazareth on September 21st and Von Sanders - the Commander of all German forces and Military Adviser to the Turks - was forced to flee in his pyjamas.

In an echo of the war in Iraq sixty years later, Turkish columns retreating from Tulkarm and Nablus were caught in the open by British aircraft in the most destructive aerial attack of the war. The Turks were spotted fleeing through a narrow, steep-sided defile and were bombed and machine-gunned by more than fifty planes who first destroyed the trucks at the head of the column, cutting off any means of escape. They dropped nine tons of bombs and fired 56,000 rounds of ammunition. The following day they returned and completed the slaughter. Sick of killing, some of the British pilots asked to be spared any further sorties.

On September 25th, 2,750 Australian and New Zealand cavalrymen of the Egyptian Expeditionary Force crossed the River Jordan and took Amman, which sat astride the Berlin-Baghdad railway. The sole rail link with Germany was finally cut. They took another 2,563 prisoners that day bringing their total for the week to over 45,000. Turkey was finished.

Just ten days after the attack on the St Mihiel Salient had ended and in a telling illustration of their growing strength, the Americans attacked again, this time along the River Meuse and through the heavily defended Argonne Forest. The attack was preceded by a massive bombardment of 4,000 guns; guns fired by Americans but made in Britain and France. One of the men firing those guns that night was a future President - Captain Harry S. Truman. Thirty years later he was to complain that he still suffered from deafness caused by the 155-millimetre battery firing over his head.

As the shelling stopped at 5.30 in the morning on September 26th American infantry left their lines and followed over 700 tanks to the German positions, pushing them back three miles. By the next morning more than 23,000 prisoners had been taken.

Meanwhile, Ludendorff had retreated to the Hindenburg Line.

# Taking the Hindenburg Line

## One of the greatest-ever British military achievements.

The German High Command had drawn obvious conclusions following the failed British attack on the Somme in 1916 and had immediately decided to build a new series of lines of defence far behind the existing Front Line which in itself stretched from the North Sea to the town of Verdun. It was planned to be the supreme achievement in German military construction on the Western Front and would incorporate all the lessons learned about troop dispersal, reverse slope positions, defence in depth and camouflage. While the German Army waited behind their new secure positions in France and Belgium there would be an opportunity for the German Navy and the German Air Force to win the war with a return to unrestricted submarine warfare and a strategic bombing campaign of London.

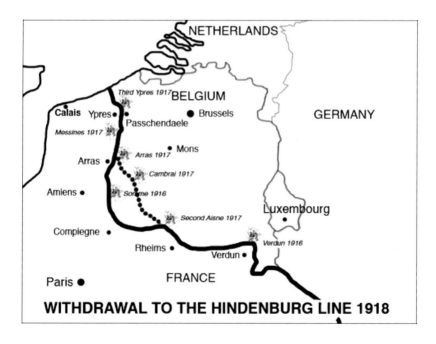

WITHDRAWAL TO THE HINDENBURG LINE 1918

Originally, the British had thought that a German retreat to a new defensive line was a sign of weakness but, in fact, it was a carefully calculated and intelligent move. By changing to a defensive line of its own choosing, rather than one where their advance had simply been halted, the Germans could shorten their line, make better use of their troops and hopefully avoid the unsustainable losses incurred at Verdun and the Somme. As part of the move they systematically destroyed every building, well, wood, road and track in the areas they were leaving as well as planting minefields and booby traps - anything to deprive the British of shelter or sustenance and to make the terrain they would be forced to cross as dangerous and uninhabitable as possible.

Booby traps were everywhere, some sophisticated ones using acid and delayed action fuses but most employed simple pressure detonators. Hidden wires were attached to useful trench 'furniture' such as stove chimneys or cooking pots which when removed would activate bundles of hand-grenades. Heavy artillery shells were buried in roads waiting for a passing lorry to detonate them. Some British troops searching for hidden devices would make German prisoners go first.

Attacking troops would need to traverse a wasteland and the Germans calculated that it would take the British more than eight weeks to rebuild roads, bridges and railways.

The German front line was made up of five operational zones (Stellungs) the most powerful being Siegfriedstellung which covered the 160 kilometres from Arras to Rheims and was named the Hindenburg Line by the British. Designed and constructed in just five months with a workforce of 500,000 forced labourers including French civilians and Russian prisoners-of-war it comprised trenches measuring five metres deep and four metres wide protecting dug-outs which had twenty metre wide bands of barbed wire placed in front of them. The carefully sited pill-boxes were built of reinforced concrete and steel. About three kilometres in front of the main defences was a line of less heavily defended outposts designed to slow down any British attack. The main battle-zone was two kilometres deep and was covered by a mass of artillery and machine-guns. When the British introduced tanks into warfare a series of anti-tank ditches were dug in front of the main battle lines.

The southern part of the line rested on the St Quentin Canal. But - and it was a big 'but' - the line had been constructed in 1916 and the advances since then in the science of attack, particularly in the British Army which was by now the centre of military excellence, meant that by 1918 parts of the Hindenburg Line were obsolescent and no longer the unbreakable prospect they once were. For a start, the line was linear in design when more recent fortifications were based on a chequerboard model to create overlapping fields of fire. It was certainly more heavily defended than the recent attack at Amiens but problems of desertion and a loss in morale among German soldiers suggested some weaknesses. To the ordinary German soldier, who had been promised victory so many times over the years, no amount of explaining and justification could change the fact that this was a retreat and took him yet further away from Paris. Nevertheless, the Hindenburg Line remained a major obstacle and a hugely difficult position to capture but, with a new belief in their own skills and professionalism, the British Army of 1918 believed it was a task well within its means.

That wasn't true of British politicians though. Lloyd-George, who disliked, distrusted and disbelieved General Haig, was determined to 'rein in' the military command and was determined never to have another Passchendaele. General Wilson, representing the War Cabinet in London, wrote to Haig:

> Just a word of warning in regard to incurring heavy losses in attacks on Hindenburg Line as opposed to losses when driving the enemy back to that line. I do not mean to say you have incurred such losses, but I know the War Cabinet would become anxious if we receive heavy punishment in attacking the Hindenburg Line without success.

This was War Office code and Haig knew perfectly well that his job was on the line. If the attack was successful he would remain Commander-in-Chief. If he failed, or even if he only partly succeeded, then not only would he be removed from his post, he would be vilified and blamed for every setback, every misfortune over the previous two years.

Winston Churchill in a memorandum to Haig dated September 5th set out the Government's war plans:

> We should be content to play a very subordinate role in France, and generally in the Allied Councils, during 1919, and count on having solid forces and conserved resources available for the decisive struggles of 1920, or held in hand for the peace situation if our Allies break down meanwhile.

In the margins Haig wrote 'What rubbish! Who will last until 1920 - only America??'

Lord Milner, an influential member of the Cabinet, visited Haig to threaten 'that if the British Army is used up now there will be no more men for next year.'

Haig was in a dilemma. He was convinced that Germany was reeling and falling apart and that the time to attack was now. Foch agreed with him, '...the German is nearing the end.'

In a hastily convened emergency meeting he explained to the War Cabinet:

> Briefly, in my opinion, the character of the war has changed. What is wanted now at once is to provide the means to exploit our recent great successes to the full. Reserves in England should be regarded as Reserves for the French Front and all yeomanry, cyclists and other troops now kept for civil defence should be sent to France at once.
> If we act with energy now, a decision can be obtained in the very near future.

So, despite opposition and threats from politicians at home and the strong possibility that he might lose his job, his career and his reputation but equally convinced that he was right that the Germans would crack, General Haig made his decision:

> ...The probable results of a costly failure, or, indeed, of anything short of a decided success, in any attempt upon the main defences of the Hindenburg Line were obvious; but I was convinced that the British attack was the essential part of the general scheme, and that the moment was favourable.
> Accordingly, I decided to proceed with the attack.

This attack of 100 divisions in total - including the French and the Americans - was to be the biggest battle of them all and the last great exploit of the British Army in the war.

Haig planned the attack as a series of sequential hammer blows against the German line, beginning with the Americans in combination with the French on Z day, September 25th. This was the Battle of the Argonne Forest. On Z + 2 the British First and Third Armies would attack two enemy sectors centred on the Canal du Nord while Generals Byng and Rawlinson directed their forces to the St Quentin Canal two days later on Z + 4.

The Germans had cleverly incorporated the water courses into their defences - partly as a guard against surprise tank attacks - and the Canal du Nord formed an intimidating obstacle. The east bank of the canal was 4-5 feet high and the west side was some 10-12 feet; for most of its exposed length it was 100 feet wide. On the east side, which was mainly marshland, the Germans had laid extensive belts of barbed wire covered by machine-guns and of course they held what little high ground there was.

The First and Third Armies were spearheaded, yet again, by the Canadians who planned a set-piece advance with infantry following closely on the heels of a creeping barrage of artillery and machine-guns. The first waves crossed a dry section of the canal successfully, bringing their own machine-guns and light artillery with them. Engineers were busy constructing bridges by lunchtime and by the evening of the first day, a breach of twelve miles deep by six wide had been made in the German line. The advance continued for the next five days before running out of steam.

Meanwhile the Fourth Army made the assault on the St Quentin Canal - thirty-five feet wide, with perpendicular brick walls rising to a height of ten feet, filled with mud and water to a depth of 7-15 feet. Any stretch of stagnant water was laced with barbed wire. Most sections of the canal sat in a steep-sided embankment, 50 feet deep and bare of vegetation. Tanks couldn't cross it and concrete emplacements on the canal banks bristling with machine-guns dominated the terrain. In Bellenglise there was a large, shell-proof tunnel capable of holding 3,000 men who could move directly into the German trench system. The whole area was protected by a continuous trench barrier and this section formed the centre of a six-line system of defence some 6,000 yards deep. German artillery had had two years to register their guns to cover all approaches and soldiers of the German 38th Division, who held this particular part of the line, were promised extra rations and pay bonuses for every British prisoner they captured. They were told that their section was '…considered to afford most favourable conditions for a stubborn defence…it is an impregnable rampart…(and) must be held absolutely intact.'

There were, however, weaknesses - three in particular: firstly, the exposed canal was only part of the line - on the northern end it ran through the Bellincourt and Bellenglise tunnels which the Germans used as troop shelters. Obviously, this was a more inviting section to assault and the

Germans had reinforced it with extensive wire and machine-gun teams but, earlier in August, in a stroke of good fortune, the Canadians had captured complete plans for the defence of the canal section - all the locations of headquarters, artillery emplacements, dugouts, railheads, and supply dumps, and, importantly, the locations of the tunnel exits. British artillery planners were delighted.

Secondly, the Hindenburg Line had been built two years previously and vital parts of it were beginning to deteriorate. This was too big a system for it to be maintained and garrisoned effectively as German forces were reduced. Barbed wire fortifications were collapsing in on themselves; artillery and machine-guns were placed too far forward making them vulnerable to counter-battery fire, instead of being distributed in depth.

And thirdly, the key to the whole position was the determination and the willingness of the individual soldier to defend it. As already mentioned in this text, a retreat is a retreat, no matter how many words were used to describe the move to the Hindenburg Line as a positive action. Morale was low and men were in poor condition. The German soldier was well aware of what was happening on the Home Front, that his family were virtually starving; that the working classes in Russia had overthrown the governing system and that, very probably, despite his sacrifices, the war was lost. First-line men were reluctant to dig trenches and only eight fresh German divisions remained on the Western Front. Losses through death, wounding or surrender meant that only thirty-two trains were now needed to move a German division rather than the normal forty-five.

Even so, the line remained a seriously strong objective, and the Germans had proved themselves time and time again as capable of determined resistance.

This time, on the St Quentin Canal, the Australians were to take the lead. There being no chance of surprise - the Germans knew perfectly well the attack was coming and were ready and waiting - the assault began with a 56-hour artillery bombardment, using 1,637 guns, nearly 600 of them heavy, on a frontage of 10,000 yards - twice the density of the Somme battle in 1916. During the final 24 hours British artillery fired a record 945,052 shells and, importantly, the 18lb shells now carried the new 106 super-sensitive fuse allowing barbed wire to be cut much more efficiently. They also delivered, for the first time, British-made mustard gas shells.

But the Australian divisions were tired and their politicians had already been pressing for them to be withdrawn from the Front Line and given extra leave. In a sign of the stress of the demands placed on them in the fighting of the previous three months, 119 men of the 1st Battalion Australian Imperial Force refused to take part in the attack.

General Rawlinson wisely ordered a compromise by allocating two American divisions to make the assault alongside the Australians. The Americans were to take the German Front Line positions before the Australians followed through. As the American forces were relatively inexperienced this was asking a lot of them and their attacks on the left and the centre went much more slowly than expected. The over-eager American 27th and 30th Divisions advanced too far and failed to 'mop-up' as they went, leaving German troops to emerge from dug-outs and attack them from the rear.

Luckily Rawlinson had insisted on a southern assault on the canal itself at the same time. This was to be carried out by an undistinguished and unfashionable British County Unit - the 46th North Midland Division, and, in truth, compared to the dashing Australian and Canadian elites, and the impressive Americans, not a lot was expected of them.

In the event, they performed one of the greatest feats of arms of any unit of the British Army during the war. The starting point and the key to a successful assault of this nature lay in the preparation. By 1918, British gunners were experienced and skilful, easily capable of delivering exactly the right intensity, duration and accuracy of bombardment to whatever target was selected. The incredibly difficult art of the creeping barrage, shifting 100 yards every two minutes, had been mastered, and it was common practice now for troops to have the confidence to be as close as 150-200 yards to the exploding shells as they advanced.

Harassing fire on known German positions (and the gunners knew all the positions) began on the 26th and the bombardment proper started 48 hours before the attack. Two six-inch batteries fired one round per minute throughout the night on the canal banks and what was left of the village of Bellenglise, while 18-pdr and 4.5 inch howitzers fired between 100 and 150 rounds each day. Mustard gas was used liberally on German trenches and on all the canal crossing points.

The decision was made for the Midlanders to advance to the Hindenburg Line - designated 'Blue Line' - under an advancing barrage where the guns would continue to fire for a few minutes before lifting to a 'safety line' ahead of the troops for 30 minutes to allow them time to consolidate the capture of the line. The planned artillery fire would be augmented by trench-mortar batteries firing high-explosive and smoke, and fifty or so machine-guns firing above the heads of the attacking infantrymen. The machine-guns had been provided with 500 boxes of Vickers ammunition and 200 boxes of German ammunition.

The Staffordshire Brigade was chosen to lead the attack on a narrow front of 2000 metres aiming to cross the canal a little to the north of the Vermand-Bellenglise road leading to the Riqueval Bridge. 137th Brigade, with 5th North Staffordshires on the left, 5th South Staffordshires in the centre and 6th South Staffordshires on the right, would lead the assault with 138 and 139 Brigades leap-frogging through as the objectives were reached. They were on their own, there would be no supporting attacks on their flanks, and the Americans and Australians were nearly a mile away to the north. To minimise the risk of mistaking allies for the enemy, 'exceptionally capable NCO's' were placed on the left of the left-hand battalion and the 5th North Staffords and the batteries of machine-guns were specifically ordered not to fire on anyone north of Riqueval Bridge unless they could be positively identified as the enemy. The Staffordshire men were to cross the thirty-five feet of the canal using ropes, empty petrol cans, cork slabs, collapsible boats and mud mats. Each man was allocated a cork life-jacket which had been requisitioned from Cross-Channel ferries and, as if to make swimming even more difficult, was weighed down with 120 rounds of small-arm ammunition, two bombs and the usual rations.

By this stage of the war major attacks were 'all-arms' affairs involving infantry, artillery, tanks and aircraft and communication between the various arms was critical. Detailed lists of the use of coloured flares were issued to battalion officers; these were used to communicate information to the rear or to aircraft overhead and ranged from 'advanced cavalry troops here', to ' tank broken down'. Advancing infantry had reflective plates fixed to the top of their backpacks that could be seen from the air and were taught to indicate enemy positions to friendly aircraft by placing three rifles in a row. Allied aircraft were easily recognised by the black rectangular board hanging from the fuselage.

The Germans, of course, weren't content to sit and watch while these preparations continued and launched a spoiling attack at dawn the day before the planned assault. They successfully seized a number of positions and it proved impossible to eject them. In the end, after some six hours of vicious trench fighting, they were left where they were but by then of course they had spotted the boats, the ladders and the life-jackets which were waiting to be issued.

Nevertheless, the attack went ahead as scheduled at 5.50 on the morning of Sunday, September 29th. The artillery barrage which had been firing for the previous two days increased in intensity for the last 10 minutes as the waiting infantry left their line and advanced into what, by most accounts, was a thick mist and visibility down to about four yards. Officers led the way using compasses and the men following broke into small groups which either accidentally or by design managed to infiltrate the German positions. Any enemy machine-gun posts were quickly subdued, including a 77mm Field gun which was firing point-blank into the advancing infantry. The 5th North Staffordshires on the northern flank scrambled down the embankment and  waited while their officers swam across the fetid water with ropes which they secured on the opposite bank. Some soldiers refused to wait and, wearing their life-jackets, half floundered and half swam to the eastern bank. Once there, they used whatever hand-holds they could find to drag themselves up the almost vertical banking to reach the Germans at the top.

At the extreme left of the attack a 5th Battalion captain, Captain Charlton, with a group of engineers from 466th Field Company, attacked Pont Riqueval. The actual details are rather confused. The most widely credited account is that Captain Charlton strode out of the mist and, using only his revolver, killed all the Germans holding the bridge, including two men who were in the process of blowing it up. A different version has it that an NCO shot four Germans as Charlton cut the wires to the explosives. Yet a third version claims that it was in fact a Corporal Openshaw who rushed at three German Pioneer troops, bayoneted two of them and persuaded the third to reveal the location of the bridge explosives. He then apparently rushed on further across the structure and eliminated a waiting German machine-gun post.

Whatever the truth, all attacking British troops were across the canal just one hour after leaving their trenches and quickly moved through the

Blue Line objectives and onto the Brown Line. The thick mist which had helped disguise and hide the attackers had severely hindered the carefully laid plans for communication. Flares and aircraft were impossible to see, runners lost their way and Lucas lamps were useless. In the end, Headquarters in the rear were reduced to questioning the passing wounded and the streams of German prisoners. When they were finally convinced that the German line had, in fact, been broken they gave the orders for the support brigades, 138th and 139th, to advance, and now the mist really began to cause trouble. As these two supporting brigades attempted to move into position aided by compasses, whole companies got lost in the maze of old trenches, gun pits and transport lines. One platoon of the 5th Leicesters was finally led into position by the battalion padre. The problem was made more difficult as leading officers were killed or wounded by German shelling leaving battalions unsure of their own position but finally word got back to Brigade HQ that they were ready to move forward through the victorious 137th Brigade. Runners were immediately sent with orders for the advance but, unfortunately, the runners got lost in the fog and it was hours before they found their way.

Eventually the follow-up troops passed through the Staffords and moved on to the Yellow Line, fighting as they went and followed by tanks. British engineers had reached the Bellenglise Tunnel which still held a large proportion of its garrison of 3,000. By now of course it was no longer a place of safety but a trap and its inhabitants soon joined the ever increasing lines of German prisoners heading westwards. The tanks had played an important role in the attack and had lost at least ten of their number between Bellenglise and the village of Magny. The padre of 5th Leicester, the Reverend Buck, who had played his part in reuniting the platoon with their unit during the morning, was killed by shellfire as he and the Medical Officer attempted to rescue some wounded tank men.

By 5.30 that afternoon the 46th North Midland Division, a Territorial division, as was the Duke of Wellington's, was relieved by one of Kitchener's New Army divisions - the 32nd. The 46th had achieved one of the most memorable feats of the war. They employed an extraordinary intense and accurate creeping barrage which destroyed the wire and smashed up the canal banks, landing 126 shells per minute on each 500 yards of German trench line for eight hours before leaving their own trenches at 5.50am. They reached their designated positions exactly on time and in less than three hours had crossed the canal - as well as capturing one complete and undamaged bridge - and were advancing deep into the Hindenburg Line. By 3.30 in the afternoon they had progressed three miles, captured the main enemy position and were moving on the German support positions. One regiment alone had captured 4,200 prisoners and seventy guns. With the help of the 32nd Division on the following day a fifty-kilometre stretch of the famed and feared Hindenburg Line had fallen and during subsequent days the gap was widened yet more.

Men of the Staffordshire Brigade on the German side of the canal after the battle.

German resistance increased steadily over the next few days and the pace of advance slowed considerably but the Midlanders could take considerable satisfaction over their day's work. Their losses had been relatively light for such a large and complicated operation against a formidable obstacle while their haul of prisoners, guns and material were astounding. They had smashed through the Hindenburg Line while their more distinguished comrades to the north were still struggling to advance and, though they may not have been particularly aware of it, they had caused absolute dismay among Germany's High Command and politicians.

Even the Official Australian War History called it an 'extraordinarily difficult task....and a wonderful achievement.' General Monash, Commander of the Canadian Forces wrote that it was 'an astonishing success…which materially assisted me in the situation in which I was placed later on the same day.'

And they had shortened the war.

# HOME NEWS 3

New Mill was having troubles.

Councillor Hiram Haigh had resigned from the board of the Military Tribunal in high dudgeon at recent events. He had, he said, been part of the tribunal when it had dismissed the claims of several young men of the town who had appealed against their conscription. These young men had gone off to the army only to claim when they were in barracks that they were, in fact, conscientious objectors and the army had sent them home. They were now to be seen, wandering the streets of New Mill while the Tribunal was sending married men of 44 to 48 years of age with wives and families off to war. The situation was made even more difficult for some members of the Tribunal by the fact that they were younger than the men whose fate they were deciding.

A typical example of the problems they faced was the case of the Thurstonland joiner and wheelwright, aged 29, married with one child and classed as A1 fit. It transpired that he was the only coffin maker left in the district. In 1918 alone he had made 94 coffins. Local farmers depended on his skills as a wheelwright and they had organised a petition to keep him. After a ballot, the members of the Tribunal were split evenly down the middle as to whether or not he should be sent away and the Chairman, with his casting vote, gave the man three months grace before he went into the army.

As it turned out, the coffin maker would be in great demand over the next few months. By the beginning of November it was recognised that influenza had become rife in the Holme Valley, as it was everywhere else. Schools were beginning to close as more and more pupils became ill - Park Head National School being the latest to shut its doors - while local mills were missing deadlines for vital orders as workers failed to turn up to operate the machines. Dr Thorp, Medical Officer for the Holmfirth and New Mill areas, gave advice on staying at home and avoiding crowds at the first sign of the disease. The New Mill District Council went as far as printing and distributing one thousand copies of a circular:

The general preventative measures available are the same for an ordinary catarrh and for the more serious influenza. An initial difficulty in securing their adoption is the serious nature of this illness. It is probable that influenza is chiefly spread during the earlier stages. If every person suffering from a feverish cold, with or without catarrh, were willing and able to stay at home for a few days, the spread of disease in factories, offices, workshops and shops, schools and other institutions would be greatly reduced. Apart from actual reduction in the number of cases, increased slowness of spread can thus be secured; and this likely to diminish the risk that successive cases will become increasingly severe…A handkerchief should always be employed to catch droplets of mucus, and the handkerchief should be boiled or burnt if of paper. Spittle should be received in a special receptacle, its contents being disinfected or burnt.

An army influenza hospital ward.

The newspapers called it 'Spanish flu' (war-time censorship prevented any mention of influenza in the war zones and Spain was a convenient neutral country which was also suffering) and by the time it finished spreading, this pandemic had affected half the world's population and claimed as many as fifty million - fifty million! - lives; double the number killed of all the belligerents during the Great War; more than any other single outbreak of disease throughout history, surpassing even the Black Death of the Middle Ages.

Recent scientific thinking believes that the virus originated in chickens and mutated in pigs before jumping to humans. People contracting the disease were killed by a massive over-stimulation of the immune system. Those people with the strongest immune systems - the young and healthy - succumbed first and there were relatively few deaths of the old or the very young. Perversely, the ones most affected were fit, hardened, front line soldiers who had survived the trenches only to catch the disease at the end of the war. It could take hold extraordinarily quickly; there were recorded cases of people waking up with a shivery cold in the morning and who were dead by the evening.

It had been prevalent in Europe for some months before reaching the U.K. in Spring, 1918 - some Holmfirth men who were prisoners-of-war in Germany had already died of the disease there - and it killed 228,000 here in Britain in the first few months. Twelve people died of influenza in Huddersfield in July and each month brought further increases. In Leeds it killed 1,400 people before it spread through every part of Yorkshire.

In Slaithwaite, where schools were closed due to the outbreak, there was disquiet that long queues of children were seen every Saturday morning outside the cinema. The children were going 'out of the daylight into the dark where infectious disease was bred'. It was proposed by members of the Colne Valley Education Sub-Committee that children should be refused admission. Mr. Farrington said that he could only support the motion if Sunday Schools were included as well as picture houses and the resolution was passed unanimously.

Huddersfield closed all its schools in October. On the 24th three soldiers collapsed in the street and were rushed by the police ambulance to the War Hospital. People began to refer to it as a 'plague' brought on by the war and there was more than a hint of panic in the air. But the Government acted quickly by publishing findings from the various medical groups that were tackling the disease. Lieut.-Col. Harvey, of the Royal Army Medical College, whose committee was analysing samples of influenza from around the country, declared that the plague bacillus had never been found. What they were finding was the influenza bacillus; the pneumococcus, the streptococcus and the meningococcus which caused meningitis. Strangely, he found that streptococcus, which resulted in severe broncho-pneumonia, was much more prevalent in sailors than soldiers.

In Parliament Mr. Hayes Fisher was able to reassure the House that, despite a considerable rise in the rate of mortality, the situation was much worse in Vienna and Paris. That wasn't particularly true. In the month of October alone, some 2,225 Londoners died of 'Spanish Flu', more than all the deaths from four years of German Zeppelin and aircraft raids. In Vienna, the painter Egon Schiele was among those who succumbed. By October 15 1,500 Berliners had died. More American soldiers died in France of influenza than were killed in action - 62,000 against 48,909.

Denmark closed all places of entertainment where people might congregate and was followed by the city of Dublin. Four policemen collapsed and died in Tottenham and nurses were beginning to fall fatally ill throughout the hospital system. In Leigh, all the cemetery staff died and council surveyors had to dig the graves. The town held the record for the highest number of funerals per head of population.

Honley issued special instructions to the Road Surveyor and the Sanitary Engineer to flush out all the drains and inspect all the manure heaps. By the end of October the Huddersfield Medical Officer reported forty-nine deaths that week; twenty-five the week before. In one house in Fartown, both father and son died - the son on Sunday and the father, Mr. Beaumont, the following morning. The Medical Officer at Storthes Hall Asylum committed suicide.

At the beginning of November the military authorities banned all men in uniform from attending events at theatres, cinemas and concerts to prevent the spread of the disease. It wasn't a popular move.

And influenza continued to spread throughout the area - apart from the tiny village of Holme, nestling below Holme Moss, where not a single case was recorded.

# Back in the thick of it

There are four grades in an infantry battalion:-
(1) A subaltern - knows nothing and does everything;
(2) A captain - knows everything and does nothing;
(3) A major - knows nothing and does nothing;
(4) The colonel .....well! The colonel thinks he is Lord God
    Almighty and does what the _____ he likes.

August and September had been a particularly busy time for the officers
and men of the 5th Battalion, Duke of Wellington's Regiment.

A staff officer arrived with orders at 4.30am on Sunday, August 25th,
1918 as they waited near Achiet-le- Grand ordering them to attack and
capture the German lines a few miles to their front, having first cleared
the small villages of Behagnies and Sapignies. They were to leave their
own trenches in just a few hours time at 9.00am and would form part
of a large scale brigade assault - one of their sister battalions, the 2/4th
Dukes, were on their left. Their objective was just to the east of the small
hamlet of Beugnatre, which nowadays if you're quick and know when to
look, can be glimpsed from the A1, the Autoroute du Nord, beloved of
British tourists heading south to the sun.

It took them an hour and a half to cover the three miles, a six minute
drive, and the Germans, who had positioned machine-guns in the village
of Fauvreuil on the Duke's right, contested every yard. As they consolidated their newly-captured positions the Germans mounted a counter
attack on the left of the line. They were being led by an officer, vainly
exhorting his men to advance, in plain view of the Yorkshire men and
against their aimed rifles and Lewis guns. When he was eventually shot
and killed his troops turned and fled. But the main attack came on the
right in Fauvreuil Wood where the enemy had quickly concentrated five
battalions - two to three thousand troops. Captain Ellis who commanded
'D' Company of the 5th saw the danger and turned his men to form a
defensive line facing South East and called up British artillery which
quickly decimated the attacking German force leaving the fields in front
of the Duke's positions full of wounded and dying men.

In a few hours of fighting they had captured one enemy officer and
forty soldiers, twenty machine-guns (four of which made their way to

Holmfirth) and huge amounts of enemy artillery shells. But they lost four officers and 180 men of their own.

> Yesterday we went up into the line and have had the roughest week I ever had. But I am away from it for a little while anyway. I was accidentally injured last night but it is nothing really serious. We went over the top in broad daylight on Thursday, but were driven back. Then we went over again on Friday at 5 am and gained our objective. We got consolidated by night time but had suffered a lot of casualties. We lost all our N.C.O's but one in our platoon. The sergeant asked me to take a party of wounded men back to our old position and bring some rations up. I was leading the way over land absolutely full of shell-holes and barbed wire, and it was black dark, when I tripped over some barbed wire and pitched headlong into a shell-hole, my ear coming into violent contact with an iron stake. I really thought I was killed, but it appears I wasn't. The stretcher bearers took me down to our aid post where my wound was dressed and I was then put into an ambulance and taken to another casualty clearing station. I hope it is a Blighty job, but am afraid, although pleased, that it is not bad enough for that.
> I am fairly tired out and want sleep badly. I have not had my boots off for a week. I should hardly care to see a looking-glass just now, as I have not had a wash or a shave for nearly a week. I never thought I could have stood what I have this week, but our officers worked with us and roughed it just like us and we all stuck it without a grouse. Still, I can't help comparing our lot out here with that of others at home.

> Holmfirth Express, September 1918

For the next few days they were leapfrogged by other units who continued to push the Germans back until they were called upon again on the 29th. This time, it was to be a two-company attack, about 400 men, led by the resourceful Captain Ellis and was a demonstration of just how professional and skilled in the arts of war the men had become. They were attacking a German trench system and following a creeping barrage which advanced 100 yards every four minutes before resting in front of the apex of the final objective and acting as a protective barrier while the troops consolidated the captured trenches and 'turned them round' using their Holmfirth shovels against enemy counter-attack.

Once they had entered the enemy defensive lines, Captain Ellis decided that two bombing parties of nine men each would work down the trenches (a bombing party would consist of 'bayonet men' in front, followed by 'bomb throwers', followed by men carrying extra supplies of grenades). These bombing parties would be covered by Lewis gun teams advancing alongside them in the open, firing down into the trench from both sides to deal with any of the enemy who might be tempted to attack the bombing groups. These gun teams kept pace with the advancing bombers. The rest of the group came on about 150 yards behind, dropping off small groups of men to act as flank guards. Other specialists dealt with German dug-outs or with isolated enemy posts.

---

A shortage of trained Lewis Gunners was seriously felt throughout operations.

The casualties of the battalion during operations were as follows –

### OFFICERS.

| | |
|---|---|
| Died of Wounds. | 1. |
| Wounded. | 6. |
| Wounded at duty. | 2. |

### OTHER RANKS.

| | |
|---|---|
| Killed. | 26. |
| Died of wounds. | 6. |
| Wounded. | 171. |
| Wounded (gas). | 36. |
| Wounded at duty. | 5. |
| Wounded & missing. | 1. |
| Missing. | 4. |

The captures of the battalion amounted to –

| | |
|---|---|
| Prisoners. | 2 Off. 250 O.R. |
| Machine Guns. | 55. |
| German Rifles. | 175. |
| Trench Mortars. | 6. |
| German Very Pistols. | 15. |
| Belt cases. | 70. |
| Anti-Tank Guns. | 3. |
| Motor Headlight. | 1. |
| German telephones. | 3. |
| Daylight signalling lamp. | 1. |
| German Bicycle. | 1. |

and large quantities of Gun ammunition, equipment etc. not recovered.

The whole assault was successful. The attack was conducted with 'great dash' and though the enemy put up stiff resistance at first he was quickly disorganised by the Lewis gun teams while the bayonet men were 'far superior' to the Germans, who lost 35 men killed, 15 machine-guns, 1 trench mortar and 93 soldiers captured. It had taken an hour.

They were preparing for action again in October and went hungry on the 17th when the ration party was hit by a random German shell which killed one CQSM, wounded two other CQSMs, killed the two soldier carriers and two mules and a horse.

On the 20th they were at Solesmes and about to take part in a multi-divisional attack. Their role was to ford the La Selle River and take the village of St. Python and La Pigeon Blanc Farm. The river was a formidable obstacle in itself being 25ft wide and up to 6ft deep with thick mud on the bottom and German machine-guns on the far bank.

At 1.30am, undetected by the enemy, the battalion engineers successfully erected eight wooden bridges across the river and in bright misty moonlight 'A' Company crossed the water in complete silence carrying five light ladders to scale the steep and very muddy eastern bank. It took them less than fifteen minutes and they formed up in the darkness about 100 yards east of the river. They were quickly followed by 'B', 'C' and 'D' Companies and the whole battalion was in position and laid down under cover in an orchard two minutes before Zero Hour.

The British barrage and overhead machine-gun cover began promptly at 2.00am directed onto the village of St. Python for exactly three minutes before lifting to the outskirts for the next twenty minutes to prevent any possible German reinforcements arriving. After that period, the guns would advance 100 yards in four minutes to the Farm.

'A' Company rushed the village, following close to the barrage, and immediately came under fire from most of the houses. The Germans had thrown two barricades across the main thoroughfare which were fought for hand-to-hand before being overcome. The village was riddled with machine-gun posts which were all taken after vicious bayonet fighting, and as the barrage lifted towards the Farm, 'C' Company leap-frogged through and continued the advance. German machine-gun posts at La Pigeon Blanc Farm were quickly subdued by Lewis gun fire and the battalion took and consolidated the position.

By 4.10am it was all over. They had taken all their objectives,, captured over 300 prisoners, 15 machine-guns and four trench mortars, along with a large quantity of rifles, signalling equipment and numerous other stores. Five men of the battalion had been killed.

And suddenly it was November, 1918.

The battalion was training at Solesmes for yet another assault when word came through on Friday, that Austria-Hungary had asked for an armistice with the Allies - Turkey had already capitulated. The weather was fine and sunny and on the following Wednesday, November 3rd, the day before they moved up to the line, everyone rested.

The Americans had already attacked in force a few days earlier on the Meuse river. They had been helped by three batteries of 14-inch naval battleship guns, which had been placed on railway wagons and then targeted on German fortified posts from positions twenty-five miles behind the American lines. During the assault, when the Americans used mustard-gas for the first time, American planes machine-gunned enemy trenches while American bombers struck at lines of communication. They broke through the German lines at every point.

On the same day, November 1st, French forces advanced beyond the Hindenburg Line.

Germany was falling apart. Newly arrived troops on the Western Front mutinied rather than go into action. Revolution was declared in Vienna and Lenin stated that 'The time is near when the first day of the World Revolution will be celebrated everywhere.' In Kiel, 20,000 army troops joined 3,000 naval mutineers and took over the city. Calls for Communist revolution spread to Berlin. People were openly calling for the Kaiser to abdicate. When he received a request from Prince Max - by now leading the government - that he should step down in order to end the war, he replied 'I wouldn't dream of abandoning the throne because of a few hundred Jews and a thousand workers. Tell that to your masters in Berlin.'

Prince Max wasn't perturbed in the slightest. He had already informed President Wilson of the United States that the German Government was simply waiting for the Allies to send them the terms of the armistice.

Meanwhile on November 4th the 5th Battalion, Duke of Wellington's Regiment, was part of a massive British assault on a thirty-mile front. Despite everything, the Germans put up a determined resistance but were pushed back, first by the New Zealanders, and then by the British.

By the end of the day they had retreated five miles, losing 10,000 men as prisoners in addition to massive casualties and two hundred guns. Wilfred Owen was killed this day - his mother received the telegram stating his death a week later on November 11, as the church bells were ringing out to celebrate the peace.

On November 5th Lieutenant Clapham was badly wounded and died hours later. Lieutenant Clapham was the fresh-faced, nineteen year old officer who had brought the news from Huddersfield, some four years previously, telling the Holmfirth 'F' Company men, waiting in the Drill Hall, to mobilise. He had then spent the whole of the war with 5th Battalion and was killed just six days before the end. When he died he was still only twenty-three.

The 5th fought and advanced for four continuous days until, exhausted, they were placed in support while other units of the brigade took over. They had fought their way forward over 25 kilometres of German-held territory, captured 11 howitzer guns, 2 field guns, 18 machine-guns, 223 prisoners and vast quantities of ammunition. In turn, their own casualties had been remarkably light considering that they were attacking a well-entrenched enemy. They had lost Lieutenant Clapham and seven other officers wounded; fifteen other ranks killed, eighty four wounded and three men missing.

On the 9th, they went into comfortable billets in the village of Louvroil, close to the border with Belgium, just south of Mons where the 'Old Contemptibles' first met the German Army four, long years before.

As they were inspecting their new billets, German armistice negotiators reached the Forest of Compiegne to begin talks on ending the war. The Kaiser was still agonising over his future. He had already been told that the Navy - his beloved Navy - had mutinied and would no longer obey his orders. But he was determined to lead his army into battle - not at the Western Front, of course, but against the Communist revolutionaries who had raised the Red Flag at Kiel, Munich and Berlin. He would remain at Spa until the armistice was signed and then return to Berlin at the head of his troops. This fantasy was quickly dispatched by General Groener (Ludendorff had resigned some time previously) :

> The army will march home in peace and order under its leaders and commanding generals, but not under the command of Your Majesty, for it no longer stands behind Your Majesty.

At that moment, almost as if to emphasise the reality of the situation, a telegram was brought in from the Commandant of Berlin 'All troops deserted. Completely out of hand.'

The Kaiser left for Holland the next day while the German delegates at Compiegne worked throughout the night on the final details of the armistice before signing them at ten past five in the morning of November 11th, 1918.

And the war ended.

The 'Dukes' weren't particularly impressed. The War Diary for the 5th, written by Keith Sykes of Thongsbridge, on the day that the war was finally over reads:

> Nov 11 Fine day. Battalion rested. News received at 8.30am that hostilities were to cease at 11am that day.
> Nov 12 Battalion did Physical Training and Close Order Drill in morning. Recreation in afternoon.

Their sister battalion, the 4th, the Halifax men, who had fought alongside them since their arrival in France in 1915, positively let their hair down:

> Nov 11 Early in the morning news was received that an armistice with Germany had been signed to take effect from 11.00 hours that day. All work was cancelled for the day and the Band paraded the streets playing. A battalion smoking concert was held in the evening which the G.O.C. attended.

The Skipton men of the 6th Battalion gave a little more detail:

> Nov 11 A succession of wires arrived in the early morning about the impending armistice with Germany. It was known that a decision was to be arrived at by 11.00 hours. Wireless messages from Germany were intercepted instructing the delegates to sign the armistice and official news was received that hostilities were to cease at 11.00. The Brigadier General Commanding immediately ordered a general holiday to be given.

The Milnsbridge men of the 7th simply recorded 'Nov 11 Armistice from 11.00 hours.' And the following day the whole battalion was sent on a route march.

# THE END OF THE WAR.

On Monday forenoon, at 10 30, Mr. Lloyd George, in front of No. 10, Downing Street, announced the acceptance of the armistice by Germany. The news spread over the metropolis and the provinces like wildfire, and rejoicings became general throughout the country. People left their work and gave themselves up to rejoicings, bells pealing forth the glad news, and flags and bunting were displayed in abundance.

When the news first broke there were no scenes of wild abandon in the streets of Holmfirth, Huddersfield and the Colne Valley. Though flags, rosettes and streamers became much in evidence as the morning wore on, there were no extravagant exhibitions of delight and no dancing in the streets. For the first few hours as the news sank in there was instead a quietness about the crowds and not a few tears. The celebrations came later in the day.

The first definite news of the armistice had arrived via the Daily Examiner. They had received a wire at 10.50 confirming the signing and had immediately put a notice outside the office. They also flew a Red Ensign flag from one of the office windows. Word spread quickly and there was much hand-shaking and shouting of congratulations. People began to congregate outside Huddersfield Town Hall to watch the hoisting of the Union Jack and a passing sailor stopped in Ramsden Street and saluted. From the balcony window came the Stars and Stripes, the French Tricolour and the Belgium flag. By lunchtime parties of school children, waving banners, singing and shouting began to appear as schools sent them home to celebrate - Holmfirth Secondary School started the trend and was quickly followed by all the schools in the valley. Inside the Town Hall the Mayor was just taking his customary place in the magisterial chair at the Huddersfield Borough Police Court when the news arrived. He looked at the cases in front of him - keeping a dangerous dog; one for breaching the Lighting, Heating and Power Order; two cases of unseemly conduct - and immediately granted a general amnesty and promptly dismissed them all. The Chief Constable of Huddersfield received a telegram from the Commander-in-Chief of the Northern Command granting permission for fireworks, bonfires and for church bells to be rung at all times for a whole week. Every church in the area took advantage and bells were heard all afternoon and evening. Just about every mill had stopped work by the afternoon. Some would stay closed for days. By mid-afternoon all shops had shut and tramway workers took their trams back to the sheds and joined in the general jubilation. Huddersfield had recently been designated a garrison town and the streets were full of uniforms - soldiers and tramway girls formed processions and paraded the town singing patriotic songs. It went on most of the night.

That week, twenty-three people of the district died from influenza.

Many people went across town to the right hand corner of Dock Street (where Aspley Sainsbury's now stands). Mr Spratt, who lived there, had built a war shrine and decorated it with flags of the Allied countries and it had recently been officially unveiled by Alderman Beaumont. Men from every house in Dock Street, bar one, were in the Army - eighty-two of them; eighteen had already been killed in action. A tiny row of houses in Watergate, next door to Dock Street, had sent sixteen men. This was an Irish Catholic part of town and Father McCarthy was on hand to move a vote of condolence to all those present who had lost members of their families. Mrs. Scally, the oldest resident, presented Alderman Beaumont with a small crucifix. She then started the singing.

The celebratory Holmfirth bonfires, the fireworks and the church bells could be seen and heard at Choppards Farm in the Holme Valley by Mr. and Mrs. Frank Bramwell. They were waiting for news of their son, Joseph, who had been gassed two weeks earlier and was in hospital in France. The first they had known about it was a letter from the chaplain at 3rd Canadian Hospital 'He is not very well at present and I will keep you informed as to his condition.'

A week later a second letter arrived from Lance Corporal Stephenson who was in the next bed to Joseph and was writing for him:

> I also am in the 10th East Yorkshires and was gassed at the same time as your son Joe. He tells me to say that he is going on well and I can assure you this is the case. He is getting well looked after and has everything he wants. He has certainly improved a good deal since coming here. I hope these few lines will relieve you of a great deal of anxiety.

As they listened to the armistice celebrations in Holmfirth on the afternoon of Monday, November 11, a third, official letter from the Infantry Record Office was delivered telling them that Joseph Bramwell, aged 20, had died of his wounds.

# Christ in Flanders

We had forgotten You, or very nearly
You did not seem to touch us very nearly
Of course we thought about You now and then;
Especially in any time of trouble
We knew that You were good in time of trouble
But we are very ordinary men…..

Now we remember; over here in Flanders
(It isn't strange to think of You in Flanders)
This hideous warfare seems to make things clear.
We never thought about You much in England
But now that we are far away from England,
We have no doubts, we know that You are here.

      Lucy Whitmell

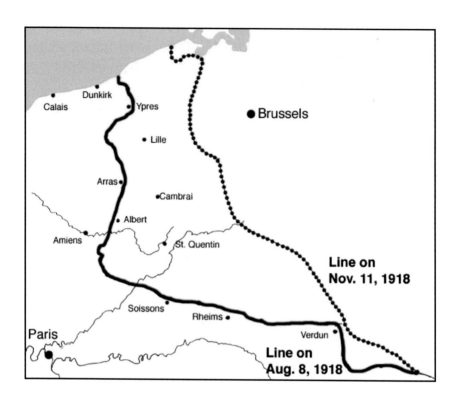

Calais ·
Dunkirk ·
Ypres ·
· Lille
Arras ·
· Cambrai
· Albert
Amiens ·
St. Quentin ·
· Brussels
Soissons ·
Rheims ·
Verdun ·
Paris ·

**Line on
Nov. 11, 1918**

**Line on
Aug. 8, 1918**

# Those who died in September 1918

2ND. LIEUT. ARNOLD I LEE

**Arnold Thomas Lee**. 2nd Lieutenant. 87th Siege Battery, Royal Garrison Artillery. Arnold had enlisted in 1915 and was commissioned in 1917 whereupon he promptly married his sweetheart Charlotte. Charlotte's father was Rev. Evans of Lydgate Unitarian Church. His last letter to his wife read: 'We are in the thick of it. We are going splendidly.'

Killed in action aged 26 years by a German shell near Arras on September 1st, 1918. Buried at Achicourt Road Cemetery.

CINDERHILLS FAMILY'S WORTHY RECORD

[HAROLD CHARLESWORTH.]

**Harry Charlesworth**. Gunner. No. 151447 87th Siege Battery Royal Garrison Artillery. Harry would have been one of the gunners under the command of Arnold Lee (above). He was born and went to school in Netherthong and, before enlisting, was a cloth finisher at Shaw Brothers in Firth Street, Huddersfield. He had been wounded exactly one year before but returned to duty and died of wounds at No 23 Casualty Clearing Station on September 7th aged 32. Buried at Duisans British Cemetery.

**Norman Hinchliffe.** Private. No 99533. 6th Battalion The King's (Liverpool Regiment).

An Upperthong man, sang with Lane Congregational Choir and, as a boy, was a member of Upperthong Sunday School. Just before he enlisted in 1917 he was an apprentice in the bakehouse at Dawson and Birch. Died of wounds received some five months after arriving in France on September 8th, aged 19. Buried at Pernes British Cemetery.

PTE. NORMAN HINCHLIFFE.

**Frank Tyas.** Guardsman. No 30471. 1st Battalion Grenadier Guards. Frank was born in Cartworth and, as a boy, attended Hade Edge Council School. He worked as a farm labourer for Mr Hinchliffe in Longley. Killed in action on September 12 aged 21. Buried at Vault Hill Cemetery.

His Lieut. Colonel wrote to Frank's parents:

> ...I am proud to tell you that he set a fine example of courage in action, and died as he lived, a fine British soldier who put his duties to his King and Country before any thought of his own personal safety.

PTE. FRANK TYAS.

251

**Fred Hardy.** Private. No 38236. 5th Battalion The Yorkshire Regiment. Fred was brought up at 25 Brownhill Lane and worked at Whiteley and Greens in Hinchcliffe Mill. He was reported missing on May 27th, taken prisoner. His parents received a letter from a comrade in the camp:

I must say, Mrs hardy, he got the best attention that could be given to him by either his comrades or the camp staff, but owing to him being too far through with dysentery and weakness, it was impossible for him to come through it.

Fred died as a Prisoner-of-War on September 18 aged 22 and is buried at Niederzwehren Cemetery, Cassel, Germany.

**Josiah Coker.** Private. No 21/804. 10th Battalion West Yorkshire Regiment. Josiah lived with his parents in Upperthong before finally enlisting in 1915 after being rejected six times. After 18 months he suffered a severe rupture and returned home to recuperate but was eager to get back to France and volunteered once more for active service. He had only been back with his regiment for five weeks when he was killed in action on September 20. Buried at Villers Hill British Cemetery.

**George Rippon Hardy**. MM. Private. No 40016. 1st Battalion Northumberland Fusiliers. George was from Durham but his family had taken over the Ford Inn and George worked just down the road at Digley Mills. He enlisted just as soon as he was eighteen and went to France in October, 1917 where he was wounded for the first time. His last letter home talked about going 'over the top' in the morning. Badly wounded in the back and arm he died of his wounds on September 21 aged 20. Buried at Sunken Road Cemetery, Boisleux-St. Marc.

FORD SOLDIER'S HOPE OF BLIGHTY.

[PRIVATE G. R. HARDY.]

**George Hubert Bradley**. First Class Air Mechanic. No 403127. 1st Aeroplane Supply Depot Repair Park Royal Air Force. George worked as a weaver at Bridge Mills in Holmfirth and was one of the original 'F' Company Territorials who marched away up Station Road in 1914. He served with the 5th Battalion Duke of Wellington's before transferring to the RAF in 1917. He had returned home to Thongsbridge just a few weeks before, crossing the Channel in an airship, before returning to France. He was injured by a 'hostile bomb' and died of his wounds on September 23 aged 22. Buried at Terlincthun British Cemetery.

THONGSBRIDGE FLYING MAN'S DEVOTI

[AIR-MECHANIC G. H. BRADLEY.]

[Seaman R Lockwood.]

**Robert Lockwood.** Ordinary Seaman. No J/87974. Royal Navy. HM Motor Launch No 247. Robert lived at Whitewalls, Austonley, the long winding track that looks down on Bilberry Reservoir, near Flush House, and worked on his father's farm and at Digley Mill in the valley bottom.

On the evening of September 29, his motor launch was caught in a storm while making for shelter at St. Ives. The boat was believed to have capsized in the heavy seas and smashed on the rocky coast. The whole crew, apart from one officer, was drowned. His body was never recovered and his name is commemorated on the Plymouth Memorial to the Missing.

[Signaller H H Kaye.]

**Herbert Holmes Kaye**. Gunner. No 176840 Royal Garrison Artillery. Herbert, his wife and their young baby lived at Glenthorpe in Holmfirth. As a boy he had attended Almondbury Grammar School and before enlisting had a career in the counting house of Messrs. Henry of Huddersfield. After just four months at the front he died of gunshot wounds on September 30. Buried at Tincourt New British Cemetery.

# Those killed in October 1918

**Harold Brackenbury**. Private. No 33222 6th Battalion York and Lancaster Regiment (formerly No 31383 Duke of Wellington's). Harold was a keen footballer and played for Burnlee. Born in Thongsbridge, he attended Netherthong National School and grew into a staunch Wesleyan. He worked at Albion Mills in Holmfirth before enlisting in 1917 and had recently been on leave.

He died of wounds received on October 1st, 1918 and is buried at Chapel Corner Cemetery, Sauchy-Lestree.

Harold Brackenbury

Lewis Harker

**Lewis Harker**. 2nd Lieutenant. 2nd Battalion King's Own Yorkshire Light Infantry.

Lewis had enlisted in the Duke of Wellington's Regiment as early as 1915 and served in the Gallipoli campaign, taking part in the Suvla landings. He took his commission in January 1918 and was granted leave in August which he spent with his parents at Ford Cottage, Holmfirth.

Killed in action on October 1, 1918 and buried at Bellicourt British Cemetery.

[Pte. G. A. Mellor.]

**George Albert Mellor**. Private. No 29/631. 12/13th Battalion Northumberland Fusiliers.

Another Netherthong man - his parents ran the Victoria Inn - and he worked as a plasterer and concreter for Haigh Brothers. Keen cricketer (Cartworth Moor CC) and footballer (St. John's Football Team). He had only recently returned to France after being gassed, and had been wounded twice before that.

He was killed in action on October 8, aged 31, and is buried at Prospect Hill Cemetery, Gouy.

ALWAYS CHEERFUL UNDER THE WORST CONDITIONS."

[Lance Corporal Luther Hartley]

**Luther Hartley.** Lance Corporal. No 267866. 1/6th Battalion Duke of Wellington's Regiment.

Luther lived in New Mill, up Sude Hill and attended Christ Church where he was sidesman, teacher and Treasurer to the Sunday School. He had enlisted in 1915 and before that worked as a weaver at Kirkbridge Mill.

His officer wrote to Luther's wife 'He was killed by a shell as he went over the top and he suffered no pain.'

Killed in action near Cambrai on October 11 aged 28 years and buried in the Regiment's own graveyard in France - Wellington Cemetery.

**John Wilfred Johnson**. Private. No 39517. 1/4th Battalion Duke of Wellington's Regiment.

John moved to Totties in Holmfirth from Keighley when he was twelve and attended Wooldale Council School. He was a Wesleyan at Lane Bottom church and a teacher in the Sunday School there.

Just one year after enlisting he died of wounds on October 14, aged 19, and is buried at Queant Communal Cemetery British Extension.

TOTTIES FAMILY'S SEVERE BLOW.

[PRIVATE J. W. JOHNSON.]

**Willie Dyson Whiteley**. Private . No 267800. 1/7th Battalion West Yorkshire Regiment (formerly 5541 Duke of Wellington's).

Born and bred in Cartworth and played cricket for them as a young man. Worked at Digley Mill as a weaver before enlisting in March 1916. He was captured by the Germans in their April offensive and died of 'lung trouble' (Influenza?) on October 19 aged 23.

Buried at Cologne Southern Cemetery.

ENGLISH INTERPRETER'S MESSAGE.

[RIFLEMAN W. D. WHITELEY.]

[LANCE CORPORAL SYKES THEWLIS]

**James Sykes Thewlis**. Lance Corporal. No 203011. 1/4th Battalion Duke of Wellington's Regiment.

James had enlisted at the beginning of the war and had served continuously for the previous four years.

His mother received a telegram saying that he had been seriously wounded followed shortly by a second telegram which confirmed that he had died of his wounds. He was 32 and had previously worked at Prickledon Mills.

Buried at Terlincthun British Cemetery.

[Ex-Pte. GAMALIEL BOOTHROYD]

**Gamaliel Boothroyd**. Private. No 23419. Durham Light Infantry.

Gamaliel was well known in Holmfirth and before enlisting in 1916 was his father's 'right hand man' in the yeast business. He was badly wounded in the left arm and thigh and spent most of the following year in a military hospital before being discharged from the Army.

Back in Holmfirth he contracted tuberculosis of the lungs and spine and died in Holmfirth Auxiliary Hospital on October 20 aged 29.

Buried in New Mill at Christ Church Churchyard Extension.

**Andrew Greenwood**. Ordinary Seaman. No 2/13436. R.N.R. Royal Navy Depot (Crystal Palace) Tyneside.

Andrew worked with his father in the finishing department of Tinkers Bottoms Mill in Holmfirth before joining the Navy but died of pneumonia in Croydon just five weeks after leaving home.

He died on October 24 aged just 18 and his body was brought back to Holmfirth. Buried in Holy Trinity Burial Ground.

HOLMFIRTH FAMILY'S SEVERE BLOW

Wireless Operator Andrew Greenwood

**Hugh Philip Ballantyne**. Lieutenant. 4th Battalion Seaforth Highlanders.

Hugh was the son of Annie Ballantyne, Headteacher at New Mill School, and had been working in London when he volunteered at the outbreak of war. He served as a private until being commissioned in 1917. He had already been wounded twice - once at Messines Ridge and again at Cambrai - before being killed in action on October 28 aged 27. His name is commemorated at the Vis-en-Artois Memorial to the Missing.

LIEUT. P. HUGH BALLANTYNE
SEAFORTH HIGHLANDERS

PTE. BOOTH BATTYE
DURHAM LIGHT INFANTRY

**Booth Battye**. Private. No 79609. 1/9th Battalion Durham Light Infantry.

Booth was a New Mill man and was employed as a weaver at Kirkridge before joining the Army. He was taken prisoner by the Germans in May, 1918, and it was an agonising five months before his family knew that he was alive when they finally received a postcard from him on October 20. That was the last they heard and it took until March 1919 before the War Office was able to tell them that he died on October 29 in a prisoner-of-war camp aged 23. Cause of death unknown but influenza was rife in that area at that time.

Buried at Worms (Hochheim Hill) Cemetery, Germany. In a very rare mistake by the Commonwealth War Graves Commission, his name has been carved wrongly.

**Raymond Tyas Brook**. Private. No 42003. 10th Battalion Northumberland Fusiliers. Raymond lived at 46 St. George's Road, Scholes and worked in the finishing department at Washpit Mills. He was killed in action in Italy on October 27 and is buried at Tezze British Cemetery, Italy.

I feel the loss very much as he was a good pal but we have one consolation in knowing that he suffered no pain as a bullet from an enemy machine gun hit him in the head.

"A BETTER PAL NEVER LIVED."

Raymond Tyas Brook

# Those killed in November 1918

**Douglas Irvine Tolson.** Cadet. No 177552. 2 Observer School. Royal Air Force.

PROMISING CAREER CUT SHORT.

Douglas Irvine Tolson

Irvine had been a talented student throughout his education and prior to his enlistment was studying in the dyeing and chemistry department of the Huddersfield Technical College. His parents received a telegram telling them that Irvine had been taken dangerously ill during his training at Manston and they took a train early the next morning to be with him. When they got there they found him dying of septic pneumonia and he died on November 1.

He was brought home to Holmfirth and is buried at Holmfirth Wesleyan Burial Ground.

PTE. LOUIS WOODHEAD

**Louis Woodhead.** Private. No 38162. 1st Battalion The Yorkshire Regiment.

Another New Mill man, Louis worked at Wildspur Mills before enlisting in September 1916. His wife received a letter from Private Green:

The poor lad must have been instantly killed by a shell during the recent advance for I came across his body two or three days after his Battalion went over the top and I may say I buried him on the field of battle as respectfully as I could.

Killed in action on November 5, one week before the end of the war. Buried at Roison Communal Cemetery.

"OUT TO DO HIS BEST."

[PRIVATE C. A. BATTYE]

**Charles Alfred Battye.** Private. No 91514 1/4th Northumberland Fusiliers. Charles Alfred was another Upperthong man who enlisted in 1917. He'd recently been employed as a butcher with Mr. Stockwell in Victoria Square and after army training was transferred to farm work until the Fusiliers sent for him after the March battles. On his way to France he fell ill and was detained at hospital in Hornsea where he died from septic pneumonia on November 8.

His remains were returned to Holmfirth and he was interred at St John's Churchyard in Upperthong. He was 19.

Also remembered.

**Herbert Wilson Brook**. Private. No 131828. 50th Machine-Gun Depot, Machine-Gun Corps. Born and grew up in Thongsbridge, Holmfirth and was killed in action on September 11, 1918.
   Buried at Harlebeke New British Cemetery, Belgium.
**Harry Brown MM**. Private. No 100192. 24th Battalion Royal Fusiliers. Harry was born and grew up in Holmfirth but his family later moved to Huddersfield. He worked as a porter in Mr. Hardy's paper warehouse in Birkby before enlisting in 1917. Awarded the Military Medal for the action in which he was killed - bravery and resourcefulness during an attack on an enemy defensive system - aged 19.
   Killed in action on October 1,1918 and buried in Anneux British Cemetery.

**Hubert Coldwell.** Corporal. No 203618. 2/5th Battalion Duke of Wellington's Regiment. Hubert was one of the Territorials in the Drill Hall on the night war was declared in 1914 and fought in France until 1916 when he was discharged as a time-expired soldier. He immediately re-volunteered and went back in 1917 where he was promptly wounded in six places and hospitalised. Returning to the trenches once more he was posted as missing on the opening day of the German offensive on March 21st. A short time later his family received a letter saying that he had been captured and was wounded in the shoulder. He communicated regularly over the following few months but complained in his last letter that he had not received a single reply or a parcel from home. He died, cause unknown, on October 7, aged 26.
Buried at Mons Communal Cemetery.

**F. Marston**. Private. No 263011. 1/4th Battalion King's Own Yorkshire Light Infantry. He was born and brought up at Holme village and worked at Whiteley and Green's Mill down in the valley bottom. He enlisted in 1916 and was taken prisoner in August 1918 and died (cause unknown) as a Prisoner-of-War on October 21, aged 24.
  Buried at Glageon Communal Cemetery Extension.

**Joseph Bramwell**. Private. No 40933. 10th Battalion (Hull Commercials) East Yorkshire Regiment. Jo grew up on Choppards Farm, just outside Holmfirth, and when he wasn't working at Bridge Mills helped his father on the farm. He enlisted in May 1917, was wounded in the hand in March 1918 and returned home to England for a few months to recover. Sent back to France in September he was wounded again, but this time much more seriously, and died in the 3rd Canadian Hospital at St. Omer on November 6, five days before the armistice, aged 20.
  Buried at Longuenesse Souvenir (St Omer) Cemetery.

# WOMEN AND THE WAR
## What happened to the Suffragettes?

They never went away.

Dora Thewliss of Huddersfield being arrested March 1907
(Courtesy of the Huddersfield Examiner)

Without the active support and involvement of women it's unlikely that the conflict could have continued for as long as it did. This was true for all the major combatants. Without the contribution of millions of women, many of them members of feminist organisations, the war could not have been fought the way it was.

Germany had the BDF - the Bund der Frauen - with some 500,000 members engaged in a variety of support roles for the war. France, initially more reluctant than Germany or Britain to involve women directly in the war effort, nevertheless had 430,000 'munitionettes' and 120,000 military nurses by 1918. Britain started the war in 1914 already possessing a women's organisation numbering hundreds of thousands that readily turned its hand to war work. This was the Women's Social and Political Union formed by Emmaline and her daughter Christabel Pankhurst in Manchester in 1903.

The WSPU was created to campaign for social reforms and an extension of women's suffrage (but only for middle-class women) which would lead, they believed, to sexual equality. To emphasise their militant stance they adopted the slogan - 'Deeds not Words' and by 1908 the movement was big enough to hold a 'Women's Sunday' demonstration in Hyde Park of over 300,000 women.

Their protests led to three Parliamentary Conciliation Bills aimed at extending the rights of women in 1910, 1911 and 1912 but all three failed to satisfy the increasingly militant disaffection of women and the movement began to adopt more extremist, and at times violent, measures. At first these measures involved targeting property and smashing the windows of public buildings. They cut telephone lines, fought with the police (there was a trained 'Bodyguard Team' of women who protected prominent members from arrest), and attacked works of art in the National Gallery. By 1913 some individuals were making pipe-bombs and committing what the newspapers referred to as 'outrages' - the same term that was used to describe the concurrent killings and bombings of the Fenians in Ireland. The Glass House at Alexandra Park in Manchester was destroyed by a bomb allegedly made and planted by Kitty Marion, one of the stalwarts of the WSPU. Parts of Kew Gardens in London - the Orchid House and a pavilion - had already been attacked and burnt down, probably also by Kitty. Bombs and incendiary devices were placed in and outside of banks, churches, even Westminster Abbey. In Dublin in 1912, Mary Leigh, Gladys Evans, Lizzie Baker and Mabel Capper made an attempt to burn down the Theatre Royal during a packed lunchtime concert which was attended by Prime Minister Asquith. They had hidden a box of gunpowder close to the stage and dowsed the projection booth with petrol, which contained highly flammable film, before throwing lighted matches.

Earlier that morning, Mary Leigh had thrown an axe at Mr. Asquith which only narrowly missed him but hit the Irish MP John Redmond on the head. Kitty, meanwhile, burnt a whole train.

The train was afterwards driven into Teddington Station, where an examination resulted in the discovery of inflammable materials in almost every set of coaches. Among the articles found in the

265

train were partly-burnt candles, four cans of petroleum, three of which had been emptied of their contents, a lady's dressing case containing a quantity of cotton wool, and packages of literature dealing with the woman suffrage movement. Newspaper cuttings of recent suffragette outrages were also found scattered about the train ... The method adopted was very simple. First the cushions were saturated with petroleum, and then small pieces of candle were lighted immediately under the seats.

An unexploded bomb found at Lloyd-George's house

Between1906 and 1914 there were 1,214 court appearances by suffragette activists. By December 1913 some 240 women had been sent to prison for militant suffragette activities where many of them promptly went on hunger strike. Force-feeding of hunger strikers developed into a major social and political  issue and the violence reached its height during the summer of that year. There were attempts by suffragettes to blow up the Bank of England, the Royal Astronomical Observatory in Edinburgh, the Theatre Royal in Taunton (painted on the side of the unexploded bomb were - 'Votes for Women', 'Judges Beware', 'Martyrs of the Law' and 'Release our Sisters').

Lloyd- George's new home had already been destroyed by one of two bombs - the other failed to go off - and, in a further blow to the Government, the Suffragettes were reported to be contemplating kidnapping Cabinet Ministers, holding them captive and subjecting them to force-feeding. The threat was taken seriously and private detectives were employed to protect the members of the Government.

The use of bombs and explosives was justified by Christabel Pankhurst:

> Perhaps the Government will realise now that we mean to fight to the bitter end…. If men use explosives and bombs for their own purpose they call it war, and the throwing of a bomb that destroys other people is then described as a glorious and heroic deed. Why should a woman not make use of the same weapons as men. It is not only war we have declared. We are fighting for a revolution.

These extreme acts dominated the newspaper headlines, as of course they were meant to, and were accompanied by a constant backdrop of women chaining themselves to railings, smashing windows in public places, damaging priceless museum pieces, placing poison in post boxes, refusing to pay taxes and marching and protesting in their thousands against a government which they felt had refused to take them seriously. In June 1913 Emily Wilding Davison threw herself under the King's horse during the Derby horse race and was killed. She was the movement's first martyr and in her honour Kitty Marion burnt down the racecourse pavilion.

Emily's headstone at Morpeth, Northumberland bears the WSPU slogan, 'Deeds not words'. It couldn't go on.

The Government finally acted, but in rather a kid-glove fashion, and proceeded only to ban the Women's Social and Political Union from holding open-air meetings. It was hardly a crack-down but the militants were infuriated and responded by burning down the homes of prominent members of society who opposed women's suffrage. Museums, churches and stately homes were closed to the public in case they suffered the same fate. Everything came to a head with the formation in 1913 of what became known as 'Mrs Pankhurst's Army'.

> A meeting was held at Bow, London, last night, for the purposes of inaugurating the projected suffragette 'army', to be known as the

People's Training Corps. About 300 persons assembled, mostly young girls and women … Miss Emerson, in an address, said that their intention was to train the corps that they could proceed in force to Downing Street, and there imprison Ministers until they conceded women's suffrage. They had all heard of bloody Sidney Street, but the bloody scenes that might be expected at Downing Street would be worse.

In these last few months before the world was thrown into turmoil, the Women's Social and Political Union had embraced the rhetoric and actions of war and danger. These were determined, dangerous and violent women and it begs the question of whether or not they should be given the more modern name of 'terrorists'. The fact that relatively few members of the public were injured by the bombings and burnings was more a matter of fortune than a deliberate plan to spare them. Certainly if this had been a 20th Century, male dominated, political movement employing the same methodology and tactics there would be little hesitation in describing them as a terrorist group. And, suddenly it all came to a halt with the declaration of war against Germany.

On the outbreak of war and in a display of patriotism, Emmeline Pankhurst instructed the Suffragette movement to suspend all violent campaigning for the duration of the war and to support the Government in every way. The Government quickly responded by declaring an amnesty for all suffragette offenders, halting force-feeding regimes and releasing all prisoners sentenced for suffragette activities.

But not all members of the WSPU agreed and there was a split in the movement between the mainstream who enthusiastically  supported the war, and the more radical members led by Sylvia Pankhurst who were against it. Sylvia went on to form the Women's Suffrage Federation which campaigned for working class women and eventually became part of the Socialist/Communist Party group before splintering even further and then disappearing.

But the Suffragette movement spoke for only one section of female society and other voices clamoured to be heard.

# The Anti-Suffrage Movement

At 15 a little pet.
At 20 a little Coquette.
At 40 Not married yet!
At 50 a suffragette.

It wasn't all straightforward. The Suffragettes hadn't had the argument for votes for women all to themselves and throughout the pre-war period they were opposed by a group of well-organised, well financed and well connected women.

Fairly primitive opinion polls taken pre-war indicated that the majority of women were against having the vote at all. How comprehensive and accurate these polls were is debatable but, as early as 1889, a protest movement, the 'Appeal Against Female Suffrage' was launched with an initial 104 signatures. This appeal grew in size until the creation of the Women's National Anti-Suffrage League in 1908 which, at the outset, was an upper-class women's group led by thirty peeresses with Lady Jersey as Chairperson. Two years later it claimed that 250,000 women had signed an anti-suffrage petition and it now boasted 15,000 paying members.

Membership cost between 1s and 5s and men were allowed to subscribe or become affiliated members. The group published the Anti-Suffrage Review, costing one penny, until 1918.

In 1910, having run out of funds, the Women's National Anti-Suffrage League amalgamated with the Men's League for Opposing Woman Suffrage to form the National League for Opposing Woman Suffrage. The first President was Lord Cromer and the executive committee was formed of seven men and seven women.

There were any number of powerful women speakers who addressed meetings throughout the country. Mary Humphrey Ward held debates at Newnham and Girton Colleges at Cambridge exhorting women not to join the pro-suffrage movement. 'The emancipating process' she said 'has now reached the limits fixed by the physical constitution of women'.

The writer and archaeologist, Gertrude Bell, argued that women's lack of education prohibited them from being able to engage in political debate and therefore having the vote was pointless and a waste of time.

At the Albert Hall, Violet Markham was addressing large crowds:

> We believe that men and women are different – not similar – beings, with talents that are complementary, not identical, and that they therefore ought to have different shares in the management of the State, that they severally compose. We do not depreciate by one jot or belittle women's work and mission. We are concerned to find proper channels of expression for that work. We seek a fruitful diversity of political function, not a stultifying uniformity.

Men spoke too. One of the leading male opponents of votes for women was William Cremer. Hansard records a speech he made in the House of Commons on April 25th, 1906:

> …had always contended that if we opened the door and enfranchised ever so small a number of females, they could not possibly close it, and that it ultimately meant adult suffrage. The government of the country would therefore be handed over to a majority who would not be men, but women. Women are creatures of impulse and emotion and did not decide questions on the ground of reason as men did. I am sometimes described as a woman-hater, but I have had two wives, and I thought that was the best answer I could give to those who called me a woman-hater. I am too fond of them to drag them into the political arena and to ask them to undertake responsibilities, duties and obligations which they did not understand and did not care for.

But by 1913 membership of the Anti-Suffrage League began to dwindle and it reverted to its original upper-class support. The movement lost its energy and drive as middle and working class women became persuaded by pro-suffrage arguments and, though it stuttered on until the end of the war, it had all but lost the battle many years before.

# Working Women

Mummie does the house-work,
Can't get any maid,
Gone to make munitions,
'Cause they're better paid,
Nurse is always busy,
Never time to play,
Sewing shirts for soldiers,
Nearly ev'ry day.
Ev'ry body's doing
Something for the War
Girls are doing things
They've never done before,
Gone as 'bus conductors,
Drive a car or van,
All the world is topsy-turvy
Since the War began.

Nina MacDonald, War Time Nursery Rhymes

All of the major protagonists in Europe employed women in the war industries. Women also took over the running of businesses or farms, filled the jobs vacated by men, managed the household finances, brought up children and looked after their families. Women worked as tram-drivers, welders, butchers and bakers, bus conductors, even blacksmiths.

The Daily Mail, in a patronising footnote by Lord Northcliffe, gave praise to the:

> …nice girls from dreary manless suburbs…delaying the marriage to which every patriotic woman looks forward, they have the great satisfaction of knowing that, whether they be women doctors, women dentists, women clerks, women ticket collectors or engaged in any other profession, they are helping the great cause of freedom.

Their physical role in the wartime economy was vital but they also maintained morale both abroad and at home and supported the fighting men. Even the French General Joffre admitted that without a women's workforce sustaining the munitions industry, France would have lost the war. Before 1914 there were comprehensive and quite strict controls on the type of employment that could be offered to women, not least because of the opposition of male-dominated trades unions. Women could certainly work in mills and some factories (and between 1914 and 1918 some two million did so) but traditional male industries - steel, engineering, chemicals and munitions - were denied them.

When the Army High Command in 1915 blamed a shortage of shells for a notable military defeat the Government founded the Ministry of Munitions under David Lloyd-George who energetically introduced a number of initiatives to increase production. One of these initiatives was an appeal for women volunteers to work in the munitions industries. Tens of thousands of women responded and by the end of the war some 700,000 women (possibly up to one million - the numbers have never been fully calculated) had become 'munitionettes'.

'Munitionettes' in their boilersuits, felt gloves and shoes.

After 1916 the situation in heavy industry became even more desperate as more and more men were conscripted into the military forces. The demand for more artillery, more explosive and more shells increased exponentially and women became an essential and vital part of the work-force; so much so, that munitions factories which primarily employed women produced 80% of the weapons and shells used by the British Army. By 1918 women were skilled workers responsible for operating machinery, making shell cases, assembling detonators, weighing powder and filling bullets and shells. The munitions factories were the largest single employer of women in the country and for many women, war work was a revelation. Nearly half a million of the 1.7 million women who before the war worked as domestic servants got jobs in factories and mills where even the low wages they received were far better than they had ever known before. Many of these factories were huge places. The Woolwich Arsenal employed 14,000 men and no women in 1914 but by 1918 had grown to 100,000 workers of whom 50,000 were women.

'Woodbine Willie' - the army vicar, Geoffrey Student Kennedy, known in the trenches for his constant supply of cigarettes for soldiers in the line, wrote in his diary after watching a British artillery barrage:

> By George, it's a glorious barrage, and English girls made 'em. We're all in it, sweethearts, mothers and wives. The hand that rocks the cradle wrecks the world. There are no non-combatants.

This was certainly true for the women and men who worked at No. 1 Filling Factory at Barnbow, between Crossgates and Garforth, just outside Leeds. The Filling Factory, begun in early 1916, was a further development of the Armley Ordnance Factory which was already in production and a massive undertaking occupying some 400 acres. When it was finished its huge canteens used a milk supply from its own cows, its own slaughter-house and butcher's shop, its bacon factory, and vegetables from its own kitchen gardens. The factory had its own fire-brigade supplied by a 300,000 gallon reservoir. Each building had built-in sprinklers and drenchers, and a steam siren to sound the fire alarm. There were fire-proof doors and protective earth-works to separate the various danger areas of the manufacturing process.

Despite having to build everything from scratch for a workforce of some 17,000 people, most of them women, the roads, railways, utilities, as well as the buildings themselves were completed within a few months and by April, the first section of the Amatol explosive plant was completed and 4.5 inch shells were being filled, 6,000 of them each day. It was quickly followed by plant and machinery for the manufacture of cartridges and another Amatol factory. Amatol was a mixture of TNT (Trinitrotoluene) and ammonium nitrate which together formed an extremely powerful, but volatile, explosive and the quantities used at Barnbow were staggering - 12,000 tons of TNT were mixed with 26,350 tons of nitrate. In the cartridge section more than 61,000 tons of N.C.T. (Nitrocellulose Tubular) and cordite were combined and used to fill millions of bullets. All these chemicals had to be carefully weighed on scales in ounces and drachms.

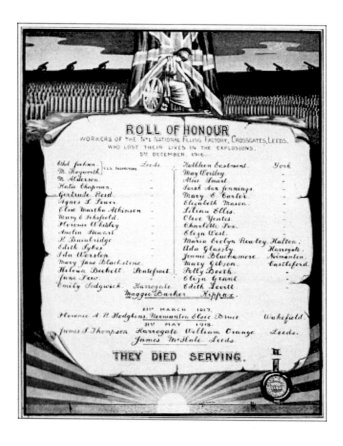

On the night of December 5th, 1916, a 4.5 inch shell exploded as the fuse was being attached. That one explosion triggered off others throughout the building and killed 35 young women and seriously injured many others. The building was totally destroyed and if it hadn't been for the protective sand-bag walls and earth mounds the same fate would have befallen most of the factory.

Mrs Mary Ann Cowell, one of the survivors that day was persuaded to talk about it in 1995:

> I worked in Room 41 shell store and opposite was Room 42. At the bottom of my room they filled the shells with two bags - one known as 'A' bag and one known as 'B' bag. My recollection of the accident was that it occurred about 10.30pm just after I had finished my 2pm-10pm shift. There was this terrific bang and we were told afterwards that the accident had occurred because instead of one 'A' bag and one 'B' bag being put into the shell, someone had put in two 'B' bags. The first did not go down sufficiently enough and the worker who picked up the shell in No. 42 Room put it into the machine and it blew up. It also burst all the hot water pipes above and many workers got scalded.

One of the heroes that night was William Parkin, a mechanic at the plant, who was passing when the explosion blew the building apart. He entered the devastated wreck, which was burning and collapsing around him, at least eleven times, each time bringing out an injured girl. He received no official recognition for his acts but later on, the girls and women at the factory clubbed together and presented him with a silver watch and chain for his bravery.

In spite of the horror of the event the work continued - this was wartime after all. Within a few hours of the explosion the girls and women of the factory were volunteering to go back to work, some of them to what remained of Room 42. At the end of the war in 1918, it was calculated that this one factory alone, of the hundreds throughout the country and the Empire, had filled 36,000,000 breech loading cartridges, 25,000,000 shells, and had filled, fused, packed in boxes another 19,250,000 shells which made for a grand total of 556,000 tons of finished ammunition for service overseas. Of the most widely used British shell of the war, the 18-pounder, Barnbow had made 9,250,000 - enough to stretch from London to New York, 3,200 miles (for further details of the above, please refer to 'Leeds in the Great War, 1914-1918').

Wages for women grew proportionately. The average female wage was 10 shillings (50 pence) before the war; 30 shillings (£1.50) by 1916 and £2 by 1918 - much more for a supervisor.

Compared to domestic service these were good wages and service was a hard life - 16 hour days were the norm - and living in the same house as your employer meant that every moment was scrutinised. Servants were given cheaper furniture, smaller beds, worse food; they were segregated in back kitchens or quarters and had to use outdoor toilets while their employers had indoor bathrooms. Privacy was limited with employers having the right to enter their rooms and go through their belongings. The Duchess of Devonshire claimed that the housemaids at Chatsworth were entitled to one afternoon and every other evening off, but in practice 'there was too much work for this to happen'.

But in war work, despite the often long hours and poor working conditions, women were far more independent than they would have ever been in service:

> When you were in service you couldn't go out when you liked. When you work in the factories you've got your own time, haven't you? You just go home of a night, wherever you live, and you can go out when you like.

Ethel Dean - left domestic service to work in a munitions factory.

Working conditions in some factories demanded special clothing and shoes. The high risk of explosion when working with some chemicals meant that no metal of any sort - no jewellery, no hair slides, no wire reinforced corsets - were allowed into 'clean' areas of the factories. Long skirts were impractical and were replaced by shorter ones and even trousers. Long hair could easily become trapped in moving machinery so women started to cut their hair into a bob. The bra replaced the corset. Almost inevitably, women's new found independence and financial security was seen to be threatening to a male-dominated society and before too long the newspapers were denouncing young working women as 'flaunting flappers'. Public morality was 'outraged' as working women enjoyed their new-found freedoms. Many women had left home and lived in hostels or lodging houses organised by the Government, where they enjoyed what was essentially a male-free environment; women smoked, went to the pub or the cinema unescorted. It was unheard-of and unprecedented and obviously immoral. Eventually the Government appointed Welfare Inspectors (the organisation grew into the first women police officers) who attempted to control morals among the female working population. These mainly middle class women in uniform patrolled parks, cinemas and alley ways and chased away young couples who were keen on privacy. They weren't popular.

This movement of 'concerned' women had begun as a small voluntary group much earlier when a group of Bishops' wives had worried about reports of large numbers of young women congregating near soldiers' barracks or railway stations where troops were assembled before departing. The worthy wives were concerned that the girls had succumbed to 'khaki fever' and were placing themselves in moral danger. As were the soldiers in fact, just as willingly, most of whom were young men separated for probably the first time in their lives from the social constraints of family, friends, church and community.

One of the first women to tackle the problem was a philanthropist and mountaineer, Margaret Damer Dawson, who had already formed a group of like-minded ladies to patrol the streets of London advising and supporting bewildered Belgian refugee women. They eventually became known as volunteer policewomen, much to the disgust of the Metropolitan Police Commissioner who, understandably, felt that patrols of educated ladies would make his constables feel stupid. Even more fearsome was Mrs. Edith Smith who was a one-woman anti-prostitution campaigner in the town of Grantham which had recently become home to an enormous military camp of machine-gunners. The camp, predictably, attracted a large number of amateur and professional girls and women and Mrs. Smith patrolled the streets and parks at night creating a black list of individuals which she then banned from the town's cinemas and theatres. 'My presence in the streets is sufficient to bring order among girls' she claimed. She became the first woman to hold a police warrant card.

There had been widespread hostility in all sectors of industry in the early years of the war from male workers who viewed the employment of women as a management strategy to reduce men's wages. Trade unionists in particular believed that women in the workplace would lead to 'dilution', where female workers would settle for lower pay and disregard all those laboriously negotiated and agreed restrictive practices which protected jobs. But there was little choice for the unions with so many men volunteering or being conscripted away and, anyway, Government legislation placated the unions by ensuring that women would always be paid less than their male counterparts, even when doing the same job. Equal pay was some way off, even as late as 1918.

Harry Smith remembered the reaction to his new workmates from the male workers at his factory in Yorkshire:

> Oh they all came in, the women, then. Well, they worked the lathes, the machines. They did quite a few jobs, the womenfolk that came in. Well, they weren't as skilled as the men that'd been brought up with the job, but they did just the job that they were told to do. And there were more repetition work then than previously in the years before the war. Well, some didn't – the older men didn't like it, but some enjoyed it because they, some went to have a drink at night with them, but not me.

But wage equality was an issue and women had already initiated, led and won strikes in London over the payment of war bonuses for those women workers employed on the buses and trams. That strike spread to the London Underground and then to towns throughout the South East.

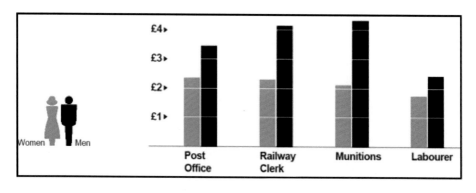

The War Cabinet eventually set up a Committee to examine the whole question of women's wages which (conveniently for the Government) released its final report after the war ended. The report agreed with the principle of 'equal pay for equal work', but as women suffered from 'lesser strength and special health problems' their output would never be equal to that of men. Despite copious evidence that women had performed effectively and efficiently in any number of what were considered men's jobs throughout the war, Government opinion was that women would always be less productive than men. Unions that included and represented women were assured that in those cases where women had completely replaced skilled men they would receive equal pay. But it was emphasised that this would apply only for the duration of the war and it would be reversed just as soon as the soldiers returned.

Machinery, chemicals and explosives were recognised as dangerous work even in an age when Health and Safety Regulations were largely absent, and accidents and illnesses were common. Those women munition workers who filled the shells with Trinitrotoluene - TNT - were not only working with a high explosive but were particularly prone to poisoning. One particular study of women workers at Woolwich Arsenal found that 37% of shell-fillers suffered from abdominal pain, constipation and nausea, one quarter had skin problems and 36% showed signs of depression. There were 149 serious cases of TNT poisoning reported during the war with 109 deaths recorded.

The Ministry of Munitions, concerned that output might be affected if women realised just how dangerous the work was, reported to the Government:

> …unless measures are taken to meet this difficulty, serious interference with output may arise as if the operatives become frightened at the number of diseases and deaths of their colleagues, greater difficulty than ever will be experienced in procuring labour.

The Government responded quickly by offering sick pay of one pound per week, insurance cover in the event of workers needing hospital treatment and an allowance for special diets. Free milk was provided.

At the beginning of a shift, women workers changed their clothing into overalls or new-fangled boiler suits and rubber shoes before being allowed to enter the work place. Nothing metal was allowed on any article of clothing - no metal buttons, no hooks or eyes and, certainly, no wire-reinforced corsets. Hair was covered by a bonnet.

But the toxins still turned skin yellow.

> Everything that that powder touches goes yellow. All the girls' faces were yellow, all round their mouths. They had their own canteen, in which everything was yellow that they touched… Everything they touched went yellow – chairs, tables, everything.

Ethel Dean who worked at Woolwich Arsenal

Some of the girls used make-up to cover the discolouration but many didn't and some took delight in their nickname of 'Canaries'. But there were others who fell ill through the effects of the chemicals, particularly the 'black powder' used to make the explosives. Lillian Miles and her sister Grace went to work at a munitions factory in Coventry in 1917. Grace fell ill within months of starting.

Well she was ill. She went to the doctor and the doctor said that she was under the influence of alcohol because she was falling about and she couldn't hold herself up, she was falling about. So the doctor told her to come back again when she was sober, he said. Well I went down to the doctor and I said to him, I said, "She doesn't drink." He said, "Well," he said, "I think she was under the influence of drink." And I said she wasn't. I said, "There's something wrong with her," I said, "because she's falling about all the while." And of course she was only 19, she wasn't 20 – she died before she was 20. Besides, she didn't drink. And so any rate, my landlady she said, "Oh," she said, "don't go down to him again," she said, "I'll send for him." So she sent for the doctor and she was ill and he had a specialist to her and they took her in the hospital. She died in terrible agony. She died in terrible pain and they said that they reckoned that black powder it burnt the back of her throat away. And the continual breathing of this black powder it sort of burnt the back of her throat away.

Women munition workers mixing TNT

281

# Women and Football

The Great War allowed women to enter into roles in society that had previously been denied them. As more and more women entered what had previously been male-dominated worlds there were profound changes in female lifestyles, expectations and even dress. Working class women with a disposable income - unheard of before the war - had, by 1918, adopted an almost androgynous 'look' - trouser suits, shorter hem-lines, cigarettes, short 'bobbed' hair - all of which reflected new defined roles. Women felt themselves much more free to become part of a man's world, and that included sport.

The need for women in the munitions industries was so pressing that the Government provided funds for day nurseries for those women with small children. By 1917 there were over one hundred creches in munitions industries and women who worked the night shift got an extra child allowance. Enlightened male management at some factories encouraged their women workers to participate in organised sporting activities and the fact that there were such large numbers of women employed meant that many new leisure and recreational opportunities were opened up to them. Many factories organised social events and even recruited and financed their own ladies' football teams.

As the game became more popular and the quality of the football improved, spectators came to enjoy the games for the skill and ability of the women players rather than simply the humorous spectacle of 'women playing football'.

In Preston, the firm of Dick, Kerr and Co. Ltd which before the war had manufactured light railway equipment was, like so many other firms since 1915, busily turning out munitions on a huge scale with a new workforce of uniformed women. These workers from disparate backgrounds were discovering comradeship and teamwork and were encouraged by the works management to kick a football around the cobbled courtyards during the short lunch breaks:

> We used to play at shooting at the cloakroom windows. They were little square windows and if the boys beat us at putting a window through we had to buy them a packet of Woodbines, but if we beat them they had to buy us a bar of Five Boys chocolate.

> Alice Norris, one of the young women who worked at the factory

Soon, the women organised themselves into teams and began playing each other; they even played against some of the men, a practice which had been officially banned by the Football Association as long ago as 1902.

One of the Works Managers, Alfred Franklin, had watched these lunch-time football sessions and had the idea of organising a charity match against another ladies team. This duly took place on Christmas Day, 1917 at the home stadium of the mighty Preston North End when Dick Kerr's Ladies beat Arundel Coulthard Foundry 4-0 watched by 10,000 paying customers.

Dick Kerr's were not long in showing that they suffered less than their opponents from stage fright, and they had a better all-round understanding of the game....Their forward work, indeed, was often surprisingly good, one or two of the ladies showing quite admirable ball control.

The Daily Post

The game raised £600 for the local hospital for wounded soldiers, equivalent to nearly £50,000 today and the team went on to become famous, playing in front of huge crowds and raising a fortune for wartime charities.

They were the first British ladies team to wear shorts and the first to go on an overseas tour when they played in France. One of their star players was the glamorous blonde centre-forward, Florrie Redford who regularly featured in the newspapers of the day. Jennie Harris was at inside-left, only 4ft 10in, but a wizard of the dribble. On the left-wing was the fourteen year old Lily Parr - 'with a kick like a Division One back'. Lily proved this in a later game at Chorley when she shot at goal from the edge of the area and broke a professional goalkeeper's arm. She later became one of the first female professional players. A smoker, part of her wages in the early days was supplemented by packs of Woodbine cigarettes and she had the distinction of being the first woman football player to be sent off for fighting. She was tall - 6ft - and athletic and scored over 1000 goals in her 31-year career. She scored 34 of those in her first ever season - aged 14.

Lily Parr

There is probably no greater football prodigy in the whole country. Not only has she speed and excellent ball control, but her admirable physique enables her to brush off challenges from defenders who tackle her. She amazes the crowd wherever she goes by the way she swings the ball clean across the goalmouth to the opposite wing.

Daily Post

In 1917 ladies' teams came together and organised the Tyne Wear & Tees Alfred Wood Munition Girls Cup - more popularly known as the Munitionettes' Cup - and the first winners were Blyth Spartans who beat Bolckow Vaughan of Middlesbrough 5-1. The winger for Blyth, Jennie Morgan, was said to have gone straight from her wedding to play in the match - she scored twice.

Huddersfield had three women's teams including 'Atlanta Ladies' who trained at Crosland Moor. Most of their players came from more genteel backgrounds, teaching and clerical work, rather than the heavy steel or munitions works and they were talented - reaching the semi-finals of the England Ladies Football Association FA Cup.

As the ladies' game became ever more popular (by 1920 there were some 150 teams in England alone) decisions had to be made as to what exactly women players should wear. It's probably fair to say that in the beginning many male spectators came to watch ladies' football games primarily for the rare sight of uncovered shapely calves. An early team from Scotland was ridiculed when it became rumoured that one of the girls played in her brother's underwear. Before the war (before women were able to feel comfortable in more 'manly' sportswear) ladies teams wore traditional jerseys that had been loosened by the addition of embroidery at the edges. Sleeves were very wide and loose-fitting while knickers, or knickerbockers, were worn very much to individual taste. London ladies' teams wore short skirts over their knickerbockers. By 1916, nearly all teams wore the traditional shirt and shorts but, for some reason, continued to wear their 'bubble-hats'.

Back at Dick Kerr's, Mr. Franklin continually improved the team by spotting talented girls and ladies and tempting them to Preston with attractive offers of employment coupled with ample opportunity for football. They became so popular that they played the National French touring team in 1920 in front of a 25,000 crowd, winning 2-0. Later that year on Boxing Day, they played St. Helen's Ladies in front of 53,000 spectators at Goodison Park, beating them 4-0. Still wearing their trademark 'bubble hats' they became the undefeated British champions in the 1920-21 season. But it couldn't last.

> Complaints have been made as to football being played by women, the Council feel impelled to express their strong opinion that the game of football is quite unsuitable for females and ought not to be encouraged.

Minutes of the Football Association meeting of December 5, 1921

The FA banned all women's teams from using league grounds and women's football ground to a halt for fifty years.

# Women in the Services

By 1918 there were 30,000 women serving as nurses with the French army and a further 90,000 with the Red Cross. The were 92,000 nurses in the German army. In Britain tens of thousands of young women volunteered as nurses and ambulance drivers with VAD - the Voluntary Aid Detachment and FANY, the First Aid Nursing Yeomanry both of which had existed before the war, as had the Queen Alexandra's Imperial Military Nursing Service. The Queen Alexandra's nurses expanded to 23,000 volunteers and served in every theatre of the conflict. There were numerous other voluntary organisations that sprang up in 1914, many of them utilising the energy and the ability of the suffragette movement - the Territorial Force Nursing Service; the Women's Hospital Corps; the Almeric Paget Military Massage Corps, (which despite its suggestive name, provided invaluable physiotherapy for wounded soldiers); the Women's Forage Corps; the Women's Forestry Corps - the 'Lumber Jills'; Mrs. St Clair Stobart's Women's Sick and Wounded Convoy Corps who worked exclusively with the Belgian Army; the Women's Army Auxiliary Corps whose uniform consisted of a small tight-fitting khaki cap, khaki jacket and skirt (regulations stated that the skirt must be no more than 12 inches above the ground); the Women's Volunteer Reserve for part-time workers; the largest of all the voluntary bodies - the Women's Legion; the Women's Volunteer Reserve founded by a militant suffragette, the Honourable Evelina Haverfield, which attracted many women who had played a central, and at times violent, role in the pre-war protest movement, and not least, the Scottish Women's Hospitals founded by the formidable suffragette Dr. Elsie Maud Inglis who had volunteered to set up a hospital for wounded soldiers at the beginning of the war but was advised to "Go home and sit still" by the military authorities. Instead of meekly following their advice she set up a mobile medical unit of women and travelled to Serbia to help the Serbian Army. By the end of the war there were 14 such units working throughout Europe with all of the Allied armies except the British. Dr. Inglis was captured by the Germans in Serbia and became a prisoner-of-war but was repatriated and immediately joined one of her units in Russia. She was evacuated from there during the fighting of the Revolution and returned to her home in Newcastle where she died the following day.

And in 1916, in a major demonstration of their continued presence, the Women's Social and Political Union marched through London in their thousands, amidst cheering crowds with Prime Minister Lloyd-George at their head in support of 'Women's Right To Serve'. The Suffragette Movement, which had caused such violence and uproar before 1914 now demanded the right to be at the heart of the war.

W.R.A.F.'s sight-seeing outside Buckingham Palace, 1918

Within a few months the country saw the formation of a number of women's services whose members were subject to military discipline - the Women's Auxiliary Army Corps to serve in non-combatant roles abroad; the Women's Royal Naval Service and, by 1918, the Women's Royal Air Force ( there is a headstone for Emily Lambert of the WRAF, dated 1918, in Beckett Street Cemetery, Leeds; it lies a short distance from a headstone for a Hussar from the Crimean War - 'one of the six hundred' of the Charge of the Light Brigade).

One of the biggest female organisations was the Women's Land Army which numbered 113,000 by 1918. Since the very early days of the war, women had worked in the fields and forests - farmers called them 'the lilac sunbonnet brigade' - but in 1917 the Government created a formal organisation complete with a quite stylishly designed, practical uniform - knee length tunic, boots, puttees, breeches and a slouch hat, as made popular by Australian troops. Most farmers were against women working the land and the Government was forced to despatch agricultural organisers to convince them of the necessity of female labour.

The Sheffield Daily Telegraph emphasised the healthy life-style in a gushing article:

> ...an open air life has built them up into strong healthy-looking Amazons, a type for which England was renowned in the days of Queen Elizabeth, when bright-cheeked and clear-eyed lasses were bred on the land, lived on the land and became mothers of the yeomen of England.

One or two of these 'Amazons' had been busily planting bombs and plotting the downfall of society just a few years previously.

# Votes at last!

There was a reward of sorts after the armistice.

  With one eye on what was happening in Russia and the fate of the Romanovs, the Government introduced and passed the Representation of the People Act, sometimes called the Fourth Reform Act. At a stroke the size of the electorate tripled. With the passing of the Bill in Parliament by 385 to 55 and the consequent enlargement of the electorate, the 7.7 million men entitled to vote in 1912 had become 21.4 million men and women by the end of 1918. Women now comprised nearly 43% of the total vote. Admittedly, only women over the age of 30 who met minimum property qualifications, or who were married to property owners, were enfranchised, compared to the age of 21 for men, but it was an important start and seen as recognition of the contribution made by women to the war effort. Had women been given equal voting ages to men they may well have formed a majority, given the war losses among male soldiers. In 1918, at war's end, women numbered 24.5 million compared to 22.7 million men:

> War by all classes of our countrymen has brought us nearer together, has opened men's eyes, and removed misunderstandings on all sides. It has made it, I think, impossible that ever again, at all events in the lifetime of the present generation, there should be a revival of the old class feeling which was responsible for so much, and, among other things, for the exclusion for a period, of so many of our population from the class of electors. I think I need say no more to justify this extension of the franchise.

> Home Secretary George Cave introducing the Act

There had been political pressure from both the Liberals and the Independent Labour Party for extending the franchise at the end of the 19th century which would have included women. The issue had been debated in Parliament before the war, spurred on by the campaign waged by the suffragettes, and there was a small, but growing, support for granting women the vote.

  The life of the 1910 Parliament had been prolonged in order to avoid holding a General Election during war-time but by 1916 it was recognised that there was a breakdown of the old electoral system caused by the wholesale enlistment of millions of men and the widespread dislocation of the population caused by the development of war industries. The structure itself needed a complete overhaul with a radically altered system of registration and voting and, possibly, new franchises. Devising such a system was entrusted to an extraordinary commission under the chairmanship of the Speaker of the House of Commons who chose thirty-six cross-party members in a 'Speakers Conference' which began hearing arguments in October 1916.

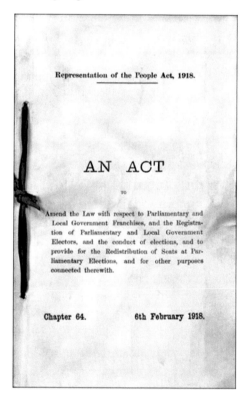

Representation of the People Act, 1918.

AN ACT

TO

Amend the Law with respect to Parliamentary and Local Government Franchises, and the Registration of Parliamentary and Local Government Electors, and the conduct of elections, and to provide for the Redistribution of Seats at Parliamentary Elections, and for other purposes connected therewith.

Chapter 64.     6th February 1918.

One of the speakers was the suffragette Millicent Fawcett who called for the voting age to be lowered for everyone to 18 (knowing full well that this would mean that women voters outnumbered men). If this wasn't possible, she suggested that women aged 30 and above should be enfranchised.

The Commission recognised that women needed to be 'rewarded' for the vital war work they had undertaken. The potentially disastrous munitions shortage had been solved by the recruitment of women 'munitionettes' while female labour in everything from farm work to collieries had saved the Home Front and contributed enormously to final victory.

Neither could anyone forget or ignore the shadow of the Suffragette movement before the war. The Government of 1919 had no desire to return to pre-1914 Suffragette militancy and was mindful of a resurgence of the violence and the reaction to the possible arrest of women who had performed important work for the country for the previous four years. This was a nation exhausted by war and, for a time at least, a nation in mourning.

# Post-war

During the war, of course, women, on all sides of the conflict, had received financial support if their husband or father was serving in the forces. As early as 1915 in Germany some 4 million families (11 million individuals) were receiving benefits, while in Britain the equivalent numbers were 1.5 million wives and several million children and dependents. Between 1914 and 1920 the cost to the British economy was £414.75 million. Unsurprisingly America was the most generous of all the combatants, offering wives both financial support and war-risk insurance giving many women better incomes than they had before the war.

The money was needed. Nine months after the first of Kitchener's volunteers had sailed abroad Britain was faced with the birth of thousands of illegitimate children. They were quickly named 'War Babies' by the Press and were patriotically viewed as being necessary to replace the losses on the battlefield. And they were certainly needed. J.M. Winter calculates that the birth rate had fallen to 660,000 by 1918 (from 880,000 before the war) including a doubling of the illegitimacy rate to about 60,000 annual births. The overall countrywide birth rate fluctuated according to when soldiers were allowed home leave or depending on numbers of battle casualties. There was a sharp decrease nine or ten months after the battles of the Somme and Passchendaele.

But one of the biggest changes affecting the lives of women and children by 1918 was that of public health. Paradoxically, Britain was a healthier country at the end of the war than it had been at the beginning. Between 1911 and 1921, life expectancy for men in England and Wales grew from 49 to 56 years, and for women from 53 to 60 years of age. In all those categories of death from diseases associated with poverty, the rates declined significantly during the war and immediately after, suggesting that public health standards had risen considerably, particularly in the manufacturing cities of West Yorkshire, Manchester, Glasgow and Birmingham. In other words, in all those areas where there was high female employment. Infant mortality fell by two-thirds during the war and women lost fewer children in childbirth. The reasons for this quite dramatic change are complex but could partly be explained by the fact that working women had control of the family budget and spending tended to be more on food and less on alcohol. With husbands away and therefore fewer children, households were smaller and, so long as wages rose faster than prices, with more disposable income.

Everything changed of course with the peace accord and the end of the war. With the gradual return of the victorious troops, working women were superfluous to requirements and by the Autumn of 1919 750,000 fewer women were employed in industry as factories and mills returned to peacetime production. Nurseries were closed, canteens shut down and accommodation for single women sold off. It was a return, for many families, to a period of economic hardship and low expectations, where women were unemployed. Many women of course were now expected to spend the rest of their lives caring for the hundreds of thousands of men who were casualties, either physically or mentally, of the conflict.

The 1919 Restoration of Pre-War Practices Act actually ordered women to vacate wartime jobs for returning soldiers. Those women who resisted, particularly married women, were vilified in public and even criticised by other women. Single and widowed women claimed priority in employment over those who were married. The Daily Herald newspaper published a letter in 1919 from Isobel M. Pazzey:

> No decent man would allow his wife to work, and no decent woman would do it if she knew the harm she was doing to the widows and single girls who are looking for work. Put the married women out, send them home to clean their houses and look after the man they married and give a mother's care to their children. Give the single women and widows the work.

In 1921, women civil servants passed a resolution calling for a ban on married ladies in the service. The ban lasted until 1946. Hospitals rejected female medical students on the grounds of upholding modesty despite the fact that they had been welcomed throughout the war. The National Association of Schoolmasters campaigned vigorously against the employment of female teachers. Women teachers were already forced to resign their posts if they married, a restriction that lasted until at least the 1950's.

The Practices Act was quickly followed by the Unemployment Insurance Act of 1920 which specifically excluded domestic service, meaning, in effect, that women who were entitled to benefit would have it taken away if they refused to accept any job offered. With few jobs available, this usually meant returning to domestic service. Placements in domestic occupations showed an increase of 40% in 1919. There was an appeal system through the courts which rarely succeeded - possibly because magistrates had wives who needed servants to clean their houses.

The change to a peacetime economy was rapid and abrupt. As there was no longer a need for munitions (even before the war formally came to an end) women were fired en masse with little compensation. Those on government contracts in the munitions industries received two weeks pay in lieu of notice and a free rail pass back to their homes. They also got an 'out of work donation' of 20s. a week for the first 13 weeks; then 15s. for the next thirteen weeks and then nothing. Within months, the 'munitionettes' who had been lauded in the newspapers for their vital role in the war effort were being subjected to media scorn. They were 'taking a holiday at public expense'; they were 'loafers' and 'dodgers':

> ...a little investigation (at the Labour Exchange) showed that since they have "been in munitions" women have acquired to a remarkable extent a taste for factory life. Many of them of course, might return at once to the domestic service from which they came, but, for the moment at any rate, they literally scoff at the idea.

> Daily Telegraph

Women had gone from heroines to pariahs almost overnight - cursed if they refused to give up their jobs and equally so if they were sacked and accepted unemployment benefits. As the numbers of the employed began to fall in 1920 the complaints rose - 'The girls were clinging to their jobs, would not let go of the pocket money which they had spent on frocks' - was a typical cry.

A reporter for the Leeds Mercury who had obviously been slighted by a working woman at some point in the war, finally got his revenge in an article welcoming the dismissal of female bus conductors:

> Their record of duty well done is seriously blemished by their habitual and aggressive incivility and a callous disregard for the welfare of passengers. Their shrewish behaviour will remain one of the unpleasant memories of the war's vicissitudes.

> Leeds Mercury

By 1922, the Government, desperate to reduce the benefits bill, ruled that married women were ineligible for the dole if the total family income exceeded 10s. per week. Most women had lost their jobs by this time. London County Council had sacked all its married female staff in 1921 and excluded them from all government-sponsored training schemes. Women bus conductors and railway guards were made redundant or offered lower paid jobs as booking clerks.

The 'temporary men' in industry were no longer needed and Woolwich Arsenal dismissed 1,500 women each week during the demobilisation period.

In all of the major economies of the West there was a psychological as much as an economic rationale for men to regain employment over women. Masculine identity, harmed and warped by four years of combat, needed to be reassured by the restoration of the social order that existed before the war. Former soldiers wanted a return to their 'natural authority' in the home and they wanted to find their wives and women as they had left them.

Unsurprisingly for nations that had endured such massive losses of men, the immediate post-war period emphasised the need to increase the birth rate and halt the decline in population. Maternity was exalted. The mother-figure was seen as the perfect model for womanhood and the best agent for reviving the demographic and moral reconstruction of the country. In France, laws were passed which banned contraception and abortion. The benefit system was rigged to favour women with families instead of childless wives or widows.

Ironically, as peace arrived, there were fresh fears that the emancipation of women along with the self-confidence brought by their new working roles and a degree of financial independence would make them virtually un-marriageable. A shortage of husbands (at the end of the war women outnumbered men by 1.9 million) coupled with a generation of 'de-sexed and masculinised' women as the Daily Mail described them, would result in a catastrophically reduced birth rate at a time when it was essential to rebuild the population. Certainly, women's appearance had changed considerably by 1918. Shorter hair, shorter skirts and even trousers became the norm and social interaction between the sexes and between classes was easier and more common than before the war. Marie Stopes published her ground breaking and massively influential book 'Married Love' in 1918 which advocated equality of the sexes and a recognition of the importance of women's sexual desire. Marie had written it, she said, to save other women from the ignorance which had doomed her own marriage. By 1925 it had sold half a million copies and been reprinted thirty-nine times. The book was banned in America until 1931 on the grounds of obscenity.

And family sizes continued to shrink despite the fact that in 1920 as an army of millions of men was discharged, 957,000 babies were born in Wales and England - a total that has never been equalled since.

Women had changed and experienced far too much for many of them to return to pre-war norms of simple home and family. They were now much more aware of their individuality, their capacity to earn, and their ability to assume responsibilities outside of family life.

The war itself had opened up the possibility of a wider range of occupations available to female workers and caused a collapse in the tradition of women in domestic employment. In 1911, between 11% and 13% of the total female population of England and Wales were domestic servants. Post-war, that proportion had almost halved. Some of the slack was taken up by the introduction, for those who could afford them, of labour-saving devices - cookers, electric irons, vacuum cleaners. There remained a clamour from the middle classes for servants but as the country slowly recovered from the economic disaster of the war, jobs for women multiplied. New industries and professions opened up opportunities. The Education Act of 1918 raised the school leaving age to 14, meaning that many women were better educated. The Sex Disqualification Act of 1919 made it easier for women to go to university. The number of women in the Civil Service rose from 33,000 in 1911 to 102,000 by 1921, though they were still confined mainly to the lower paid clerical and administrative grades. Some new industries came to be dominated by women workers - assembly work in engineering and the electrical, food and drink industries in addition to the more traditional clerical work, typing and shop sales.

But most of these jobs were to be found in the Midlands and the South East and London. The great industrial heartlands such as West Yorkshire faced declining industries and shockingly high unemployment throughout the 1920's. Unemployment statistics show that those out of work never fell below a million and figures of 40%, 60% and even 80% in some blighted areas were commonplace.

Women had joined Trades Unions in their hundreds of thousands during the war years and membership peaked in 1920 when 1,342,000 women, some 25% of the total female workforce were unionists. But the union leadership was male dominated, even in those areas where women formed the majority of workers and, in a general climate of cost cutting, closures and unemployment, women workers were seen as a threat to men's jobs. Many unions worked to restrict the employment of women by insisting on the application of the marriage bar - jobs for single women only. Just about all unions refused to pursue the issue of equal pay or campaigned for wage claims that increased the pay differential between men and women. Some went even further and demanded an end to the employment of women altogether.

By 1931, despite gaining the vote, a working women's weekly wage had reverted to the 1914 situation of half the going rate for men.

# AFTERMATH
## TYKE-LAND

Let other men sing of "Lovely Kent",
Or rave of "glorious Devon".
As if these counties had been sent
Down here direct from Heaven.

Old Yorkshire is the place for me,
She is England's greatest county;
From "Peak-land" downward to the sea
We have her for her bounty.

Her sons are hardy, brave and strong,
In war they win renown;
They are "sports", love joke and song,
That also is well known.

Then here's to every loyal "Tyke",
And to her bonnie lasses;
Let other men say what they like,
Not a county her surpasses.

T. Otty
By kind permission of the Hudds. Exam. January 1919

Butchers' shops in Holmfirth were busier than ever as more meat became available in January. There were still shortages as the New Year opened but things were getting better and there was talk of relaxing some of the rules on rationing.

The divorce courts were busy too, as husbands returned home after enforced absences and wives rediscovered their husbands. The results weren't always ideal. Many marriages that had been celebrated in the heat of wartime failed to survive the coldness of peace and couples began to turn to the recent reforms of the divorce laws. Reform of long established and previously sacrosanct institutions was in the air and there was a mood in the country that was eager to embrace 'the new'. The word itself was fashionable. Nowhere was this more obvious than in the loosening of the laws governing divorce and men and women who had married during the war, but who now regretted the decision for whatever reason, took advantage. The number of recorded divorces jumped sixfold from 512 in 1900 to 3090 in 1919, and, in a display of the new independence of women, nearly one third of them were actions brought by wives. Sylvia Pankhurst came to speak at New Mill in January to spread the word.

Holmfirth was scandalised by the divorce of Mr. and Mrs. Leggatt who had married in haste after knowing each other for just a few weeks before Mr. Leggatt went off to war. When he finally returned home he discovered that his wife had led a lively social life while he was away and they separated. She then wrote him a letter asking how much he was prepared to pay her if she agreed to a divorce. She 'would have to pay the price (of the stigma of divorce) all her life and it was necessary for her to have some money to fall back upon'. Mr. Leggatt was granted a divorce on the grounds of infidelity.

Other returning men with marital problems solved them differently. A naval officer was found naked, covered in tar and feathers and tied by a stout chain and two padlocks round his neck to a tree. His uniform was rolled in a bundle by his feet. The tree was opposite the Y.M.C.A. where a certain married lady lived while her husband was serving abroad and the streets around were littered with printed leaflets explaining in graphic detail the naval officer's 'offences'. After releasing the man, the police went to speak to an army officer who had recently returned from Salonika.

Weddings were still popular, though. Norman Caldwell married Alice Smith at the Wesleyan Church in Holmfirth. Alice was 'daintily attired in a dress of cream crepe de chine, with chiffon and pearl trimmings. She also wore a veil with real orange blossom and carried a bouquet of white roses, lilies and sweet peas'.

Some of the biggest beneficiaries of the end of the war and the relaxation of travelling restrictions were the coastal resorts of Blackpool, Scarborough, Bridlington and Whitby. Visitor numbers peaked at Whitsuntide when 250,000 people went to Blackpool - the railways ran fifty trains a day into the town while the roads were crammed with cars and charabancs. Some people arrived by aeroplane and before long holiday makers could enjoy a flying 'flip' from the South Shore sands. Bridlington boasted 2,000 bathers in the town's Spa pool, and Scarborough had so many visitors that bathrooms and billiard tables were converted to beds. People flocked to hear Mr. Alick MacLeans Orchestra at the Spa while Miss Dorothy Morley sang with her Band on Marine Drive.

In Holmfirth the pressing need, in common with just about every town, village, city and hamlet in the country, was to decide just how they were to remember the war. Talks had begun almost as soon as the guns stopped firing and by January, suggestions from the public were sought as to the most appropriate form of memorial. There was no shortage of ideas - a public hospital, public library, public baths, cottage homes for soldiers' widows, a drinking fountain and publicly owned picture palaces. In the first public meeting held at the Drill Hall on Tuesday, January 7th, 1919, to discuss the proposed memorial, Major Trotter, who had been in charge of the Holmfirth Auxiliary Hospital throughout the war, suggested a new hospital for the people of Holmfirth and District, including New Mill and Holme Village. Not a soul present disagreed. Within hours a committee had been set up and plans for a public subscription scheme outlined. Major Trotter thought that the initial cost would be about two thousand pounds.

Hospitals were very much on people's minds as the influenza pandemic was still raging through the district. Dr. Thorp, Medical Officer of Health for Holmfirth and New Mill, was asked to report to the District Council and stated that, since Christmas, there had been twenty-four deaths caused by influenza in New Mill alone, ten men and fourteen women. All were adults aged between 20 and 45 - no children or elderly had suffered fatal doses. With a death rate calculated at 12 per thousand, New Mill had the highest influenza fatality rate in the area, compared with Holmfirth at 6 per thousand, Honley's 2 per thousand, and no deaths at all in Holme village. A typical death was that of Charles Hirst from Gully, Holmfirth, aged thirty, and working as a packer. He had suffered from influenza but returned to work on Tuesday, fell ill again on the Wednesday, and died before the doctor arrived on Thursday morning. In one week alone in Holmfirth the deaths were reported of the solicitor Fred Hampshire; the caretaker of the Liberal Club, Fred Shore; young Willie Robinson who collapsed and died in the offices of Sykes and Son, and Albert Whiteley, a well known hunt enthusiast whose funeral was attended by the Holmfirth, Honley and Meltham packs. All from influenza.

Dr. Thorpe ended his report by declaring that fortunately he had only received three notifications in the last few weeks of the more normal infectious diseases - typhoid fever, diphtheria and pulmonary thrombosis!

Industrial unrest hadn't ceased with the war's end and the textile unions in particular were clamouring for wage increases. Eventually the dispute went to arbitration and the Court decided that:

> Willeyers, fettlers, blenders and carbonisers should receive a basic rate not less than sixpence farthing an hour. All other adult male workers over the age of twenty-two should receive sixpence an hour. Scribblers' feeders and women workers over the age of eighteen should be paid 17s per week.

Messrs. James Watkinson and Sons of Washpit Mills gave every worker a 'thanks offering' to celebrate the end of the fighting. Those under the age of 18 received 10s each; those 18 - 25, 15s each; and those over 25, 20s.

Most unions were demanding pay increases. Even teachers were up in arms. At a packed meeting of the National Union of Teachers in Leeds so many turned up to hear the speakers that the numbers overspilled into an adjoining room where the speeches were relayed to them. Many of them, it was claimed, couldn't afford to educate their own children and some of them were paid less than 'colliers' lads'. Local teachers were further disappointed when Huddersfield Town Council, led by the Mayor rejected their plea for a war bonus of twenty pounds.

They were followed by the Board of Guardians who were demanding a rise in the old-age pension from 7s 6d per week to 12s 6d. One Labour member stunned the room by insisting that the pension should be raised to £1.

Further afield, there were complaints from ship-owners that their boats, which were full of foodstuffs, were having to leave port without being unloaded. Liverpool dock-workers were busily occupied in organising and attending workers' meetings and refused to unload the boats. In South Wales three thousand mine workers went on strike when two of their members were arrested for non-payment of income-tax and there were race-riots in Liverpool and Cardiff when white British ex-soldiers, unemployed since being discharged, attacked black workers.

The fighting may have stopped but families were still grieving. It took twelve months for the War Office to confirm to his parents that James

Albert Senior had died in April the previous year after being wounded and reported missing.

And as the now-quiet battlefields were searched, re-searched and searched again, news filtered back to Holmfirth of all the others whose fate had been unknown - among them, Walter Rogers and Turner Thorpe - there were more to come as the year progressed.

Others were still dying of wounds suffered during the fighting. Albert Bailey died at Royds Hall Hospital after coming home on leave and falling ill. He was yet another member of the Harriers and a stalwart of Holmfirth Parish Church. His coffin was carried by some of his recently discharged comrades, accompanied by a squad of wounded soldiers from the Holmfirth Auxiliary Hospital.

It wasn't a good start to the Peace and it was about to get much worse.

Fred Charlesworth

**Fred Charlesworth.** Lieutenant. 2nd Battalion Duke of Wellington's Regiment. Fred had been born and brought up at Smithy Place in Brockholes but had been a Sheffield teacher for over twenty years when war broke out. He served first in Egypt with the Sheffield 'Pals' and then with the 'Duke's' in France and during that time was wounded twice and gassed in April, 1918. He was sent home to Sheffield for treatment but he never recovered and died on February 1, 1919, aged 41.

He's buried at St. George's Churchyard, Brockholes where buglers played the Last Post at his funeral.

**Walter Shaw Rodgers**. Private. No 30394. 'A' Company, 11th Battalion East Yorkshire Regiment (Hull Tradesmen).

Walter grew up at 197 Woodhead Road in Holmbridge and was employed as a motor-man with Messrs. Henry Mitchell and Sons. He departed for France just three days before his 19th birthday and was reported missing at the Battle of Hazebrouck just a few days after arriving in the trenches on April 12, 1918.

His family finally received official confirmation of his death on February 6th 1919. His body was never found and his name is carved on the Ploegsteert Memorial to the Missing.

AT THE FRONT UNDER A FORTNIGHT

Walter Shaw Rodgers

# Peace
# June 28, 1919

The official end to the 'War to End All Wars' was finally declared In the Hall of Mirrors in the palace of Versailles, some seven months after the fighting had stopped the previous year.

After the Armistice of 1918, politicians began to gather in January to argue over the terms of the peace treaty - the Treaty of Versailles. Representatives of all the countries involved in the conflict, with their vast numbers of supporting economists, geographers and bankers, arrived from all over the world to stake their claim to reparations and to take their revenge on Germany and what was left of the Austro-Hungarian Empire.

In the end, though, most of the major decisions were made in private by the Big Three - Lloyd-George of Britain and the Empire; President Wilson of America and Monsieur Clemenceau of France. All three countries wanted Germany punished but France wanted much more. Having been invaded twice in fifty years, she wanted Germany weakened to such an extent that it would never threaten war again. The French also wanted revenge and they got it.

Germany lost a tenth of its territory and population. Alsace and Lorraine went back to France; Poland was resurrected and given most of West Prussia and a corridor to the sea, leaving East Prussia geographically separated from the rest of Germany. Three small bits were given to Belgium, even Denmark benefited. All of Germany's overseas colonies in China, Africa and the Pacific were taken and divided between Britain and France. Under Article 231 (the 'War Guilt' clause) the Central Powers were forced to accept responsibility for:

> …all the loss and damage to which the Allied and Associated Governments and their nationals have been subjected as a consequence of the war imposed upon them by their aggression.

Germany was left squirming under legal sanctions, deprived of any military power, economically destroyed and politically humiliated, leaving a population burning with a sense of injustice and deeply resentful. It was a recipe for future disaster.

Holmfirth celebrated the war's final end by holding a children's Sports Day. The event took place at Cliffe Recreation Ground, lasted all afternoon, and featured a full round-up of running races, skipping races, needle-threading races, obstacle and sack races. Edith Armitage won the Egg and Spoon race and in the Girls Tug-of-War contest St. John's beat Underbank and the Holmfirth Wesleyans Boys conquered the Choppards Boys' team after a strenuous and long drawn-out trial of strength. They said that when it got dark, people on Cliffe Top could count nineteen bonfires between there and Huddersfield.

Back in the previous November as the celebrations ran their course and slowly died down, whole populations shook their heads, set their shoulders and began to turn their faces to the future. Those here who thought life would simply return to the halcyon days of pre-war Britain would be bitterly disappointed. Far too many sacrifices had been made, too many promises believed; things that had been set in stone before the war now appeared temporary and trivial; beliefs that had been previously unquestioned were now open to debate. Change wasn't merely an option anymore - it was a necessity and a demand.

And the first priority was to get the men home. As soon as possible after the Armistice, plans that had been drawn up in 1917 were put into practice to return over 3,000,000 soldier/civilians back to their homes and families. But there were no easy solutions:

> To put back an army of millions of men, scattered over 3 continents, into civil life is just as difficult as it was to raise that giant Army. In fact, in some ways it is more difficult. It involves - quite inevitably - just as many complications, hardships, inequalities. One man will be luckier than another, whatever you do, and however you set about it. The difference is that while war is on, people mind less. The sense of national danger, national necessity, submerges complaints. Men are ashamed to nurse grievances when their country is in peril. But when danger is over, or thought to be over, there is at once a reaction. Men are, quite naturally, less patient, more critical, more exacting. Grievances are made the most of, and there are plenty of people about who make a business of stimulating the sense of grievance, collecting instances of everything that goes amiss, exaggerating it, and putting it all down to the negligence, or slackness or mismanagement of officials, to red-tape, to departmental dawdling and so forth.

Demobilisation speech extract - War Secretary Lord Milner Dec 1918

Lord Milner had been War Secretary before Winston Churchill sacked him from the Cabinet following the electoral victory of the Lloyd-George Coalition Government in December 1918. Milner had urged patience on the millions of servicemen waiting to come home and he supported Lord Derby's reasonable point that the priority was 'to demobilise in the way most likely to lead to the steady resumption of industry'.

Lord Derby had proposed that the first men to be released from service should be those skilled workers who would be most use to industry. Many of these skilled workers, however, had only been conscripted late on in the war in response to the German attacks in 1918, meaning that those men who had volunteered in 1914, 1915, and who had served the longest would be the last to leave.

It was asking a lot for these hardened veterans to wait patiently and quietly, while newly enlisted men who might only have served a few months were discharged before them. It was a recipe for widespread un-rest. Churchill recognised the political and social dangers in a slow, de-liberate, demobilisation process and scrapped Milner's plans, replacing them with a much more rapid response based on age, length of service and the number of times a man had been wounded - essentially a 'first in, first out' system.

Under this new regime, any soldier who had enlisted before December 31, 1915, or was over 37, or had three wound stripes would be dis-charged immediately. The crisis of a lengthy demobilisation process was delayed for a few more months.

One of the many difficulties faced by the War Office was the fact that this had been a World War and British and Commonwealth servicemen were fighting in far flung places. Some of these war zones would require an Army of Occupation for years to come and, in addition, there were military commitments to Germany, North Russia and various garrisons of the Empire that all needed to be fulfilled.

Mesopotamia, for instance, held 92,000 British and 260,000 Indian troops at the Armistice; Egypt held 140,000 British, 22,000 ANZAC sol-diers and 100,000 Indian troops; there were 160,000 British and Indian forces in Salonika and 92,000 Chinese in France. All of whom were demanding to be sent home.

The trouble was, of course, that nearly everyone wanted to go home at once, if for no other reason than that the available and choicest jobs back in Britain would go to the first-comers. Those discharged last, some of whom had made the biggest sacrifices, would be at the end of the queue again.

Not all soldiers though - those men who were part of the Regular Army and who were still serving their period of service simply remained at their posts. There was also a considerable number of men who, for a variety of reasons, opted to remain in the Army. These soldiers who were either volunteers or who had been conscripted, married or single, aged between 18 and 35, in fitness categories of A or B1, could re-enlist for either 27, 39 or 51 months and receive a very generous bounty - £50 paid in five instalments for those opting for the longest period.

> The pay ... is on such a scale that the lowest rank can at present expect to put 21 shillings (that is, £1 and 1 Shilling) per week into his pocket clear of all expenses of living. This compares more than favourably with the average man in civil life.

Added to this was the awarding of two months home leave on full pay which, wherever possible, was granted immediately. The families of married men were paid separation allowances. The Scotsman newspaper reported that men were re-enlisting at the rate of 700 per day.

But that still left millions clamouring for and demanding early release. Those servicemen identified by Churchill's instructions went first, followed quickly by men with valuable and scarce industrial skills, including mining. Those who had volunteered early on in the war and had served longest came next. Finally, the conscripts were discharged, starting with the men of 1916, then 1917 and finally the young and the old ones of 1918.

By April 17 the Ministry declared that 76,609 officers and 2,145,307 other ranks had been demobilised; 119,202 had been discharged as medically unfit and all the Reserves had been sent back home - a grand total of 79,609 officers and 2,408,950 men. Most servicemen were back in civilian life before the end of 1919.

It was a remarkable piece of planning, and testament to the organisational skills of the Civil Service. In November 1918, the British Army had numbered almost 3.8 million men. Twelve months later, it had been reduced to slightly less than 900,000 and by 1922 to just over 230,000.

All demobilised men followed the same procedure. Before leaving his unit every soldier was medically examined and handed (in true British

Army fashion) a number of official forms - Army Form Z22 with which he could make a claim for any type of disability arising from his military service; Army Form Z44 for his civilian clothing allowance and a Certificate of Employment explaining what he had done or learned in the Army. His personal and military information was on his Dispersal Certificate, Z18, which also recorded the state of his military equipment; his rifle, uniform, and any specialist tools (anything that went missing after this date, would be deducted from his outstanding pay).

No local currency of France, Belgium or Italy could be brought home, only official government-issue banknotes which could be exchanged for Sterling at any Military Post Office. Currency from any other Theatre of War could be converted into a Postal Order at an Army Post Office.

The first move for a soldier about to be discharged was to a Transit Camp near the French coast, and from there a homeward sailing, followed by a period in a Dispersal Centre, which was usually a hutted or, at worst, tented, barracks. More forms - Z3, Z11 or Z12 - and a railway warrant to his home, ration book, back pay for his time on leave, and either an allowance of 52s. 6d to pay for civilian clothes or the issue of a demob suit ( for which the Government had stockpiled enormous quantities of low grade material). He could either sell his greatcoat back to the Government for one pound or he could keep it. In addition he would receive unemployment insurance, worth 29s. per week for himself, 6s. for his first child and 3s. for each additional child subject to a time limit of twenty weeks.

Best of all was the war-service gratuity which started to be distributed shortly before Christmas, 1918. Privates received £20; Corporals £28; Lieutenants, up to £226, and, at the top of the scale (some would argue completely off the scale) Field Marshal Haig and Admiral Beatty were awarded £100,000 each.

**WARNING.**—*If you lose this Certificate a duplicate cannot be issued.*

Certificate of discharge of No. 4645 (Rank) Pte

(Name) Thomas Ashworth

(Regiment) North Staffs Regt

who was enlisted at Stoke-on-Trent

on the 8. 3. 12 19 .

He is discharged in consequence of No longer physically fit
A.6.1550 of 1917 for War Service
A.C.11038 of 1917 (K.R. 392 (XVI))
after serving Five years 67 days with the Colours, and
_____ years — days in the Army Reserve.

(Place) Lichfield    Signature of ) _____
(Date) 13. 5. 17    Commanding ) for 6½ Infy Regt.
                    Officer

*Description of the above-named man on 13. 5. 17 when he left the Colours.

Age 24 yrs 5 mths.          Marks or Scars, whether on face
Height 5 ft 3½ ins.              or other parts of body.
Complexion Pale.            Tattoo marks
Eyes Brown.                  both arms.
Hair Black.                   Scar r. shin
                             r. side forehead

* Should agree with the description on Character Certificate, Army Form B. 2067.

A2077  Wt.W8212/2755  500,000  8/15  D. D. & L.  Sch. 44  Forms/B.2079/21

# What had they left behind ?

The sad truth is that at the beginning of the 20th Century the majority of working class people in the towns and cities of Britain lived in conditions now associated with the worst of desperate Third World countries. Ill health, particularly among children, grinding poverty, and poor housing were commonplace. The appallingly low standards of health in many urban working class districts meant that many men when called for conscription simply didn't even reach the minimum physical standard for military service, let alone being fit and capable enough for combat duty.

Before the war, only men aged between 18 and 30 who were of good physique and character and free from disease or physical defects were accepted into the army. That all changed with the avalanche of recruits on the declaration of war. Regimental Medical Officers, who had been used to more leisurely examinations, found themselves having to inspect over 200 men per day. As examiners were paid one shilling for every man they passed and nothing for the men they rejected, it is perhaps not surprising that many men were accepted for army service when they were patently unfit.

The army medical boards of 1914 were guided by two assumptions - the first was that if a man was fit enough to be in full-time employment, he was fit enough for the army; the second was that medical boards would often pass a man not on his level of fitness at the time of the examination but on what his fitness would be after three or four months of wholesome army life. Army life, it was believed in 1918, was particularly good for tubercular or syphilitic cases.

Even with such a relaxed approach to diagnostics, nearly one third of recruits in 1917 were classed as Grade IV, the lowest category - men who were in such poor health that they were totally unable to fulfil military duty of any description whatsoever.

In June 1917, General Bedford and the G.O.C. of Northern Command inspected a large contingent of a Labour Battalion, or Grade III men, and were shocked by the physical condition of many of them. The General immediately issued a directive to his medical boards to stop passing 'the lame, the halt and the blind', all of whom he had just seen in uniform.

The whole system of medical inspection of recruits had come into disrepute and it was finally reformed towards the end of 1917, the first step being to remove military doctors from the process. From now on, each recruit was examined by four civilian doctors. The first took basic measurements and recorded distinguishing features; the second made a general assessment of condition, physique and any deformities such as flat feet; the third tested vision, hearing, and nerve reflexes, while the fourth and final doctor inspected the man's chest and stomach and questioned him about his medical history before making a judgement about his mental health. The expected rate of inspection was twelve men an hour - an average of five minutes with each doctor.

SPECIMENS OF MEN IN EACH OF THE FOUR GRADES.

A new four part classification system was introduced:

Grade I recruits were front-line men - usually young, fit and capable soldiers.

Grade II were men who had some disability but who were able to march six miles 'with ease' (though how doctors could be certain of that after just five minutes is debatable); these men could do garrison duty either at home or abroad.

Grade III recruits were unfit for most duties but could still serve as auxiliary troops - sanitary inspectors, batmen, cooks, clerks, butchers, grooms, drivers or orderlies; or they could serve in the Labour Battalions as bricklayers, carpenters, navvies or masons; if they were unable to march five miles they were assigned to more sedentary duties as typists or book-keepers.

All others were Grade IV men and were rejected.

Countrywide, over 41% of recruits were placed in Grades III and IV.

One man in ten was completely unfit for military service of any description. In the last year of the war over one million men were deemed unfit and unable to fight. Compared to the rest of the nation Yorkshire recorded the lowest rates of Grade IV classification. Under the new system 388,479 Yorkshire men were examined and 158,839 were deemed Grade I; just 28,927 were graded at the lowest level - 7.5% (London had 12.5%).

A four-year survey of urban working class life published in 1913 ('Round About A Pound A Week' - Maud Pember Reeves) illustrated the plight of the poor. The families surveyed were by no means at the bottom end of the poverty scale. The majority were in work and largely sober and thrifty. Nonetheless, the survey showed a death rate of one in four children - more than double the death rate of serving soldiers between 1914-1918. Of the thirty-one families who took part in the survey, twenty-two families had lost at least one child to disease or illness. Their housing was generally damp, under-heated, poorly ventilated and frequently infested with vermin. Accommodation usually consisted of three rooms for a typical family of eight. Families would have no more than two beds so parents, children and sometimes, grandparents, would sleep four to a bed. The two meals each day would consist of bread with a scraping of margarine, jam or dripping. Meat was reserved for Sunday, and then only for the man of the house. Most families would rarely see eggs or milk. Professional medical care had to be paid for and, for most, was non-existent.

As a purely personal example of the author, the 1901 Census for the Ashworth Family reveals a family of nine, including a widowed grandfather, living in the relative luxury of a 'two-up, two-down' terraced house. The Maguires, a few streets away in a similar house had ten children (nine of them girls) and two parents.

These, it must be stressed, were average families. There were countless others much worse off. Jack London, writing in 1902 about the hundreds of thousands of the desperately poor in London in his book 'The People of the Abyss' said:

> How do they live? The answer is that they don't live. They do not know what life is. They drag out a sub-bestial existence until released by death.

But, surprisingly, people of the early 1900's believed that their lives were improving. Certainly, they were better off than their parents and grandparents had been. Trade deals during the previous century had resulted in cheaper food for all; links between poor or non-existent sanitation and outbreaks of deadly diseases such as typhoid and dysentery had been identified and measures taken to dramatically improve the situation. By 1914 there were the first glimmers of a state benefits scheme for the needy and elderly.

A survey into the conditions of the working class of Bradford and District, including Huddersfield, in the 1880's gave details of wage levels. These figures would have remained pretty much the same until the 1900's.

The best paid workers were those in the iron, steel and engineering industries - boilermakers, for instance, were paid 38 shillings a week. Worst paid were shop assistants, mainly women, who earned 13s. 6d for a seventy hour week (men earned 15s.). The majority of workers in the Huddersfield area were employed in the textile industry. An overseer might get 28s. to 30s. a week, while a female carder would get as little as 12s. for working fifty-six hours. A fortunate skilled man with two working children adding perhaps another 15s. between them might have a combined family income of £2 - £3 each week, £100 - £150 per annum. The average income for a middle class man of the same period was about £5000 and this kind of spending power was reflected in the fact that 132,015 motor cars had been licensed by 1914. A new car cost about £200 to buy but was much more economical and cheaper to run than a horse and carriage which, including the wages of the groom and stabling, would run to £600 - £650 per annum.

For those literally at the bottom, there was always the dreaded workhouse. Deanhouse Workhouse in Holmfirth had been purpose-built and opened in 1862. It housed 600 inmates amalgamated from the decrepit and collapsing Workhouses of Almondbury, Golcar and Honley, and cost £10,000 to build.

Just four years later, in 1866, conditions in this sparkling new building had deteriorated sharply, and a Poor Law Inspector published his report:

Inspector regrets that a…..so ill-arranged and incomplete a building was ever erected…the vagrant wards had been converted into men's sick wards. The female receiving ward had been made into a bath room for female idiots and the male receiving ward was used as an infirm ward. The children, 24 in number, had no day rooms. The boys associate with the adult male paupers and the girls with the able-bodied women, with no separations at night. All the water closets were constructed such that the foul air was drawn inward and into the main body of the house. The sick wards were small square rooms with only three or four beds in each.

None of this came as a surprise. An Overseers Report on the conditions at Huddersfield Township Workhouse at Birkby, published a few years earlier was far worse:

…the sick poor have been most shamefully neglected; that they have been and still are devoid of the necessary articles of clothing and bedding; that they have been suffered to remain for weeks at a time in the most filthy and disgusting state; that patients have been allowed to remain for nine weeks together without a change of linen or of bed clothing; that beds in which patients suffering in typhus have died, one after another, have been again and again and repeatedly used for fresh patients, without any change or attempt at purification; that the said beds were only bags of straw and shavings, for the most part laid on the floor, and that the whole swarmed with lice; that two patients suffering in infectious fever were almost constantly put together in one bed, that it not infrequently happened that one would be ragingly delirious when the other was dying; and that it is a fact that a living patient has occupied the same bed with a corpse for a considerable period after death; that the patients have been for months together without properly appointed nurses to attend to them; that there has been, for a considerable time, none but male paupers to attend female patients; that when the poor sick creatures were laid in the most abject and helpless state - so debilitated as to pass their dejections as they lay, they have been suffered to remain in the most befouled state possible, besmeared in their own excrement, for days together and not even washed.
…that there are forty children occupying one room eight yards by five; that these children sleep four, five, six, seven and even ten in one bed; that thirty females live in another room of similar size; and that fifty adult males have to cram into a room seven and half yards long by six yards wide.
…that four shillings' worth of shin of beef, or leg offal, with forty-two pounds of potatoes have been made to serve as 'soup' for 150 inmates; that the quantity, in gallons, required of this wash, for the household is 27.

Leeds Women's Workhouse

It has been said before that one of the first consequences of the Declaration of War in 1914 was to empty the workhouses. Unemployed men, with no other chance of work, took the opportunity to be part of an emotional surge of patriotic pride and volunteered in their thousands. Suddenly, they were the heroes. Four years later they were returning, expecting a country and homes fit for them.

Many serving soldiers were better fed in the army than they had ever been in civilian life. To eat meat every day was an unheard of luxury, even if it was bully beef or Machonochie stew. They may have been uniformed but the uniforms were well made, hard wearing and warm, despite the roughness. Few working class men in civilian life could have afforded anything like an army greatcoat or as stout a pair of boots as army issue ones. The lack of privacy and the smell and the dirt of active service which many more middle class recruits found so difficult would not have been a particular problem to  men brought up in  overcrowded city slums. Nor would the constant call for hard monotonous manual labour - the men of the four Battalions of the Duke of Wellington's Regiment spent far more time digging trenches and railway cuttings than engaged in mortal combat. And, without minimising or trivialising the danger and the constant fear that characterised life in the Front Line, many of those soldiers had come from backgrounds where death or injury were also present.

Ticket men at the Salvation Army Citadel

Miners, for instance, who formed the largest single block of the male workforce before the war, and volunteered and served in their tens of thousands, (by February 1916, 25% of the pre-war workforce involved in mining and quarrying were enlisted) had grown up living and surviving in a highly dangerous environment of cave-ins, explosions and accidents, let alone the tragedy and prevalence of pneumoconiosis. Between 1860 and 1914 one miner had been killed every six hours. The chances of a miner being killed at the pit during his working life were roughly the same as those of a soldier on the Somme on July 1, 1916.

In some mining communities the chances were far worse. The worst English mining disaster occurred on December 12, 1866 at Barnsley when some 383 miners and rescuers were killed in a series of explosions. The youngest was aged 10 and the eldest 67. Even this was eclipsed in 1913 at the village of Sengennydd in South Wales which had already been hit by an underground disaster in 1901when seventy-nine miners died. Twelve years later, on October 14,1913, calamity struck again when 440 men and boys died in a pit explosion - nearly 10% of the total village population. The subsequent inquest established that the workings had high levels of airborne coal dust but the mine owners had missed two deadlines for installing compulsory extraction fans, the last one just a month earlier. The most likely cause of the explosion was thought to be a spark from some form of underground signalling system, probably the electric bell signalling gear, which ignited firedamp in the Western section of the pit. The first blast ignited the coal dust in the air and produced a shock wave which raised yet more dust which also combusted. The force was so great that the explosive wave travelled up one of the shafts and killed the winder on the surface and badly wounded his deputy. Those not killed immediately died of suffocation caused by the afterdamp. It took six weeks to recover most of the bodies and to put out the fires.

Sengennydd pit disaster, 1913

Charges of negligence were brought against Edward Shaw, the Colliery Manager, and the owners. Both parties were found guilty and fined - Shaw the sum of £24 and the owners £10, or 5 1/2 pence per miner lost. (Just as a side note, ninety men from Sengennydd were also killed in the Great War).
Safety standards improved considerably in the five years following the war but there were still 2,385,766 notified industrial injuries in Great

Britain (i.e. serious enough to warrant some kind of external medical attention) compared with 1,693,262 men wounded in the war. Admittedly, 'only' 20,263 were killed at work which is slightly lower than the horrendous losses on the opening day of the Somme.

If conditions at the pits were extreme they weren't unique. Building workers, metal workers, fishermen and quarry workers were all familiar with industrial death, disease and injury.

None of this is to deny that for many, if not most, of the men in the services the war was an appalling experience. The traumatic effect of combat, the sheer terror of surviving under artillery fire, army discipline, living outdoors, often in mud, and the emotional burden of separation from family and friends meant that few viewed the war as anything but a situation that had to be endured and with a fervent wish for it to finish.

Moreover, having given so much, there was a general desire for things to be better when they finally got home - and hadn't politicians already promised them just that! Many men weren't prepared for their lives to be simply the same. The war had generated a sense of entitlement - they didn't just desire a higher standard of living back home, they were entitled to it! They knew about the high wages workers had been earning compared to their own army pay and for those soldiers who had volunteered at the very beginning of the war, there must have been a tinge of regret that they hadn't waited just a little longer and taken advantage of full employment. They were special, they felt, having sacrificed so much, and they were looking for their just rewards. They had the example of what was happening in Russia in front of them, where the workers, the working class just like themselves, had taken power and were busily, according to Russian propaganda, redistributing the wealth of the country. And they had seen something of the wider world; their horizons weren't limited anymore to the end of their own street.

Conscription, which had eventually been introduced in Britain in 1916, implied a contract between a man and the State, and the man expected something in return for fulfilling his part of it. The very relationship between civilian/soldiers and the country had changed with the introduction of compulsory military service. Field Marshal Haig hated it and was scathing about this new attitude among working class men:

> ...under the Military Service Act a leaven of men whose desire to serve their country is negligible has permeated the ranks. The

influence of the men and their antecedents generally are not such as to foster any spirit but that of unrest and discontent, they come forward under compulsion and they will depart from the Army with relief. Men of this stamp are not satisfied with remaining quiet, they come from a class which likes to air real or fancied grievances.

It was a volatile situation.

# But what were they coming home to?

What is our task? To make Britain a fit country for heroes to live in. I am not using the word 'heroes' in any spirit of boastfulness, but in the spirit of humble recognition of fact. I cannot think what these men have gone through. I have been there at the door of the furnace and witnessed it, but that is not being in it, and I saw them march into the furnace. There are millions of men who will come back. Let us make this a land fit for such men to live in. There is no time to lose. I want us to take advantage of this new spirit. Don't let us waste this victory merely in ringing joybells.

Lloyd-George, 1918

This was an important promise to the millions returning home and to the memory of those who never would. It was a cornerstone policy of the new government coalition of Liberals and Conservatives under Lloyd-George. He was determined to 'lift the shadow of the workhouse from the homes of the poor' and create a 'land fit for heroes'.

It wasn't a question of simply rebuilding society as it had been before the war, but of 'moulding a better world out of the social and economic conditions which have come into being during the war.'

A 'better' world. This 'moulding a better world' began with the reform of the political voting system and the granting of the vote to all men, of whatever class, over the age of 21 and to women who had some kind of property qualification and who were over the age of 30. This increased the parliamentary vote from just under 8 million men before the war to a total of over 21 million in 1918, including the 8.4 million eligible women.

It also effectively created a large working class majority of voters and an electorate much younger than any previously. Women comprised forty per cent of the total available votes.

Extending the franchise was quickly followed by the introduction of Unemployment Insurance to cover a further twelve million workers and shortly afterwards a Ministry of Health was created.

The old order of politics was forced to change by the greatly increased electorate, the continuing rise of the Independent Labour Party, female voters and the impact of the war on middle and upper class men who later became Members of Parliament.

Many of these men had been relatively junior officers during the war and had come into close contact with the working class where they had been deeply affected on learning at first hand of the poverty and hardship. Anthony Eden, later to become Foreign Secretary (he succeeded Winston Churchill as Prime Minister in 1955) had enlisted at the age of 18 and had won the Military Cross for carrying his wounded sergeant across no-man's land under enemy fire in 1917. After the war he had been ear-marked for the diplomatic service but rejected that for a career in politics. He was elected as a 'progressive Tory' in 1923 and earned a reputation as a 'man of peace'. Harold McMillan, Prime Minister from 1957 - 1963, enlisted in 1914 at the age of 20 and was wounded three times during the war. He became M.P. after the war for Stockton-on-Tees and fought hard for the unemployed of the region throughout the 1920's. He was known as a left-wing rebel Tory. Even Sir Oswald Mosley, who had been a professional soldier and later served in the Royal Flying Corps, was a parliamentarian advocate of 'socialist imperialism'. He was bitter and angry at what he saw as the betrayal of working class troops by the old men of politics who had retained their grip on power and bungled the peace process. Throughout his career he argued for policies to counter the evils of unemployment, which led him to join the Labour Party in 1924 and eventually become a Fascist in 1932.

Unfortunately, few of the government promises of 1918-1919 were really fulfilled, least of all those concerning housing. The poor physical health of many young urban recruits in 1914 was a shocking indictment of the nation's neglect of its people, and a wake-up call for government action.

The first post-war initiative was the Addison Act of 1919 which required local councils to provide housing for the working classes for which there was a huge demand, and awarding subsidies to help them do so. Not just any old housing, these were to be 'of such quality that they would remain above the acceptable minimum standards for at least 60 years'. Social housing that was uncrowded, well-built, on secure tenancies and at reasonable rents to working class people.

But it was proving harder to deliver on the promises. Most of the pre-1914 bricklayers had been killed or disabled during the war and those that were left were waiting to be demobilised. Builders found it far more profitable to build commercial buildings rather than houses and the price of small homes rose alarmingly - from £250 in 1914 to £900 by 1918.

One bonus of the government initiative was the beginning of a system of Council Housing where, for the first time ever, housing quality was recognised as being of national importance. The essential features of each house would be:

- a minimum of three rooms on the ground floor (living room, parlour and scullery)
- three bedrooms above, two of these capable of containing two beds
- a larder and a bathroom

The first of them to be built were in Chesterfield on St. Augustine's Road in 1920, costing nearly £1,000 each. The Government promised to build 500,000 of them but failed dismally. Six months after the house-building programme had begun there were only 10,000 under construction and a pitiful 180 actually occupied. The programme finally petered out after 170,000 had been built and Mr. Addison was dismissed.

There was better news on the issues of health and poverty. Two of the surprising effects of the war were that the poorest became less poor and the unhealthiest became more healthy.

Infant mortality, usually the yardstick of public health and economic well-being, declined overall by about 10% during the war, which is note-worthy in itself but the most dramatic improvement was in the poorest city and town districts where the number of deaths of children was re-duced by 33%. The most obvious explanation was better nutrition for mothers and babies, though some argued that it was partly due to the fact that, because of the war, doctors were few and far between. This wasn't so silly as it sounds - in an age when causes of infection were not properly understood, doctors, who were moving from patient to patient would rarely wash their hands and were the first suspects in the spread of disease.

Mortality rates among adult females over the age of 30 dropped by as much as 12%. Rates rose for women below 30 during the latter stages of the war principally because they were hit particularly hard by the influenza outbreak in 1918. This awful pandemic killed by stimulating and overloading the body's immune system - those with the strongest immune systems, young healthy people, died first - 200,000 civilians in Britain alone and some 10,000 soldiers.

Mortality rates for the most common diseases - measles, whooping-cough, bronchitis, tuberculosis and meningitis - all dropped after 1915. As did those for diarrhoeal infections which affected the very young and the very old. Shortages of sugar helped to accelerate a decline in diabetes and restrictions on the sale of alcohol resulted in deaths from cirrhosis of the liver declining by over 30%.

J.M. Winter concludes that, paradoxically, the period between 1914 - 1919 was one of major gains in the battle for survival of the urban working class civilian population.

# Money

Despite the fact that the cost of living more than slightly doubled during the war it was more than countered by full employment, extensive overtime and the regular awarding of 'war bonus' which meant that earnings usually outstripped price rises. Moreover, because there were so many jobs on offer, every member of the family unit - exhausted older men, young girls and boys, married women - were in work and earning. Skilled men were paid considerably more than the minimum wage.

A working class woman in Leeds in 1917 found herself in court for a minor offence where it was revealed that she was receiving £3 each week in Army separation allowance; another £3 working in a munitions factory and a further £2 from her employed 13 year old son. The magistrates and the local media were outraged that a working woman could have so much wealth -'Four hundred pounds a year. It sounds like a fairy-tale'.

A common labourer in 1860, working a ten hour day, six days a week, earned 3s. 9d a week.

Families were smaller during the war, with men in uniform and usually abroad leading to a plummeting birth-rate resulting in more food to go around. And finally, the imposition of social changes - rationing, industrial canteens and nurseries, limited pub opening hours and shortages of alcohol, the payment of separation allowances which supported the families of servicemen - all meant that working class civilians saw a steady improvement in their living conditions. Those who had been bottom of the scale and had the least to lose in 1914 had gained the most. An achievement they were determined to hang on to.

The post-war Government of 1919 was faced with an avalanche of expectations. One of its first priorities was to financially support those civilians and soldiers who had been deeply and seriously affected by the war. Top of the list of claimants were the families of the men who had been killed in the war and who were all entitled to pensions. By March 1919, these numbered 190,000 war widows and 10,000 orphans. Further benefits were provided to another 350,000 children whose fathers had died. Far more sums were needed for the 1.2 million men - one quarter of the total who had served - who qualified for disability pensions. Two-thirds of this number were classed as having a relatively minor disability, such as the loss of fingers or toes, but 40,000 received pensions on the basis of their total or near-total disability. This was officially defined as the loss of two limbs, or two eyes, or both feet, or those men who were totally paralysed, permanently bed-ridden, rendered insane, having an incurable disease, or suffering from severe facial disfigurement. Proportionately, more officers than men were in this category. The full weekly disablement pension was 25s. and 2s. 6d for each child - about the wage of an unskilled labourer. This small sum was then reduced according to the scale of the disability - a man missing a whole arm would receive 16s. If the amputation had been above the elbow it was reduced to 14s.; below the elbow, 11s. 6d. Unless the man was left-handed, the left arm was valued lower than the right. Officer's rates were higher. The Government expressed the hope that charities would step in to help but its suggestion was treated with scorn and public pressure eventually forced an increase to £2 per week and 26s. 8d for a widow.

While the largest single cause of disability was due to wounds or amputations, more pensions were awarded for various diseases or complaints contracted during service. These were mainly tuberculosis, respiratory problems through gassing, malaria and heart problems. Some 230,000 of these unfortunates remained permanently disabled for the rest of their lives and a total of 80,000 died soon after returning home.

Harry Roberts served in the Royal Field Artillery as a gunner in India where he contracted Sandfly fever in 1918 and was discharged from the service. Six years later he collapsed and died of pulmonary embolism at the age of 34. Before the war he had been one of the foremost amateur players at Oldham Athletic Football Club and the trainer there testified at the inquest that Mr. Roberts was one of the fittest men in the club. His employer said that Harry had been a 'robust' man in 1914 but prone to illness after his return in 1918. His widow applied for a State pension. It was denied.

# Homecoming - Reality

Send the boys home. Why in the world the delay? The war is not officially 'over' but everyone knows that in fact it is over. Munition making has stopped; motorists can joy ride; the King has had a drink; Society has had its Victory Ball and is settling down... Danger of too rapid demobilisation? Bunkum! There are thousands of men for whom jobs are waiting but the Army won't let them go. And - even if a man hasn't a job - why not let him go home at once?

The Daily Herald, December 7, 1918

The period of demobilisation was followed by a post-war economic boom. Unfortunately it was short lived and over by the Autumn of 1920. In order to protect Sterling the Government had introduced deflationary policies (as had America) which had a drastic effect on living standards. Unemployment doubled in the three months between December 1920 and March 1921 and wages fell sharply. Strikes broke out everywhere and in every trade and industry. In 1919, 35 million working days had been lost to industrial disputes; in 1921 the figure had risen to 86 million. By the Summer of that year, the number of unemployed reached 2 million. Homes for heroes had been promised but it was an impossible task - 822,000 new homes were needed just to cover the basic housing shortage - let alone to replace the millions of urban slum dwellings.

The economic cost of the war was jaw-dropping. Government debt was six times higher in 1918 than it had been four years earlier. Britain, which before the war had been the world's biggest investor ended it owing America £1,150 million. The National Debt had gone from £650 million in 1914 to £8,000 million in 1919 - simply to service the debt consumed one quarter of all government expenditure. Income tax had risen to the unheard-of six shillings in the pound. The answer to all these economic woes was, of course, the resumption of international trade and the export markets. Unfortunately, these no longer existed as each trading country imposed its own import tariffs. British industry was still capable of producing but no-one was buying. Bit by bit, the industries shut down and unemployment figures began to rise.

There were other effects of the war which took a little longer to become apparent. The Dominion countries, particularly Australia, finished the war in some bitterness about the conduct and professionalism of British generals and their handling of those countries' troops. Australia, which had suffered the highest casualty rate, was angry at what they regarded as the incompetence of the British High Command.

In Asia some 800,000 Indian troops returned home disillusioned, with their confidence in Britain as the dominant world power shattered, realising for the first time that the Mother-country was only one of four or five equal powers. Ironically, the victory over Germany saw the transfer of many of Germany's African territories to Britain - territories which no-one particularly wanted and which were to prove a drain on what little resources and finances were available.

And then there was the problem of the Royal Navy - the country's pride and first line of defence, the biggest in the world (and the most expensive). The Navy had fought only one major battle at Jutland during the whole war, and even that was not really a victory, despite the claims. It had also shown itself to be extremely vulnerable to enemy mines and submarines and had failed to protect the East coast of England from German shelling. People's confidence was shaken and the very raison d'être of why we went to war was questioned. Some people pointed out that there had been no direct threat to Britain or its Empire in 1914 and, while defending 'gallant little Belgium' was a morally defensible reason for going to war the consequences of doing so had been disastrous. Only gradually did people begin to realise the true, and much more complicated reasons. Quite simply, Britain and the Dominions had declared war on Germany because it was necessary to preserve France as a major European power and counter-weight to German aggressiveness. If France had lost (and it came very close to losing - even with the help of Britain and Dominion troops) Germany would have been the dominant military and economic superpower of the Continent and capable of threatening Britain and her trade routes and the Empire. At the time, it was viewed as too big a risk to take.

The post-war situation was no better throughout Europe, and in many countries far worse. Inflation wrecked the economy of Germany which had a thirtyfold rise in its National Debt while the currency lost half of its value. In Poland, Austria and Russia price-inflation grew out of control and the currency was ruined totally. In Britain, as in most of the former European powers, countless former soldiers were living in dire poverty, selling matches on the streets or begging, living off food kitchens and sleeping in doorways. They were no longer 'heroes', they were the unemployed and they frightened the Government.

During the first year following the Armistice, 1919, more than 2.4 million British workers were involved in strike action - 300,000 more than in Germany. Germany was in the first throes of what was close to a civil war and was widely regarded as being the next country likely to succumb to a Communist revolution. There was a distinct fear in Britain that the same thing could happen here and returning soldiers began to be regarded by the authorities as possible rallying points for serious labour unrest. Many of them were suspected of showing support for the dreaded Bolshevism. Quite quickly, the middle class public vision of dependable, patriotic, Tommy Atkins was replaced by that of an anarchic-revolutionary demanding unrealistic wages and social change.

What was particularly worrying for the authorities was that for the first time in the history of civil unrest in this country, the rioters were often better trained and more experienced than the troops sent to contain them.

There was a particular concern about the various Ex-Servicemen's Associations that had sprouted during the war. The first to be organised was the National Association of Discharged Soldiers and Sailors formed in 1916 which had links to the Liberal Party. Holmfirth had its own branch which opened a social club in the Newtown district in January 1919.

It was soon followed by the National Federation of Discharged and Demobilised Soldiers and Sailors which allied itself with the Labour Party from 1917. Neither of these two groups were against working within the political system but much of their support for peaceful agitation was interpreted as revolutionary activity by a nervous government quick to see 'reds under the bed'. As late as 1920, the War Office was working on a plan to counter the threat of a 'Soviet Government in Liverpool'.

There were two further associations influenced by the Russian situation that campaigned for complete and profound changes to British Society - the National Union of Ex-Servicemen (NUX), and the International Union of Ex-Servicemen (IUX). But a completely different and far more dangerous movement was the Soldiers', Sailors' and Airmen's Union formed in February 1919 with the sole intention of stirring up discontent among servicemen chafing at the bit of demobilisation. The very real prospect of being kept in the Army and then sent to Russia to fight the Bolsheviks was continually raised. Under the terms of the Derby Scheme of enlistment a few years previously, it was widely believed that those men who had volunteered to serve for the duration of the war could only be retained by the Army for no more than six months after the termination of hostilities. The SSAU took that as meaning that the War Office had no legal jurisdiction over these men after May 11, 1919, and advised them to leave the Army of their own accord. They even urged sailors to take control of the ports and encouraged them to join a general strike.

This was tantamount to inciting mutiny and the Government took the threat seriously. On May 8th Churchill responded to the crisis by publishing an explanation of the phrases 'duration of the war' and 'termination of hostilities'. They meant the same thing, he said, and the Armistice was simply a suspension - not the end - of the war, hostilities could well be resumed at any moment. His statement averted widespread mutiny, but only just. Many of the 'Derby' men, who had served since 1915, were already ear-marked as forces for the occupation of Germany.

Any army, particularly a conscript one, carries all the faults as well as the virtues of the population as a whole and the British Army was no exception. Military discipline was tight throughout the war but not over harsh compared to other nations.

A total of 5,952 officers and 298,310 other ranks were court-martialled between 1914 and 1919. This amounts to just over 3% of the total of men serving. Of those tried, 89% were convicted, 8% acquitted and the rest were either convicted without the conviction being confirmed or with it being subsequently quashed. Of those convicted, 30% were for absence without leave; 15% for drunkenness; 14% for desertion (although only 3% were actually in the field at the time); 11% for insubordination; 11% for loss of army property, and the remaining 19% for various other crimes. The main punishments applied were : 3 months detention in a military compound – 24%; Field Punishment Number 1 – 22%; Fines – 12%; 6 months detention – 10%; reduction in rank – 10%; Field Punishment Number 2 – 8%.

3,080 men (1.1% of those convicted) were sentenced to death. Of these, 89% were reprieved and the sentence converted to a different one. 346 men were executed. Their crimes included desertion – 266; murder – 37; cowardice in the face of the enemy – 18; quitting their post – 7; striking or showing violence to their superiors – 6; disobedience – 5; mutiny – 3; sleeping at post – 2; casting away arms – 2. Of the 346, 91 were already under a suspended sentence from an earlier conviction (40 of these a suspended death sentence).

These figures demonstrate little evidence of widespread mutiny in the British Army during the war, unlike two of the other main protagonists, Russia and Germany, who were brought to a standstill because they could no longer rely on their armies to continue fighting. France came very close to a similar disaster, firstly in 1917 when 3,427 Courts Martial for mutiny were carried out with a resulting 629 death sentences (43 were actually carried out) and later, towards the end of the war, when 20,000 cases of mutiny were recorded. There is an argument to be made that if the war had continued into 1919/1920 France may well have gone the way of Russia and Germany.

It may be worth mentioning at this point the very real legal and constitutional differences between members of the armed forces and police officers, compared with the population as a whole. From the Prime Minister downwards - Government ministers, all civil servants, officers in the services, all members of the police force - owe their allegiance to the Crown and not to any political party or any other group. There is a tangible difference between a miner in dispute with the mine owner over the amount of wages paid and a soldier disobeying his officers. The miner is in opposition to his employer but still loyal to the State, and the soldier is rebelling against the Crown. This is also true for police officers, which is why it is illegal for them to strike or even to belong to a trade union today - a consequence of events that took place in 1919.

# As mutinies go it was quite peaceful….

British soldiers first mutinied in an army camp at Shoreham near Brighton just weeks after the signing of the Armistice. This was the London Command Depot and the vast majority of servicemen there were conscripts. The immediate spark was caused when a Major gave a 'dressing down' to a soldier and then pushed him into the mud. Within hours, word of the incident had spread throughout the camp and a mass walkout was organised by the men who believed that with the ending of the war they should be demobilised at once. An estimated 7,000 troops left camp and marched the six miles to Brighton, without officers and in good order. There they held a rally outside the Town Hall, and were addressed by the Chief Constable and the Mayor, both of whom promised to support their demands. The next day a General was sent from London to talk to the men and restore a sense of military discipline. He failed; his orders were ignored and none of the men returned to their posts. The local newspaper reported that the men particularly resented being 'Confined to Camp' to wash and to clean and do 'women's work' when they should be at home finding employment. They sent a telegram directly to Lloyd- George who had made extravagant promises about rapid demobilisation during the recent elections. He replied quickly and the day following the General's visit some 1000 men were released. More were sent home during the next few days.

General Wilson, Chief of the Imperial General Staff and Head of the British Army was appalled at Lloyd-George's actions. He had already prepared plans for armies of occupation in Germany, and a British presence was required in India, parts of Europe, Africa and the Middle East. In addition, the politicians had decided on a new military adventure in northern Russia. Most of the troops that were to be involved in that campaign were the 1918 conscripts, men who had only recently left well-paid jobs - a great number of them with promises that their jobs would be kept open for them. Prolonged service in Russia and the very real possibility of disease, injury or death was not part of their career plan. Later on in the year, when military mutinies were almost commonplace, Wilson wrote in his diary 'The whole trouble is due to Lloyd- George and his cursed campaign for vote-catching.'

# SPECIALS CALLED OUT !

SPECIAL Constables were ordered to report themselves for duty yesterday morning, as troops from Shoreham were expected to pay a visit to the town, similar to the orderly march to Brighton on Monday, to demand more rapid Demobilisation. But owing to the wet weather they did not arrive and the Specials were dismissed.

Worthing Gazette

A similar crisis had already arisen in the highly important military port of Folkestone. Large numbers of soldiers had been given leave in December 1918 in order to spend Christmas with their families. Most of them expected to be demobilised while they were back in Britain but instead, as soon as their leave ended, they were ordered back to France. Rumours soon spread that their ultimate destination was to be the Arctic to fight the Bolsheviks in Russia. Over the following few days thousands of discontented, non-cooperative and sullen soldiers arrived by troop trains in Folkestone where tensions finally exploded and, in an orderly and disciplined fashion, 2,000 British soldiers - N.C.O's and Privates - took over the port. Pickets were placed on the dockside to prevent any troop ships leaving and trains were met at the station by representatives of the mutineers and asked to join the protest - most did.

By Saturday, January 4, 1919, in the absence of officers, some 10,000 soldiers had organised themselves into a collective, running their own affairs, patrolling the quayside, holding meetings and setting up committees. This was no undisciplined, rampaging rabble. This was a large, armed, organised group of trained soldiers who obeyed orders only from the men they had themselves elected to lead them. The parallels with the situation in Russia the previous year were obvious to everyone, from King George down. There, as the revolution unfolded, the Russian Army

331

had refused to fight or to support the monarchy and had elected their own soviets to lead them. It was one of these soviets - the Ural Soviet - with the full approval of Lenin, that butchered Czar Nicholas with his whole family and their loyal servants on the night of July 17, 1918.

General Sir Willie Robertson, Commander-In-Chief of Home Forces (Robertson had started his military career as a trooper in the Queen's Lancers at the age of 17; he was the first and only British Army soldier to rise from private soldier to Field Marshal) was sent down from London to reason with the mutineers. He promised them that there would be no reprisals for their disloyalty and that their leave would be extended. Not surprisingly, while he dampened down the unrest in Folkestone, the trouble spread to the port of Dover and to a number of army camps in the South of England over the next few weeks.

It even reached the heart of government in Downing Street itself. Men of the Army Service Corps had heard that they would be among the last to be demobilised so they promptly commandeered regimental lorries, used them to blockade Downing Street, and demanded to see Lloyd-George. Four days later most of them were discharged.

On the same day there was an attempt at revolution in Berlin which was widely reported in British newspapers. Huge crowds gathered to hear speeches by leading members of the Spartacists - later to become the German Communist Party. They proclaimed the birth of the German Soviet Republic and raised red flags across the city. It was only the loyalty of the army to the newly-formed Republic that stopped the country becoming the latest 'Dictatorship of the Proletariat' after Russia. Having faced-down the left-wing revolutionaries and restored order, the Army then stepped aside as right-wing, armed militias attacked and hunted down the Communists.

The nightmare scenario for the Government here in Britain was that mutinous, armed and war-experienced troops would eventually seek common cause with striking workers. There was cause to believe that social unrest and widespread industrial action could reach a level where the civil forces - the police - would be unable to cope. In that perilous situation, the authorities would be forced to call upon the Army to restore order, as it had done on numerous occasions for the past few hundred years. But if the Army itself couldn't be relied upon - what then? The police themselves were already suspect, having gone on strike in 1918 when 12,000 Metropolitan Police Officers walked out in a dispute over a number of issues, including pay. Lloyd-George quickly returned from France and arranged a meeting with representatives of the police union, the National Union of Police and Prison Officers, where he immediately acceded to all their demands.

The military problem though was a situation that couldn't be allowed to continue. The Army was simply melting away and eventually, as everyone recognised - including Lloyd-George - a stand would have to be made on the mutinies. Not only was the Army essential for the occupation of Germany and all other international commitments, but as the civil situation here at home deteriorated alarmingly there would soon be a desperate need for a national military force that could be relied upon to obey orders, support the Government and the police and be available to counter growing civil unrest.

The next crisis for the Government, which occurred at Southhampton, provided the opportunity for them to take control of the widening unrest. Following the example of their comrades at Folkestone, some 5,000 soldiers refused to board troop ships taking them back to France at the end of January and instead took over the docks. This time, General Willie Robertson took the decision to act firmly. Instead of opting to deal with the situation himself, the general sent a colleague with orders to deal with the problem as he saw fit. The colleague was General Hugh Trenchard, lately of the Royal Flying Corps and a career soldier, used to having his orders obeyed.

Arriving at Southampton, he interviewed and then dismissed the commander of the camp for his incompetence in allowing what he described as 'a minor problem' to escalate into a crisis. Believing that a few stern words from a general officer would be enough to resolve the problem he set off to the docks accompanied only by his aide-de-camp and a clerk. His reception at the dock gates came as something of a shock to the three of them. Not only did the soldiers greet him with boos, whistles and abuse, but he was grabbed, roughly man-handled and thrown out:

> It was the only time in my life I had been really hustled. They did not want to listen to me. They told me to get out and stay out.

> Trenchard's memoirs.

In a cold fury Trenchard immediately phoned the garrison commander at Portsmouth and demanded 250 armed troops and military police to be sent to him at once. They arrived the next day and were met at the station by the general who ordered them to fix bayonets and load their weapons. They were then marched to the docks where they were drawn up in line and ordered to cock their rifles and be prepared to open fire on command. The soldiers they were facing were unarmed. One sergeant from the crowd shouted an obscenity at Trenchard and was quickly seized by the military police and taken away. The rest surrendered, apart from some 100 men who barricaded themselves into a dock building. Trenchard ordered the windows to be smashed and fire hoses turned onto the men inside, before they too gave themselves up.

An even more serious event was taking place in the British Army's most important continental port of Calais. There, men of the Royal Army Ordnance Corps and the Army Service Corps had refused to operate the port and had been joined in their 'strike' by French railway workers. Army units, waiting to move back to the Front Lines, disobeyed orders and stayed put.

This was a critical moment for Britain. The cease-fire with Germany was just that - a cease-fire. Germany hadn't yet signed any surrender documents, its Army was still in place and there remained the possibility that hostilities might start all over again. Being unable to use one of its few major supply ports was a major problem for the British war machine and General Haig was incensed. This time there was not even a pretence at negotiation. Two divisions, some 30,000 fighting troops, were sent to Calais and surrounded those parts of the camp that contained the mutineers. Machine-guns were set up and the rebels were ordered to lay down their arms and surrender. They did;

Churchill as Secretary of State for War

four ringleaders were identified and Haig wanted them shot for mutiny. He was overruled by Churchill - 'I do not consider that the infliction of the death penalty would be justifiable.'

Increasingly in 1919 the Government believed that the mounting number of strikes by workers throughout the country were less to do with wages and working conditions than an organised push to change the political system of the nation on the lines of the Russian Revolution. Desperately needing a force of military units that could be relied upon, it recalled the Guards Divisions - the Scots, Grenadiers, Coldstream, the Welsh and the Irish - from active service in France. They were needed as early as February when badly organised army travel arrangements had left large numbers of troops at Victoria Station in London without accommodation or food. Tempers rose over the course of the next day and the mood of the men changed to one of belligerence and abuse of their officers. Scots Guards, with bayonets fixed, were marched to the station where they cleared the area of civilians and corralled one group of the potentially rebellious soldiers in the yard. They were disarmed, arrested and taken to Wellington Barracks.

Meanwhile, unobserved in another part of the station, over a thousand armed soldiers had decided to take things further and set off along Victoria Street to the Houses of Parliament. Word was sent to the War Ministry where the Secretary of State for War - a young Mr. Churchill - was at his desk. Eventually, the men arrived at Horse Guards' Parade where they were confronted by a troop of the Household Cavalry and a unit of the Grenadier Guards. They also were arrested and taken to Wellington Barracks, where rather than spend months court-martialling a thousand cases, the military quickly sent them back to France.

Military riots multiplied throughout the country. Canadian soldiers rioted for two days in their camp just outside Rhyl, North Wales. The unrest culminated in a bloody gun battle between officers and men where five were killed and twenty suffered bayonet and knife wounds. A serving police officer, Sergeant Green, was killed in Epsom by a rampaging mob of Canadians who besieged and attacked the police station. Ex-soldiers burnt down Luton Town Hall after a demonstration turned violent, ironically on Peace Day. There was trouble in Wolverhampton, Bilston and Birmingham and race riots in Liverpool and Cardiff involving razors, knives and guns. A policeman was shot in the face in Liverpool and a black sailor was thrown into the dock and drowned.

London wasn't spared. There, anyone from an ethnic-minority background - black, Chinese, Arab, Asian - was likely to be the target of angry mobs:

Last night there was a serious riot in the East End, arising out of a feud which has existed for some time between white and coloured seamen arriving at the Port of London. Trouble occurred in a number of cafes in Cable Street, near Leman Street. About half past nine o'clock the neighbourhood was startled by the noise of firearms and the breaking of glass, and in a few minutes a crowd of men were engaged in a violent fight in Cable Street.

The Times, April 16, 1919

Three days of racial rioting in Cardiff resulted in a number of deaths of black sailors. There were reports of Australian soldiers, in uniform and armed with rifles, taking part in the attacks. White ex-servicemen headed lynch mobs that terrorised the city's black community during a week of violence that left three men dead and dozens more injured. In the aftermath the Government repatriated hundreds of black people, over 600 by mid-September.

The police, worried that they were unable to contain the disorder, asked for military help and two hundred men of the Welsh Regiment were secretly brought into the city. The unrest spread to Newport and Barry. It was at this point that the police went on strike.

The National Union of Police and Prison Officers had been formed, almost in secret, in 1913 and by 1918 had some 12,000 members, most of them members of the London based Metropolitan Police Force. A successful strike in 1918 had led to an increase in wages and better working conditions, and membership of the illegal union had soared to some 50,000 countrywide by 1919. In Sheffield, for instance, 346 of the 366 rank and file officers were members of NUPPO. The Government were particularly concerned that the Police Union was allied to the TUC and the Labour Party and in the event of a general strike it was likely that the TUC would ask for NUPPO's support. This time though, the authorities intended to be much better prepared.

They set up the Desborough Committee in March to report on police pay and conditions and that group's recommendations, which included pay increases, retirement on half pay and free housing, were immediately accepted by the Government. They also suggested the setting up of a body to represent police officers and negotiate on their behalf. This body would replace the union.

If that was the carrot, the stick was soon made obvious. Membership of a trade union was to be made a sacking offence and it would be illegal for any police officer to strike. Accumulated pension rights would be forfeit.

The Union, confident that it had numbers on its side, decided to fight, and the Executive Committee in a surprise move called for a national police strike to begin on August 1st. Unfortunately for them, they had completely misread the mood of rank and file officers and the response was poor - in London only 994 out of 18,200 participated - one inspector, one station sergeant, 27 sergeants and 965 constables. In Manchester, during a meeting of policemen discussing the strike, one member said:

> There is a force somewhere in this country which is trying to lead
> the National Union of Police to become the thin end of the wedge
> for social revolution. This must not be in Manchester.

The government also cleverly agreed to an immediate advance of £10 on the proposed wage increase. Apart from London, only two other areas of the country showed some support for the strike - Liverpool and Birmingham. In Birmingham 119 officers failed to report for duty out of a workforce of some 1,340, but in Liverpool nearly 50% of the total went out on strike. The result there was widespread civil unrest over a number of days and nights when crowds took advantage of the lack of policemen. Shops were looted and burnt and troops were attacked by violent mobs. In a show of force, the Government sent warships into the Mersey, where sailors took over the ports. Soldiers fired into crowds of rioters and at one stage attacked a mob with a bayonet charge. Machine-guns were set up, tanks were stationed in St. George's Square and 400 people - men, women and children - were arrested and tried. Finally, on the Monday evening, the weather turned to a downpour and the riots fizzled out.

One outcome of the police strike, however, proved to be a bonus for the authorities. Every single one of the strikers was immediately sacked - none was ever reinstated - and as these men had tended to be the instigators and agitators of the strike, the force had effectively dismissed those they regarded as the malcontents and troublemakers.

Meanwhile, workers continued to strike, particularly in the major industrial cities. Glasgow was brought to a halt when 40,000 men walked out and began to picket those shipyards, engineering works and factories that continued to work. Many of them were still wearing their army greatcoats and other items of uniform. Belfast followed suit and in that city the workers seized control of the electricity supply. They were demanding a 40 hour working week and calling for a general strike in defiance of their own trades unions who were viewed as tools of the Government. Lloyd-George had no intention of intervening between employers and strikers but had already made plans to bring in large forces of troops and armoured vehicles. On Friday, January 31, the Glasgow strikers congregated in large numbers in George Square and after fiery speeches by some of their leaders - Manny Shinwell and Willie Gallacher - they began to get restless and disruptive. Soon they blocked the roads with disabled trams. At this point, the police, including mounted units, moved into action using their truncheons enthusiastically. It had quickly degenerated into an ongoing battle when the Sheriff Principal, Sheriff McKenzie, appeared on the steps of the City Chambers and read out the Riot Act:

> Our Sovereign Lord the King chargeth and commandeth all persons, being assembled, immediately to disperse themselves and peaceably depart to their habitations, or to their lawful business, upon the pains contained in the Act made in the first year of King George the First for preventing tumults and riotous assemblies. God save the King.

Despite the measured language, the 1714 Riot Act (which remained in force in the U.K. until 1973) was a serious piece of legislation. Once the Act had been publicly read to a crowd by a magistrate and one hour had elapsed, the authorities could take any action they deemed suitable, up to and including ordering armed troops to open fire. In Glasgow's case, the reading of the Act provoked the very riot it was meant to prevent. A bottle thrown from the crowd hit the Sheriff, the Chief Constable was attacked, windows everywhere were smashed, trams damaged and shops looted. The Government responded by declaring what was almost martial law on the city. Some 10,000 troops in full battle kit, steel helmets and fixed bayonets, were sent (there were actually troops available in the city, but being composed of mainly local men they were felt unreliable and likely to side with the rioters). They set up machine-gun posts on rooftops, a 4.5 inch howitzer outside the City Chambers, and positioned tanks just outside the city centre. There they stayed for a week.

No-one involved needed particularly long memories to know where this unrest was heading. Twenty five years earlier the precedent had been set in Yorkshire where miners went on strike in 1893 and riots and looting took place in Barnsley and Dewsbury. Fighting broke out at Ackton Hall Colliery in Featherstone between striking and non-striking miners and the Deputy Chief Constable of Yorkshire contacted the General in charge of the Army's Northern Division, based in York, and asked for military assistance in putting down the disorder. Eventually twenty-nine men of the 1st Battalion, South Staffordshire Regiment were paraded in front of the striking miners who responded with stones. The Riot Act was read to the crowd but the officer in charge insisted on being given written orders before telling his men to fire warning shots into the dead ground between them and the rioters. When this failed to deter, the order was given to fire into the crowd. Two men, James Gibbs and James Duggan, were killed immediately. The rest dispersed.

In Belfast, the strikers had formed 'Soviets' and had organised a 'Worker's Parliament'. Having complete control over the electricity supply to the city meant that they had the power to decide who could, and who could not, have power - hospitals could, but factories couldn't. When electricity workers in London declared that they would be striking in solidarity with the men of Glasgow and Belfast, the Government acted quickly and decisively. They introduced legislation which made it an

Joint patrols of police and soldiers in Liverpool

offence to deprive the community of light and power or to encourage others to do so. Offenders were liable to six months imprisonment with hard labour or a fine of £100.

It signalled the end of the strike in Belfast. Troops were brought in and took over the gas and electricity supplies:

> The only important development in the labour situation yesterday was at Belfast, where the gas and electricity supplies of the city, which had been cut off for three weeks owing to the strikes, were resumed under military protection. There was no excitement. Infantry detachments were posted inside the stations at an early hour, while machine-guns commanded the entrances to the gasworks and a Lewis gun was mounted at the electricity works.

The Observer, February 16, 1919

But there was much more trouble to come. Early in 1914, three of the country's biggest trades unions had combined to form the Triple Alliance - the National Union of Railwaymen, the Mining Federation of Great Britain and the National Transport Workers' Federation. Each union had the option, in the event of a strike, to call on the other two to come out in sympathy and to support them. This one agreement, if put into action, had the potential to paralyse the whole country.

Despite the crippling number of days lost to strike action in Britain during the war (80,000,000 days lost between 1914 and 1918) the battle between unions and owners and employers had generally been postponed while the country was in crisis. With the ending of the war that struggle began again, but this time the stakes were far higher. All three of these industries had been nationalised during the conflict and remained nationalised in 1919. Any dispute now - a general strike - was between worker and State, not worker and employer.

It began with the London Underground drivers who went on strike over whether or not their half-hour meal break should be included in their eight-hour working day. Some of those drivers drove steam trains and were members of the National Union of Railwaymen. The miners, meanwhile, were restless over proposed plans to return the industry to the owners, a move that the miners bitterly opposed. They were also asking for a 30% increase in wages, improvements in working conditions and a six hour working day (miners were only paid for the time they spent actually producing or processing coal, not for the hours spent at the pit getting to the coalface and back). The possibility of the Triple Alliance being activated and thereby provoking a major national crisis brought Lloyd- George rushing home from the Paris peace talks. He had already set up the Industrial Unrest Committee which had been charged with formulating plans to maintain order if industrial action and subversion reached a point where the State would be unable to function normally. He decided to meet the leader of the Triple Alliance, Robert Smillie, who also represented the Miners' Union, alongside James Henry Thomas of the N.U.R., and Robert Williams of the Transport Workers for a straight talking session at No. 10 and lay the Government's cards on the table.

Many years later, Robert Smillie was able to recount, word for word, Lloyd-George's speech to them:

> Gentlemen, you have fashioned, in the Triple Alliance of the unions represented by you, a most powerful instrument. I feel bound to tell you that in our opinion we are at your mercy. The Army is disaffected and cannot be relied upon. Trouble has occurred already in a number of camps. We have just emerged from a great

war and the people are eager for the reward of their sacrifices and we are in no position to satisfy them. In these circumstances, if you carry out your threat and strike, then you will defeat us. But if you do so, have you weighed the consequences? The strike will be in defiance of the Government of the country and by its very success will precipitate a constitutional crisis of the first importance. For, if a force arises in the State which is stronger than the State itself, then it must be ready to take on the functions of the State, or withdraw and accept the authority of the State. Gentlemen, have you considered, and if you have, are you ready?

Robert Smillie in conversation with Aneurin Bevan.

Robert Smillie was a trade unionist, not a politician, and he and his fellow union leaders had no desire to run the country nor lead a revolution. The threatened general strike was averted. For the moment.

# Something must be done…

The war had politicised large sections of the population. The vast majority of people had shown complete loyalty to the national cause and final victory throughout the war, but when the conflict ended there was an outpouring of bottled-up anger and resentment - anger at the huge profits made by the increases in food prices and at the preferential treatment of businesses by government policies. Strikes multiplied from 1917 onwards and peaked in 1921 when they were only stopped by the onset of the slump and mass unemployment.

But the most dangerous moment for the country came towards the end of 1919. For months the Government had lurched from crisis to crisis, each one being more serious than before when, starting at midnight on September 26th, the railwaymen went on strike.

This wasn't simply a case of a union in dispute with an employer but a body of men, half-a-million strong, in a nationalised industry, employed by the Government, who had the capacity to do something that Germany was never able to do in four years of warfare - to bring the whole country to its knees. Railways, far more than now, provided the means to feed and move the population, and that included troops. They carried the coal that powered most of the industrial base - without the power that coal provided, trade, manufacturing and commerce would be brought to a halt. So too would power stations and winter was approaching. As most food was distributed nationwide by rail there was a very real danger of countrywide famine. At the back of it all remained the threat of a general strike under the terms of the Triple Alliance. As it was, without the means to move the coal from the pits to the docks, coal miners and dock workers would soon be standing idle anyway.

The Government invoked DORA, the Defence of the Realm Act, which allowed them almost unlimited powers to pass any legislation they saw fit. As Parliament was in recess, this effectively meant that Lloyd-George was granted dictatorial powers. His first act was to deploy 23,000 soldiers (Haig had assured him that there were enough loyal soldiers to deal with any uprising or attempt to overthrow the lawful government of the country); a further eighty-six infantry battalions were placed on standby and the Navy used ten destroyers, twenty minesweepers and six sloops to land sailors to secure and guard docks, power stations and other vitally important sites. Sailors were landed at Grimsby to operate the dock gates.

The Government also returned to the recommendations made by Sir Eric Geddes earlier that year. Geddes had been charged with formulating national policy to cope with a complete breakdown of authority. He had proposed that the country should be split into regions ruled by District Commissioners with extensive powers and backed by the Army and Navy. Commissioners would appoint Food Controllers who had the authority to declare a state of emergency and commandeer any lorries, vans, cars, buses or horses.

But the most contentious, and frightening, recommendation of all was the suggestion that a paramilitary force of 'Citizen Guards' be recruited who would be available to help the police and the military. These would be men loyal to the Government and opposed to Bolshevism. In the event, 70,000 volunteers signed up, many of them ex-soldiers:

> The government, therefore, invite all Lords Lieutenant, Lord Mayors, mayors, Chairman of County councils, Chairmen of Standing Joint Committees and Watch Committees, and Chief Constables, Town Clerks, and other local officers to take steps for the formation in all counties, cities, and boroughs of Citizen Guards to undertake to act in co-operation with the police in the duty of protection and maintenance of order. They request that in each county, city, and borough the officers above-named should form forthwith a committee for the organisation and recruitment of such a Citizen Guard.

> Part of a Government newspaper proclamation, October 3, 1919

In the beginning the Government insisted that the Citizen Guards were there simply to assist the military in guarding food supplies. By the end of the year there were secret discussions in Downing Street on the possibility of arming them as the best means of tackling strikers and suppressing political dissent. Bonar Law, soon to be the next Prime Minister, discussed the proposal that 'All weapons ought to be available for distribution to friends of the Government.'

The First Lord of the Admiralty noted that 'The peaceable manpower of the country is without arms…a Bill is needed for licensing persons to bear arms', and Sir Robert Horne, Labour Minister, urged the police to compile confidential lists of men who could be relied upon to support the Government in the event of a crisis - an armed militia.

Let's be perfectly clear here. This is a government that is discussing the very real possibility of arming one section of the population to fight another - in any other context, a civil war - or, as most of the volunteer Citizen Guards were likely to be professional men - a class war against the workers.

The railwaymen felt that they had been treated badly by a government that had promised to reward the efforts they had made during the war. Instead of the longed-for wage increases at war's end the railway workers were faced with reductions in both pay and in the workforce itself as the country struggled with insolvency and its inability to pay off its international debts. All negotiations between the Union and the Government failed and a strike was called:

> The short issue is that the long made promise of a better world for railwaymen which was made in the time of the nation's crisis, and accepted by the railwaymen as an offer that would ultimately bear fruit has not materialised .

> NUR General Secretary J.H. Thomas

The NUR was both powerful and well organised and some 400,000 of its own members plus members of the Associated Society of Locomotive Engineers and Firemen ceased work on the night of Friday, September 26. Their aim was to paralyse the internal transport structure, but after nine days, realised that they had failed. They agreed to further talks with Lloyd-George who offered to maintain existing wages for one more year and the introduction of an eight-hour day. It was enough for both sides to declare a victory and the strike was abandoned.

So too was the concept of Citizen Guards. They were not needed once the immediate crisis had passed. Moreover, informed public opinion had begun to recognise the dangers in having a middle class militia on the streets in opposition to working class protest.

# End of the war with Russia

Britain had never actually declared war on Russia. The Allies had intervened in the fighting on behalf of the 'Whites' against the 'Reds' of Lenin and the Communist Party (there was also a 'Green' Army which fought against both of them, and an anarchist 'Black' Army in Ukraine which fought everybody). By 1919 it was obvious to everyone that the Bolsheviks had fully consolidated political and military power in the country and Lloyd-George, ever the pragmatist, decided that the time was right to withdraw. Unfortunately he neglected to tell his Secretary of State for War, Mr. Churchill, who fully believed in the ideological struggle and spoke frequently in Parliament in support of Britain's involvement in the Russian war. At a banquet in the Guildhall on November 8th, with Churchill present, the Prime Minister declared:

> We cannot, of course, afford to continue so costly an intervention in an interminable civil war. Our troops are out of Russia. Frankly, I am glad. Russia is a quicksand.

From Revolution and War, Stephen M. Walt

He was right of course, despite Churchill's protests. None of the Western Powers had any great interest in helping to create a united and peaceful Russia. It was much more important to keep Russia weak - a strong Russia could threaten Britain's Indian Empire. And Britain had enough problems of its own - constant industrial action, war weariness, the arguments over the spoils of victory with wartime allies, the Paris Peace Conference and coping with the economic turmoil of defeated European countries. The brief intervention in northern Russia had been costly - the British alone sent one hundred million pounds worth of military equipment to the Whites. The contribution of a few thousand troops actually setting foot in the country was negligible. Though there were some casualties from sickness or accident none were killed in action. Two years later Britain and Russia signed a trade agreement.

There were concerns elsewhere in the world. Britain had only just ended the fighting in Afghanistan with a victory in the Third Anglo-Afghan War in 1919 but had now become militarily involved in Iraq and was fighting for control of the oil-fields at Mosul. The burden of maintaining, protecting and developing a worldwide Empire as well as providing troops to guard domestic ports or patrol cities was troubling the services:

> I think you know that during the month of August we sent 10 Native Battalions from India to Basra, and in this month of September we are sending 6 more Native Battalions and 3 British Battalions from India, making a total reinforcement from India for Mesopotamia of 19 Battalions, plus a few guns, sappers, etc. On the top of this comes a telegram from Haldane asking for yet another two divisions and two cavalry brigades. These, of course, we cannot supply, because India has warned us in the most solemn manner that she has reached the limit of her possibilities. In looking round the dish, the only bit of food I see is your three Battalions at Constantinople. There is nothing worth talking about either in Palestine or Egypt. There is obviously nothing on the Rhine or in Ireland, and we have not nearly enough troops here in England in view of the danger of this miners' strike which is now hanging over us…The fact, of course, is that the Cabinet policy has completely outrun their military power, and although we have repeatedly told the Cabinet that this course of action is bound to lead to disaster, I have never been able to change their headlong course.

Field-Marshal Henry Wilson, Chief of the Imperial General Staff.

On 28th June, 1919, a treaty was signed between Germany and the Allies formally ending the war. In a final humiliating gesture for her former enemy, France insisted that the ceremony be held in the Hall of Mirrors at the Palace of Versailles - the place where fifty years earlier the unification of Germany had been declared. There had been extensive discussion regarding the prosecution of the Kaiser and Austro-Hungarian Emperor Karl as war criminals - 'a supreme offence against international morality and the sanctity of treaties' was the proposed charge - but in the event both were allowed to retire and to disappear. The Kaiser had fled to Holland the night before the Armistice was signed and grew a beard to make himself less recognisable. Whenever the Dutch talked of repatriation back to Germany he feigned madness, until finally they reluctantly agreed to allow him to stay. He bought a very pretty moated villa near the village of Doorn where he terrorised the neighbours by insisting on having Imperial privileges. He was sixty-three when his wife died in 1921 and he quickly married the thirty-five year old Princess Hermine of Schonaich-Carolath. He lived long enough to witness the Second World War German victories in Europe, dying in 1941.

Grave of Lieutenant George Dancey who died in the military hospital at Archangel in 1919

Emperor Karl never actually abdicated but gave up all right to be involved in the government of Austria. He was exiled by the Allies to Switzerland but irritated his hosts by twice trying to reclaim the Hungarian Crown of St. Stephen until eventually he was expelled to Madeira where he promptly died of influenza at the age of thirty-four. Somehow, puzzlingly, since his death, despite failing to protect his people from death and destruction, he has become a figure of veneration in the Catholic Church and has been credited with curing a Brazilian nun of varicose veins. Pope John Paul II beatified Karl, the last of the Hapsburg Emperors, in October 2004 and at some point in the future he will be canonised and become, presumably, Saint Karl.

# Taking stock - November 1919

Twelve months of peace had given the country time to take stock of the previous four years. The losses, the costs and the changes to what had been the solid foundations of the state had shaken the nation to its very core and, on a few occasions, come very close to destroying it.

The situation in Britain, dismal as it seemed to many domestic observers, was far from being the worst in Europe. Casualties had been higher in most of the other belligerents. As the missing bodies were recovered and recorded from the destroyed landscapes and battlefields, the British figures became more accurate and settled. By the end of 1919 it was accepted that Britain's military dead numbered 750,000, and a further 180,000 troops of the Empire. Russia suffered 1.8 million killed; Italy, half a million; France, 1.3 million; Austria-Hungary 1.5 million; Germany had to cope with the shocking loss of 2 million men. The disabled, wounded or incapacitated outnumbered even these figures. Later on, when the world deaths from the influenza pandemic during 1918-1919 were added up they were found to be twice as many as all those caused by four years of European war.

The economic cost to Europe was devastating - it was more than six times the sum of all national debts since the end of the Eighteenth Century up to 1914. Britain owed America an immense debt which grew to over 4.5 billion dollars by 1922, and would be forced to rely on American credit for years to come. In fact, Britain only finally repaid the last of its WW1 American war loans in 2015 when George Osborne redeemed the last £1.9 billion (it has been calculated by the Government's Debt Management Office that the country has paid some £5.5 billion in total interest on the WW1 loans from America since 1917).

British soldiers returning home had no problems in recognising the country they had left behind. That wasn't particularly true of many parts of Europe. In the western regions, most of the devastation was confined to parts of France and Belgium, but the destroyed houses, villages and towns, the poisoned land and the dead livestock were largely to be found in a strip measuring between nineteen and forty miles wide running through both countries.

More than 3,430,000 hectares of land was ruined. Some 4,926 towns and villages in France along with 866,844 houses and farmsteads needed rebuilding. There was less damage in Belgium but even there 100,000 public and private buildings, including 24,000 farms, needed reconstruction.

  Outside that strip, the countries had suffered little damage. Back home, apart  from shelled towns on the East Coast and some Zeppelin or Gotha bomb damage in London and a number of other places, Britain was largely untouched. In eastern Europe though it was a different matter - Poland particularly, but also Ukraine, Serbia and Belarus had been invaded, conquered, re-invaded and devastated by advancing and retreating armies. The suffering didn't end with the signing of the Armistice. Hundreds of thousands of refugees fled towards the west from the fighting in Russia, fleeing to countries that were themselves experiencing great hardship. Over half of the population of Warsaw was unemployed and on a starvation die:

> The country had undergone four or five occupations by different armies, each of which had combed the land for supplies. Most of the villages had been burnt down by the Russians in their retreat (of 1915); land had been uncultivated for four years…The population here was living upon roots, grass, acorns and heather.

Sir William Goode, British Relief Mission to Eastern Europe, 1919

Soldiers returning home to Vienna, Berlin, Budapest and Munich would find themselves confronted with economic and revolutionary chaos. Inflation affected most countries but hyperinflation ruined the currency of Austria, Poland, Russia and later Germany, who had gambled on winning the war and recouping its costs from the countries it conquered:

> If anyone sold anything and did not at once buy something else with the money, he would lose heavily. There were many who sold house or field, or part of their cattle, only to keep their money either at home or in some bank. These lost all they had and became beggars. On the other hand, those who borrowed money and bought things with it made fortunes. There were endless heaps of money. One had to carry it in briefcases or baskets. Purses  and the like were useless. For things for the house one paid in thousands, then in millions, and finally in billions. Officials were paid fortnightly, for the amount received had a far different value in the first half of the month from what it did later...

Jan Slomka, From Serfdom to Self-Government: Memoirs of a Polish Village Mayor, 1842-1927

There began a clamour from French households who had suffered the loss of a loved one to have the bodies returned home to be interred in their own village churchyards. Eventually, after much prevarication, the French Government (secretly appalled by the cost) agreed and some 300,000 of the identifiable dead were exhumed and reburied in a huge logistical and bureaucratic operation. Those who were left had their battlefield cemeteries rebuilt to a uniform plan, each country somewhat differently. The French refused to share their cemeteries with any of the enemy so the bodies of German soldiers were exhumed and reburied separately.

Exhumations from the battlefield and repatriation home were banned from the start of the conflict by Britain and the Dominion Governments. The reasons were many and varied. Chief amongst them was the simple one of hygiene, no-one could face the prospect of hundreds of ferries crossing the Channel packed with mutilated and decaying bodies. But there was a strong feeling among the armed forces as well as the general public that the dead should have equality of treatment, that they should dwell together in unity, regardless of rank or social class. Many, if not most, families could not afford the cost of repatriating loved ones and it would be unfair if those who could afford to do so were allowed. The argument applied through all the theatres of war where soldiers had fought and died and post-war repatriation of the dead was forbidden under Article 3 of the Anglo-French Agreement of November 26th, 1918.

Military Cemetery 1919

Tyne-Cot British and Commonwealth Cemetery, Belgium.

The British had begun the war without any formalised way of recording battle casualties let alone having the resources to cope with far greater losses than anyone had foreseen. In 1914 they turned to a Mr. (later Sir) Fabian Ware who was neither a soldier nor a politician but had been Editor of the Morning Post and in 1914 was a director of Rio Tinto Zinc. At 45 he was too old to join the Army but, by pulling a few strings, he obtained command of a mobile ambulance unit provided by the British Red Cross. After just a few weeks at the Front he was appalled at the lack of any official mechanism for marking and recording the graves of fallen soldiers and formed his own unit to oversee this task. As early as 1915 the group were given official recognition and support by the War Office and transferred from the Red Cross into the Army as the Graves Registration Committee. By October 1915, they had over 31,000 graves registered, and 50,000 by May 1916.

As the war went on and the losses increased, their job became an immense task. Rudyard Kipling called it 'The biggest single piece of work since the Pharaohs and they only worked in their own country'. It continued in earnest after the Armistice and by 1919 some 587,000 graves had been identified and a further 559,000 casualties were registered as having no known grave.

All British war dead are commemorated uniformly and equally, titled officers next to privates, irrespective of military rank, civil rank, race or creed. Headstones are carved in Portland stone (apart from in Russia where granite is used) and are laid out in straight lines to represent men on parade.

Worldwide, the Commonwealth War Graves Commission is responsible for 23,000 burial sites of war dead and more than 200 memorials. The bodies of missing Great War soldiers are still being found today and are added to the total. Some can even be identified.

Three of the finest architects of the day were chosen to design the larger cemeteries and Kipling was asked to advise on the wording of the inscriptions - it was Kipling, who had lost his only son in the war (his body was only found and identified in the 1920's), who suggested 'Known unto God' for the headstones of unidentified soldiers.

In 1919, Sir Edwin Lutyens, who had worked with the Imperial War Graves Commission ( now the Commonwealth War Graves Commission) was asked to design one of the temporary structures that were to be erected along the route of the London Victory Parade - the Peace Day Parade. This procession was to mark the formal end of the war that had taken place with the signing of the Treaty of Versailles on June 28th. His structure was one of the last to be commissioned and he was given just two weeks to design it but it was to be one of the most prominent in Whitehall between the Foreign Office and Richmond House.

Lloyd- George wanted a catafalque design, similar to Abraham Lincoln's Memorial in Washington or the one that was about to be unveiled in Paris on the Arc de Triomphe, but Lutyens decided on a Cenotaph, an empty tomb, a monument to someone who is buried elsewhere. Like all the other temporary structures along the route it was made out of wood and plaster and for weeks after the parade it was covered with flowers and wreaths that had been left by the general public. It was a popular design that reflected the quiet dignity of mourning and pressure mounted for it to be made permanent. On 23 October 1919 the War Cabinet announced that a permanent memorial should replace the wooden version and be designated Britain's official National War Memorial. It was to be made in Portland stone and would be a 'replica exact in every detail in permanent material of the present temporary structure'.

There are deliberately no names or religious symbols on the monument but the words 'The Glorious Dead' are carved below the stone wreaths on each side. These wreaths are 5 feet in diameter and the one on top of the Cenotaph measures 3.6 feet. Above the side wreaths are inscribed the dates of the war, MCMXIV - MCMXIX. There is not one single straight line in the whole structure and none of the sides are parallel. Lutyens designed it so that if the sides were extended, they would meet at a point about 980 feet above the ground. Similarly, all of the horizontal surfaces are sections of a sphere whose centre would be 900 feet below the ground. It is 35 feet tall and weighs 120 tonnes. The builders were Holland, Hannen & Cubitts, and Lutyens waived his fee so that the cost was reduced to £7,325 (equivalent to some £256,000 today). Work started on January 19 and it was unveiled by King George V on the very first Armistice Day - November 11, 1920.

This muted, restrained and understated design was so successful that it was duplicated on smaller scales throughout the country and in Australia, Canada, New Zealand, Bermuda and Hong Kong.

In Russia, there is no monument to World War 1. The "Great War' was subsumed into their civil war and edited out of collective memory.

The Cenotaph in Whitehall at the dedication on November 11, 1920.

# Who Cares?

In April 1919, the Holmfirth Express published details of the reparations expected to be presented to the German Government by the victorious Allies. Top of the list was a demand for a first payment of £1,000,000,000. As this enormous sum was four hundred millions more than the whole German budget for 1920 there were obviously going to be problems. Both Britain and America were keen to punish Germany for the war, and Britain in particular was desperate for financial reparations, but neither country wanted to see their recent enemy completely and permanently destroyed as a nation.

But France did. French Senators called for:

* Full restitution
* Full reparation for injuries and damages
* All war costs to be paid by Germany
* Exemplary punishment of of German 'war criminals'
* Territorial and legal guarantees to prevent the renewal of war.

And they looked to their Prime Minister, Clemenceau, to give them their retribution. Clemenceau's nickname in French politics was 'Tiger'. That name alone summed up his approach to how Germany was to be treated post-war. The French were still smarting about the collapse of Russia, not least because Tsarist Russia owed them 25,000 million francs (1,000 million pounds) and half as much again in war loans. French businesses also had substantial investment in Russian banking, oil, coal and the railway system. There was little chance that Lenin would compensate them or repay any loans.

So Clemenceau wanted revenge on Germany and demanded the major share of the reparations to come no matter what hardship that might cause to German civilians. When French troops seized control of the railway system in Germany it was pointed out that without the means to transport food supplies to Germans east of the Rhine they would, inevitably, starve. General Foch replied that that 'was their affair'.

Like the rest of Europe, Britain spent the next two decades coming to terms with its own changed circumstances. Within the space of ten years it had been transformed from an Edwardian superpower to a country mired in debt and economically damaged; from a country with Victorian certainties to a situation where everything was questioned and challenged; from a proud country with an Empire 'where the sun never set', to one that struggled to contain the pressures for freedom for those States.

For some people during the 1920's, the only recourse was to adopt an air of cynicism and disenchantment, which became fashionable in the arts and high society. T.E. Lawrence (Lawrence of Arabia) carved Ou Phrontis - Who Cares - in the beam above the front door of his cottage. But for the majority of the population - the working class - life remained a struggle and many features of daily living hadn't improved.

There was a short lived economic boom in 1919-20 that collapsed into a slump the following year. The great pre-war industries - coal, iron and steel, shipbuilding and cotton - had been stimulated during the war and the country enjoyed full employment. This continued for the first few months of peace as industry worked to satisfy a pent-up domestic demand but soon the market became oversupplied and by the Summer of 1920 demand had collapsed. Foreign markets wanted fewer British products as they expanded their own domestic industries or applied tariffs on imported goods, and the cotton mills of Lancashire, which before the war provided Britain's largest single export, were particularly hard-hit. A country like Britain which depended on exports and a buoyant world market was one of the first to suffer and unemployment soared.

This was to be the pattern for the next twenty years as bust followed boom. There was a partial recovery in 1921 where unemployment fell to 1.1 million but by 1933 it had almost tripled again.

Heavy manufacturing, including textiles, suffered considerably after 1918 but the war itself had created and stimulated new industries including chemicals, motor vehicles, electrical goods, medicines and aviation. The massive expansion of the electricity supply, culminating in the setting up of the National Electricity Grid meant that the country as a whole benefited enormously but it also meant that manufacturers were no longer dependent on a local source of power - coal - and were able to locate their industries more or less wherever they desired. This was not good news for the traditional heartlands of heavy industry - the North of England, South Wales and Central Scotland. In 1921 national unemployment rates peaked at 17%, but reached 36% in shipbuilding regions and 27% in engineering areas. These regional disparities continued for the next decade so that by 1934 there were unemployment rates of 50% in Bishop Auckland, 57% in Jarrow, 61% in Cumberland and 67% in Merthyr Tydfil. In that same year the unemployment rate in St. Albans reached 3.9%.

There developed in 1919 an understandable fear of impending class-conflict as the contrast between the poverty of the majority and the affluence of the middle and upper class sections of the population became more obvious. Pessimists pointed to the massive rise in trade union membership and the ever-increasing tidal wave of strikes and protests. By 1919 the middle classes had formed the Middle Class Union which campaigned against extravagant government spending on benefits for the working class and fought for a reduction in Income Tax. All eyes were on the political and economic turmoil in Europe, particularly in Germany, and many feared that it would be repeated in Britain.

Nowhere was discontent more evident than in the housing situation. In 1914 the housing shortage had been estimated at 120,000; by 1918, as a result of deterioration, neglect and lack of any new construction, it had risen to 600,000. During the war, thousands of men and women had left home to find work in the munitions industry thereby greatly increasing local shortages of accommodation and allowing landlords to raise rents alarmingly. There were rent strikes in most of the country's major cities and the Government finally responded by introducing drastic rent controls and forbidding landlords to evict tenants except for non-payment.

With Lloyd-George's promise of 'homes for heroes' in mind, the 1919 Housing Act required local councils to assess the housing needs in their areas and to propose plans to eliminate shortages with the help of government grants. Labour councillors, who were being elected in growing numbers after the reforms to the franchise, were particularly keen on these subsidies and made a point of listening to their various women's groups as to what was most needed. Women wanted indoor lavatories, a hot water supply, extra bedrooms and gardens, not yards. The result was that council houses were built to high standards.

The Government, in fact, was listening more and more to women who now formed 40% of the electorate. The expected political chaos and revolutionary change resulting from giving women the vote hadn't occurred, despite numerous forecasts of disaster. In fact, women probably made a substantial contribution to political stability during this period. It had only been a few years since leading doctors had argued that women were physically and emotionally unfit to take any part in politics - including voting - and that their roles as mothers would be damaged if they became involved. This kind of medical opinion lasted well into the 1930's. Sir Arbuthnot Lane, an eminent British surgeon and physician, argued forcefully to ban women from participating in sport - 'a craze for athletics is sweeping over women…Any excess in this direction is bound to have a serious effect on the motherhood of the nation'.

Women and motherhood were inextricably bound together. Young wives were lectured by well-meaning G.P.s who refused to advise them on contraception and instead stressed the need to repopulate the Empire. In fact, the British Medical Association opposed the provision of any form of birth control up until 1930. The Daily Mail and the Daily Express railed against 'flappers', young girls who had learned to be financially independent during the war and now devoted themselves to pleasure, leisure and emancipation, shunning the responsibilities of marriage and motherhood:

> Many of our young women have become de-sexed and masculinised with short hair, skirts little longer than kilts, narrow hips, insignificant breasts; there has arrived a confident, active, game-loving, capable human being who shuns the servitude of household occupations.

Arabella Kenealy

This 'new' woman was also highly unlikely to enter domestic service. Thirty years previously there had been 1.7 million women working as domestic servants but the lure of well paid work in the munitions industries had taken hundreds of thousands of them away and they were extremely reluctant to return. Servants, particularly in small households, were expected to be at work by 6.30am where they would clean the grates, make the fires, take up early morning tea, cook breakfasts and scrub the front steps before being allowed to eat their own meal. Munitions work meant strictly defined hours, not being at someone's beck and call throughout the day; factory work often allowed for sitting down to do the job, not running up and down stairs all day carrying buckets of coal. Newspapers raged against those young women who, instead of accepting 'proper and natural employment' as domestic servants competed for jobs with men or languished on unemployment benefits. One year after the Armistice some 775,000 women had lost their jobs - Sir

Herbert Austin, the motor manufacturer, declared that all women should be sacked as a solution to the unemployment problem. The textile industry, which traditionally employed a high proportion of women workers, was hit particularly hard.

And the Unions, despite having 1.2 million women members in 1918, did nothing for them preferring instead to campaign for higher wages for men so that their wives would have no need to work.

As war ended and the privations, the shortages and the anxieties began to fade from people's minds there was an explosion of pent-up demand for enjoyment and entertainment, not just among the young. The number of cinemas had increased dramatically during the war but now the craze was dancing and dance halls blossomed everywhere. The London rich had their own favourites - the Grafton Galleries which had black musicians and required all the dancers to wear gloves; the Kit-Kat Club with a dance floor holding 400; Murray's Club, owned by the racketeer Jack May, which always had a plentiful supply of cocaine. Entrepreneurs built chains of dance halls across the country and village halls and church halls held regular Saturday night sessions.

The craze had started with the arrival of American troops who brought and played jazz and ragtime music. By the time peace arrived the pre-war waltzes and oompah bands had been replaced by the foxtrot, the tango, the shimmy, the Black Bottom and, most famously, the Charleston. Many people were outraged and clergymen in particular railed against what was thought to be a moral decline - 'the morals of the pigsty would be respectable in comparison'. But critics were ignored and eventually even the BBC had its own dance band - the London Radio Dance Band.

By June 1919 the campaign to raise funds for the Holmfirth Memorial was in full swing and the list of subscribers had reached hundreds of names. The estimated cost of the planned hospital had now risen to fifteen thousand pounds but it was to rise further before the appeal ended. The Holme Valley Memorial Hospital and the Holme, Holmfirth and New Mill Memorial Cross were built together to commemorate the men and boys of the District who fell in the Great War. There are three hundred names recorded there, each one carved in granite with inlaid, black-painted metal letters. Recent research has unearthed a considerable number more who, for whatever reason, failed to be included.

And finally.

A newspaper cartoon was printed in 1919 as the Versailles Conference was coming to an end. It showed the French Premier, Clemenceau, leaving the Hall of Mirrors and telling a colleague, 'Curious, I seem to hear a child weeping'. In the background, hidden by the pillars, is a weeping child called 'Peace' and labelled 1940.

For the following twenty-one years Europe lived on borrowed time.

# The Holmfirth War Memorial

There are nearly three hundred names on the memorial erected in 1922 for a small West Yorkshire town. Extensive, recent research has revealed at least another fifty names that were never included for one reason or another.

The following four maps show the names and home locations of those who died.

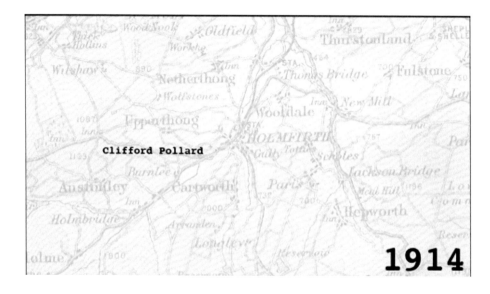

At the end of 1914 Holmfirth had suffered its first casualty - this was young Clifford Pollard of Park Head, Holmfirth. After leaving Secondary School at 14 Clifford had first worked at Lower Mills before being apprenticed to Mr Cockroft the chemist in Huddersfield. In 1913, just two days after his sixteenth birthday Clifford joined the Royal Navy and spent a year training at the Shotly Naval training barracks gaining first class marks on graduating. His first posting was to HMS Hawke which was a designated training ship but on the declaration of war on August 4, 1914, reverted to its proper role as a fighting ship. One month later on October 15 the Hawke was torpedoed by a German U-boat and sank immediately, taking 526 crew with her - including Clifford Pollard. He has no known grave and his name is commemorated on the Portsmouth Naval Memorial to the Missing.

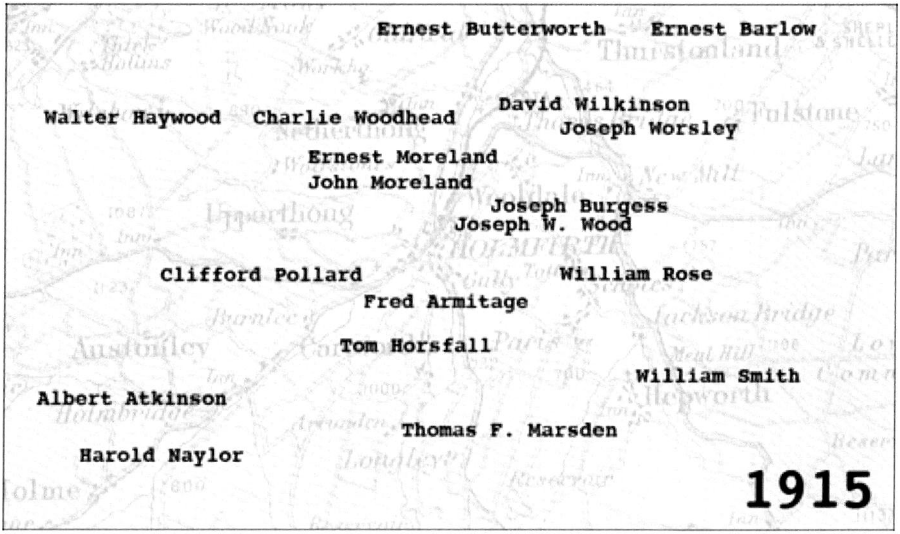

Ernest Butterworth    Ernest Barlow

Walter Haywood   Charlie Woodhead   David Wilkinson
                                     Joseph Worsley
                 Ernest Moreland
                 John Moreland
                              Joseph Burgess
                         Joseph W. Wood

    Clifford Pollard              William Rose
              Fred Armitage

         Tom Horsfall
                                        William Smith
Albert Atkinson
                    Thomas F. Marsden
    Harold Naylor

# 1915

By the end of 1915 another seventeen names had been added to the list. Of the seventeen, nine had been killed in Gallipoli and thirteen of the names were Duke of Wellington's men. The nine who lost their lives in the fighting in Turkey were New Army soldiers, young men of the area who had responded to Kitchener's call - 'Your country needs you' - and had been enlisted in the 8th and 9th Battalions of the 'Dukes'.

Their names can be found on the Helles Memorial to the Missing, or the Chunuk Bair Memorial, Lone Pine Cemetery, or Twelve Tree Copse.

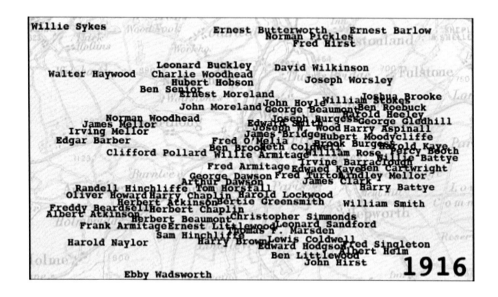

Willie Sykes    Ernest Butterworth  Ernest Barlow
                Norman Pickles
                Fred Hirst

        Leonard Buckley    David Wilkinson
Walter Haywood  Charlie Woodhead
        Hubert Hobson      Joseph Worsley
Ben Senior
        Ernest Moreland
        John Moreland George Beaumont William Stokes Joshua Brooke
Norman Woodhead                       Harold Heeley
James Mellor              Joseph Burgess George Gledhill
Irving Mellor            Joseph W. Wood Harry Aspinall
Edgar Barber             James Bridge Hubert Moodycliffe
        Fred O'Melia     Seth Coldwell
Clifford Pollard  Ben Brook          Brook Burgess Harold Kaye
        Willie Armitage William Rose  Percy Booth
                      Irvine Barraclough  Willie Battye
        Fred Armitage Edwaed Kaye Ben Cartwright
        George Dawson Fred Turton Lindley Mellor
        Arthur Dawson        James Clark
Randell Hinchliffe  Tom Horsfall              Harry Battye
Oliver Howard Harry Chaplin Harold Lockwood
        Herbert Atkinson Bertie Greensmith  William Smith
Freddy Beardsell Herbert Chaplin
Albert Atkinson
        Herbert Beaumont Christopher Simmonds
Frank Armitage Ernest Littlewood Leonard Sandford
        Sam Hinchliffe  Thomas F. Marsden
Harold Naylor           Harry Brown Lewis Coldwell
                      Edward Hodgson Fred Singleton
                      Ben Littlewood Albert Holm
                           John Hirst   **1916**

        Ebby Wadsworth

The fighting on the Somme between July 1st and November 19th, 1916 added another fifty-two names. A further ten local men were killed or died of wounds on other battlefields.

Fourteen of the names were men of the 1/5th Battalion, many of whom would have been in the Holmfirth Drill Hall the day war was declared.

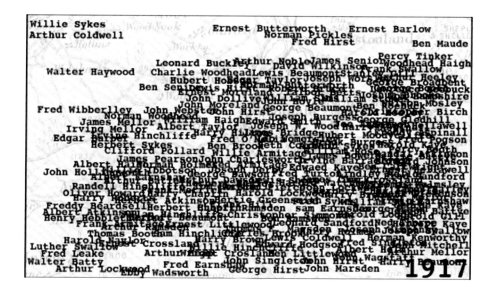

There are a total of 102 names on the memorial of men who either died in action or of wounds or disease during 1917.

Of these, thirty three were killed in the battle of Third Ypres or Passchendaele. Sixteen of them have their names on either the Menin Gate or the Tyne Cot Memorials to the Missing.

## War's end.

The massive German attack in March followed by the British Advance after the Battle of Amiens resulted in yet another butcher's bill of nearly 100 Holmfirth men and boys. Among them were the last of the original volunteers of 1914 and 1915.

I've tried to end this book where I started - telling the story of ordinary people living through quite extraordinary times.
Thank you for taking the time to read it.

IN
PROUD AND GRATEFUL MEMORY
OF THESE,
OUR SONS, WHO DIED FOR
ENGLAND
IN THE GREAT WAR
1914-1919
THE PEOPLE
OF HOLME, HOLMFIRTH, AND
NEWMILL
HAVE ERECTED THIS
MONUMENT & HOSPITAL
A.D. 1920.

✝

Oh England, sometimes think of them,
As once they thought of you.